Financial Accounting: Tools for Business Decision Making

Financial Accounting: Tools for Business Decision Making

Theon O'Brien

Clanrye International
www.clanryeinternational.com

Clanrye International,
750 Third Avenue, 9th Floor,
New York, NY 10017, USA

ISBN: 978-1-63240-899-0

Cataloging-in-Publication Data

Financial accounting : tools for business decision making / Theon O'Brien.
p. cm.
Includes bibliographical references and index.
ISBN 978-1-63240-899-0
1. Accounting. 2. Financial statements. 3. Business-- Decision making. I. O'Brien, Theon.
HF5636 .F56 2019
657--dc23

For information on all Clanrye International publications
visit our website at www.clanryeinternational.com

CLANRYE INTERNATIONAL

Printed in China.

Contents

Preface

Financial accounting is a sub-field of accounting, which deals with the diverse aspects of summarizing, analyzing and reporting of data related to financial transactions in a business. Preparing financial statements for the public is an important aspect of this field. Financial accounting is subject to local and international accounting standards. The standard framework of guidelines is provided by the Generally Accepted Accounting Principles or GAAP. Financial accounting is of use to stockholders, bankers, suppliers, business owners and government agencies among many others. This book is a valuable compilation of topics, ranging from the basic to the most complex theories and principles in the field of financial accounting. This book studies and analyzes the financial accounting tools for business decision making and their utmost significance in modern times. It is an essential guide for both academicians and those who wish to pursue this discipline further.

A detailed account of the significant topics covered in this book is provided below:

Chapter 1- The analysis, reporting and summary of financial transactions in a business is under the scope of a branch of accounting called financial accounting. The drafting of financial statements for public information is an important function of this domain. This is an introductory chapter, which will discuss in brief the different principles of accounting and financial accounting for a comprehensive understanding.

Chapter 2- Financial statement is a formal record of the financial transactions and the financial position of an enterprise. Financial statements can be of different types, such as balance sheet, an income statement, cash flow statement or an equity statement. This chapter closely examines the different forms of financial statements such as balance sheet, cash flow statement, statement of changes in equity, etc.

Chapter 3- An income statement is a financial statement, which reflects a company's revenues and expenses for a given period. This chapter has been carefully written to provide an introduction to the varied concepts of income statement such as profit and loss, income and expense, etc.

Chapter 4- A cash flow statement is a financial statement, which shows the way in which any change in balance sheet accounts and income has an impact on cash and cash equivalents. This chapter discusses in elaborate detail the significant aspects of cash flow statement such as cash flow and cash flow activities for an extensive understanding.

Chapter 5- A balance sheet is reflective of the financial position of a business. It is a summary of the balances of an organization or an individual and consists of consolidated information of assets and liabilities and ownership equity. These aspects of the balance sheet have been carefully analyzed in this chapter.

Chapter 6- A financial audit is performed to provide an insight into the authenticity of the financial statements of a company. It ensures that all accounting standards have been met. The topics covered in this chapter address the varied aspects of financial audit and reporting, which include quarterly finance report, annual report, director's report, auditor's report, etc.

Chapter 7- Accounting cycle is the process of identifying, recording and analyzing the accounting events of a company. The cycle starts when a transaction occurs and ends once it is included in the financial statements. Accrual accounting is the method which determines the performance and position of a company. This chapter closely examines the fundamental aspects of the accounting cycle and accrual accounting, such as transaction analysis, accounting cycle, cash basis and accrual basis of accounting, etc.

I would like to make a special mention of my publisher who considered me worthy of this opportunity and also supported me throughout the process. I would also like to thank the editing team at the back-end who extended their help whenever required.

Theon O'Brien

1

Introduction to Financial Accounting

The analysis, reporting and summary of financial transactions in a business is under the scope of a branch of accounting called financial accounting. The drafting of financial statements for public information is an important function of this domain. This is an introductory chapter, which will discuss in brief the different principles of accounting and financial accounting for a comprehensive understanding.

Accounting

Accounting has been hailed by many as the "language of business". There are many quotations like "A pen is mightier than the sword but no match for the accountant" which tell us about the power and importance of accounting.

The definition of accounting states that it includes recording, summarizing, reporting and analyzing financial data.

Even if you're new to accounting, you may have noticed some use of accounting in your daily life.

A mother, for example, is the chief accountant of a family. At the start of each month, she prepares a budget that lists all expected payments and income for the month. She then records all payments and receipts in her personal diary such as groceries, utilities, taxes and so on. Tracking home expenses against the monthly budget helps her avoid overspending and also gives her peace of mind knowing where the money was spent in case she forgets. She keeps all the invoices and bank statements in a shoe box. Once every year she files her taxes and this is where all her hard work in maintaining the financial record pays off as she has all the required information on her finger tips (and a shoe box). Even though she doesn't know, she is performing basic functions of an accountant to manage the home finances.

Accounting is just a more formal and efficient version of such processes in the context of a business. Businesses use accounting to keep their financial information organized which helps them in making sense of their financial data and also keeps them compliant of financial regulations.

Components of Accounting

Book-keeping, which is also known as financial accounting, is the process of recording and summarizing financial information. Book-keeping involves the recording of transactions (e.g. sales, purchases, and expenses) which are then summarized and presented in the form of financial statements which show the overall health of the business.

Book-keeping helps to organize the financial data which facilitates the effective management of the business by providing key information such as:

- How much they owe to suppliers, tax authorities, banks, employees and others?
- How much each customer owes the business?
- How much capital is invested by the owners in the business?
- How profitable is the business?

Bookkeeping is the backbone of an accounting system and forms the basis of analysis in management accounting.

- Management accounting, also known as managerial accounting, provides information to management for analysis, decision making, planning and control of the business. For example, information relating to investment decisions, budgeting and performance measurement.
- Recording

  The primary function of accounting is to make records of all the transactions that the firm enters into. Recognizing what qualifies as a transaction and making a record of the same is called bookkeeping. Bookkeeping is narrower in scope than accounting and concerns only the recording part. For the purpose of recording, accountants maintain a set of books. Their procedures are very systematic. Nowadays, computers have been deployed to automatically account for transactions as they happen.

- Summarizing

  Recording for transactions creates raw data. Pages and pages of raw data are of little use to an organization for decision making. For this reason, accountants classify data into categories. These categories are defined in the chart of accounts. As and when transactions occur, two things happen, firstly an individual record is made and secondly the summary record is updated.

  For instance a sale to Mr. X for Rs 100 would appear as:

  - Sale to Mr. X for Rs 100
  - Increase the total sales (summary) from 500 to 600

- Reporting

  Management is answerable to the investors about the company's state of affairs.

The owners need to be periodically updated about the operations that are being financed with their money. For this reason, there are periodic reports which are sent to them. Usually the frequency of these reports is quarterly and there is one annual report which summarizes the performance of all four quarters. Reporting is usually done in the form of financial statements. These financial statements are regulated by government bodies to ensure that there is no misleading financial reporting.

- Analyzing

Lastly, accounting entails conducting an analysis of the results. After results have been summarized and reported, meaningful conclusions need to be drawn. Management must find out its positive and negative points. Accounting helps in doing so by means of comparison. It is common practice to compare profits, cash, sales, assets, etc with each other to analyze the performance of the business.

Importance of Accounting

Legal

Accounting helps organizations to determine their financial rights and obligations. Without proper accounting, it would be very difficult for a business to calculate, for example, the exact amount a supplier needs to be paid taking into account cost of purchase, discounts, sales tax, withholding tax, duties, refunds, etc. Accounting is therefore necessary for a business to fulfill its legal obligations and asserting its own legal rights.

Maintaining accounting records and preparing financial statements is also often a legal responsibility for businesses above a certain size.

Performance

Accounting information is summarized to produce financial statements. Financial Statements provide an overview of the financial activities of a business during a period (e.g. cash flow, income and expenses during the year) as well as information about its financial position on a specific date (e.g. amount of cash and inventory at the end of the year).

Financial Statements help owners in assessing the performance and position of their business which can guide their investment decisions (e.g. whether they should invest more in the business, diversify or dispose their investment).

Planning and Control

Accounting helps organizations to plan their finances by developing budgets and forecasts. Variance analysis provides a mechanism for the monitoring of expenses incurred by organizations by comparison with the budgeted expenditure. This process helps organizations in planning their finances ahead and controlling any deviations from the budget.

Decisions

Accounting provides a basis for managerial decisions. Examples of such decisions include:

- Investment Appraisal
- Make or Buy decisions
- Pricing Decisions
- Limiting factors analysis

Financial Accounting

Financial accounting is a specialized branch of accounting that keeps track of a company's financial transactions. Using standardized guidelines, the transactions are recorded, summarized, and presented in a financial report or financial statement such as an income statement or a balance sheet.

Companies issue financial statements on a routine schedule. The statements are considered external because they are given to people outside of the company, with the primary recipients being owners/stockholders, as well as certain lenders. If a corporation's stock is publicly traded, however, its financial statements (and other financial reporting) tend to be widely circulated, and information will likely reach secondary recipients such as competitors, customers, employees, labor organizations, and investment analysts.

It's important to point out that the purpose of financial accounting is not to report the value of a company. Rather, its purpose is to provide enough information for others to assess the value of a company for themselves.

Because external financial statements are used by a variety of people in a variety of ways, financial accounting has common rules known as accounting standards and as generally accepted accounting principles (GAAP). In the U.S., the Financial Accounting Standards Board (FASB) is the organization that develops the accounting standards and principles. Corporations whose stock is publicly traded must also comply with the reporting requirements of the Securities and Exchange Commission (SEC), an agency of the U.S. government.

Double Entry and the Accrual Basis of Accounting

At the heart of financial accounting is the system known as double entry bookkeeping (or "double entry accounting"). Each financial transaction that a company makes is recorded by using this system.

The term "double entry" means that every transaction affects at least two accounts. For example, if a company borrows $50,000 from its bank, the company's Cash account increases, and the company's Notes Payable account increases. Double entry also means that one of the accounts must have an amount entered as a debit, and one of the accounts must have an amount entered as a credit. For any given transaction, the debit amount must equal the credit amount.

The advantage of double entry accounting is this: at any given time, the balance of a company's asset accounts will equal the balance of its liability and stockholders' (or owner's) equity accounts.

Financial accounting is required to follow the accrual basis of accounting (as opposed to the "cash basis" of accounting). Under the accrual basis, revenues are reported when they are earned, not when the money is received. Similarly, expenses are reported when they are incurred, not when they are paid. For example, although a magazine publisher receives a $24 check from a customer for an annual subscription, the publisher reports as revenue a monthly amount of $2 (one-twelfth of the annual subscription amount). In the same way, it reports its property tax expense each month as one-twelfth of the annual property tax bill.

By following the accrual basis of accounting, a company's profitability, assets, liabilities and other financial information is more in line with economic reality.

Accounting Principles

If financial accounting is going to be useful, a company's reports need to be credible, easy to understand, and comparable to those of other companies. To this end, financial accounting follows a set of common rules known as accounting standards or generally accepted accounting principles (GAAP, pronounced "gap").

GAAP is based on some basic underlying principles and concepts such as the cost principle, matching principle, full disclosure, going concern, economic entity, conservatism, relevance, and reliability.

GAAP, however, is not static. It includes some very complex standards that were issued in response to some very complicated business transactions. GAAP also addresses accounting practices that may be unique to particular industries, such as utility, banking, and insurance. Often these practices are a response to changes in government regulations of the industry.

GAAP includes many specific pronouncements as issued by the Financial Accounting Standards Board (FASB, pronounced "fas-bee"). The FASB is a non-government group that researches current needs and develops accounting rules to meet those needs.

In addition to following the provisions of GAAP, any corporation whose stock is publicly traded is also subject to the reporting requirements of the Securities and Exchange Commission (SEC), an agency of the U.S. government. These requirements mandate an annual report to stockholders as well as an annual report to the SEC. The annual report to the SEC requires that independent certified public accountants audit a company's financial statements, thus giving assurance that the company has followed GAAP.

Financial Statements

Financial accounting generates the following general-purpose, external, financial statements:

- Income statement (sometimes referred to as "results of operations" or "earnings statement" or "profit and loss [P&L] statement").
- Balance sheet (sometimes referred to as "statement of financial position").
- Statement of cash flows (sometimes referred to as "cash flow statement").
- Statement of stockholders' equity.

Financial Reporting

Financial reporting is a broader concept than financial statements. In addition to the financial statements, financial reporting includes the company's annual report to stockholders, its annual report to the Securities and Exchange Commission (Form 10-K), its proxy statement, and other financial information reported by the company.

2

Types of Financial Statements

Financial statement is a formal record of the financial transactions and the financial position of an enterprise. Financial statements can be of different types, such as balance sheet, an income statement, cash flow statement or an equity statement. This chapter closely examines the different forms of financial statements such as balance sheet, cash flow statement, statement of changes in equity, etc.

Financial statements are written records of a business's financial situation. They include standard reports like the balance sheet, income or profit and loss statements, and cash flow statement. They stand as one of the more essential components of business information, and as the principal method of communicating financial information about an entity to outside parties. In a technical sense, financial statements are a summation of the financial position of an entity at a given point in time. Generally, financial statements are designed to meet the needs of many diverse users, particularly present and potential owners and creditors. Financial statements result from simplifying, condensing, and aggregating masses of data obtained primarily from a company's (or an individual's) accounting system.

Major Financial Statements

The basic financial statements of an enterprise include the 1) balance sheet (or statement of financial position), 2) income statement, 3) cash flow statement, and 4) statement of changes in owners' equity or stockholders' equity. The balance sheet provides a snapshot of an entity as of a particular date. It list the entity's assets, liabilities, and in the case of a corporation, the stockholders' equity on a specific date. The income statement presents a summary of the revenues, gains, expenses, losses, and net income or net loss of an entity for a specific period. This statement is similar to a moving picture of the entity's operations during this period of time. The cash flow statement summarizes an entity's cash receipts and cash payments relating to its operating, investing, and financing activities during a particular period. A statement of changes in owners' equity or stockholders' equity reconciles the beginning of the period equity of an enterprise with its ending balance.

Items currently reported in financial statements are measured by different attributes (for example, historical cost, current cost, current market value, net reliable value, and present value of future cash flows). Historical cost is the traditional means of presenting assets and liabilities.

Notes to financial statements are informative disclosures appended to the end of financial statements. They provide important information concerning such matters as depreciation and inventory methods used, details of long-term debt, pensions, leases, income taxes, contingent liabilities, methods of consolidation, and other matters. Notes are considered an integral part of the financial statements. Schedules and parenthetical disclosures are also used to present information not provided elsewhere in the financial statements.

Each financial statement has a heading, which gives the name of the entity, the name of the statement, and the date or time covered by the statement. The information provided in financial statements is primarily financial in nature and expressed in units of money. The information relates to an individual business enterprise. The information often is the product of approximations and estimates, rather than exact measurements. The financial statements typically reflect the financial effects of transactions and events that have already happened (i.e., historical).

Financial statements presenting financial data for two or more periods are called comparative statements. Comparative financial statements usually give similar reports for the current period and for one or more preceding periods. They provide analysts with significant information about trends and relationships over two or more years. Comparative statements are considerably more significant than are single-year statements. Comparative statements emphasize the fact that financial statements for a single accounting period are only one part of the continuous history of the company.

Interim financial statements are reports for periods of less than a year. The purpose of interim financial statements is to improve the timeliness of accounting information. Some companies issue comprehensive financial statements while others issue summary statements. Each interim period should be viewed primarily as an integral part of an annual period and should generally continue to use the generally accepted accounting principles (GAAP) that were used in the preparation of the company's latest annual report. Financial statements are often audited by independent accountants for the purpose of increasing user confidence in their reliability.

Every financial statement is prepared on the basis of several accounting assumptions: that all transactions can be expressed or measured in dollars; that the enterprise will continue in business indefinitely; and that statements will be prepared at regular intervals. These assumptions provide the foundation for the structure of financial accounting theory and practice, and explain why financial information is presented in a given manner.

Financial statements also must be prepared in accordance with generally accepted accounting principles, and must include an explanation of the company's accounting procedures and policies. Standard accounting principles call for the recording of assets and liabilities at cost; the recognition of revenue when it is realized and when a transaction has taken place (generally at the point of sale), and the recognition of expenses according to the matching principle (costs to revenues). Standard accounting principles further require that uncertainties and risks related to a company be reflected in its accounting reports and that, generally, anything that would be of interest to an informed investor should be fully disclosed in the financial statements.

Elements of Financial Statements

The Financial Accounting Standards Board (FASB) has defined the following elements of financial statements of business enterprises: assets, liabilities, equity, revenues, expenses, gains, losses, investment by owners, distribution to owners, and comprehensive income. According to FASB, the elements of financial statements are the building blocks with which financial statements are constructed. These FASB definitions, articulated in its "Elements of Financial Statements of Business Enterprises," are as follows:

- Assets are probable future economic benefits obtained or controlled by a particular entity as a result of past transactions or events.
- Comprehensive income is the change in equity (net assets) of an entity during a period from transactions and other events and circumstances from nonowner sources. It includes all changes in equity during a period except those resulting from investments by owners and distributions to owners.
- Distributions to owners are decreases in net assets of a particular enterprise resulting from transferring assets, rendering services, or incurring liabilities to owners. Distributions to owners decrease ownership interest or equity in an enterprise.
- Equity is the residual interest in the assets of an entity that remains after deducting its liabilities. In a business entity, equity is the ownership interest.
- Expenses are outflows or other uses of assets or incurring of liabilities during a period from delivering or producing goods or rendering services, or carrying out other activities that constitute the entity's ongoing major or central operation.
- Gains are increases in equity (net assets) from peripheral or incidental transactions of an entity and from all other transactions and other events and circumstances affecting the entity during a period except those that result from revenues or investments by owner.
- Investments by owners are increases in net assets of a particular enterprise resulting from transfers to it from other entities of something of value to obtain or increase ownership interest (or equity) in it.

- Liabilities are probable future sacrifices of economic benefits arising from present obligations of a particular entity to transfer assets or provide services to other entities in the future as a result of past transactions or events.
- Losses are decreases in equity (net assets) from peripheral or incidental transactions of an entity and from all other transactions and other events and circumstances affecting the entity during a period except those that result from expenses or distributions to owners.
- Revenues are inflows or other enhancements of assets of an entity or settlement of its liabilities (or a combination of both) during a period from delivering or producing goods, rendering services, or other activities that constitute the entity's ongoing major or central operations.

Subsequent Events

In accounting terminology, a subsequent event is an important event that occurs between the balance sheet date and the date of issuance of the annual report. Subsequent events must have a material effect on the financial statements. A "subsequent event" note must be issued with financial statements if the event (or events) is considered to be important enough that without such information the financial statement would be misleading if the event were not disclosed. The recognition and recording of these events often requires the professional judgment of an accountant or external auditor.

Events that effect the financial statements at the date of the balance sheet might reveal an unknown condition or provide additional information regarding estimates or judgments. These events must be reported by adjusting the financial statements to recognize the new evidence. Events that relate to conditions that did not exist on the balance sheet date but arose subsequent to that date do not require an adjustment to the financial statements. The effect of the event on the future period, however, may be of such importance that it should be disclosed in a footnote or elsewhere.

Personal Financial Statements

The reporting entity of personal financial statements is an individual, a husband and wife, or a group of related individuals. Personal financial statements are often prepared to deal with obtaining bank loans, income tax planning, retirement planning, gift and estate planning, and the public disclosure of financial affairs.

For each reporting entity, a statement of financial position is required. The statement presents assets at estimated current values, liabilities at the lesser of the discounted amount of cash to be paid or the current cash settlement amount, and net worth. A provision should also be made for estimated income taxes on the differences between the estimated current value of assets. Comparative statements for one or more periods should be presented. A statement of changes in net worth is optional.

Development Stage Company

A company is considered to be a development stage company if substantially all of its efforts are devoted to establishing a new business and either of the following is present: 1) principal operations have not begun, or 2) principal operations have begun but revenue is insignificant. Activities of a development stage enterprise frequently include financial planning, raising capital, research and development, personnel recruiting and training, and market development.

A development stage company must follow generally accepted accounting principles applicable to operating enterprises in the preparation of financial statements. In its balance sheet, the company must report cumulative net losses separately in the equity section. In its income statement it must report cumulative revenues and expenses from the inception of the enterprise. Likewise, in its cash flow statement, it must report cumulative cash flows from the inception of the enterprise. Its statement of stockholders' equity should include the number of shares issued and the date of their issuance as well as the dollar amounts received. The statement should identify the entity as a development stage enterprise and describe the nature of development stage activities. During the first period of normal operations, the enterprise must disclose its former developmental stage status in the notes section of its financial statements.

Fraudulent Financial Reporting

Fraudulent financial reporting is defined as intentional or reckless reporting, whether by act or by omission, that results in materially misleading financial statements. Fraudulent financial reporting can usually be traced to the existence of conditions in either the internal environment of the firm (e.g., inadequate internal control), or in the external environment (e.g., poor industry or overall business conditions). Excessive pressure on management, such as unrealistic profit or other performance goals, can also lead to fraudulent financial reporting.

The legal requirements for a publicly traded company when it comes to financial reporting are, not surprisingly, much more rigorous than for privately held firms. And they became even more rigorous in 2002 with the passage of the Sarbanes-Oxley Act. This legislation was passed in the wake of the stunning bankruptcy filing in 2001 by Enron, and subsequent revelations about fraudulent accounting practices within the company. Enron was only the first in a string of high-profile bankruptcies. Serious allegations of accounting fraud followed and extended beyond the bankrupt firms to their accounting firms. The legislature acted quickly to fortify financial reporting requirements and stem the decline in confidence that resulted from the wave of bankruptcies. Without confidence in the financial reports of publicly traded firms, no stock exchange can exist for long.

The Sarbanes-Oxley Act is a complex law that imposes heavy reporting requirements on all publicly traded companies. Meeting the requirements of this law has increased the workload of auditing firms. In particular, Section 404 of the Sarbanes-Oxley Act requires that a company's financial statements and annual report include an official write-up by management about the effectiveness of the company's internal controls. This section also requires that outside auditors attest to management's report on internal controls. An external audit is required in order to attest to the management report.

Private companies are not covered by the Sarbanes-Oxley Act. However, analysts suggest that even private firms should be aware of the law as it has influenced accounting practices and business expectations generally.

Auditing

The preparation and presentation of a company's financial statements are the responsibility of the management of the company. Published financial statements may be audited by an independent certified public accountant. In the case of publicly traded firms, an audit is required by law. For private firms it is not, although banks and other lenders often require such an independent check as a part of lending agreements.

During an audit, the auditor conducts an examination of the accounting system, records, internal controls, and financial statements in accordance with generally accepted auditing standards. The auditor then expresses an opinion concerning the fairness of the financial statements in conformity with generally accepted accounting principles. Four standard opinions are possible:

1. Unqualified opinion: This opinion means that all materials were made available, found to be in order, and met all auditing requirements. This is the most favorable opinion that can be rendered by an external auditor about a company's operations and records. In some cases, a company may receive an unqualified opinion with explanatory language added. Circumstances may require that the auditor add an explanatory paragraph to his or her report. When this is done the opinion is prefaced with the term, "explanatory language added."
2. Qualified opinion: This type of opinion is used for instances in which most of the company's financial materials were in order, with the exception of a certain account or transaction.
3. Adverse opinion: An adverse opinion states that the financial statements do not accurately or completely represent the company's financial position, results of operations, or cash flows in conformity with generally accepted accounting principles. Such an opinion is obviously not good news for the business being audited.
4. Disclaimer of opinion: A disclaimer of opinion states that the auditor does not express an opinion on the financial statements, generally because he or she feels

that the company did not present sufficient information. Again, this opinion casts an unfavorable light on the business being audited.

The auditor's standard opinion typically includes the following statements, among others:

The financial statements are the responsibility of the company's management; the audit was conducted according to generally accepted auditing standards; the audit was planned and performed to obtain reasonable assurance that the statements are free of material misstatements, and the audit provided a reasonable basis for an expression of an opinion concerning the fair presentation of the audit. The audit report is then signed by the auditor and a principal of the firm and dated.

Consolidated Financial Statement

Consolidated financial statements combine the financial statements of separate legal entities controlled by a parent company into one set of financial statements for the entire group of companies.

For example, let's assume that Northern Electric Power (NEP) is an electric utility with its stock traded on a stock exchange. NEP acquires all of the stock of Midwest Gas Corporation (MGC). Both NEP and MGC continue as separate legal entities. NEP is the parent company and MGC is the subsidiary company. Each of these corporations will continue to operate its respective business and each will issue its own financial statements. However, the investors and potential investors in NEP will find it helpful to see the financial results and the financial position of the economic entity (the combination of NEP and MGC) that they control.

The consolidated income statement of NEP will report all of the revenues that the economic entity earned from outside customers. (Since the sales of electricity from NEP to MGC and the sales of gas from MGC to NEP are not earned outside of the economic entity they are eliminated.) The consolidated income statement will also report all of the expenses that were incurred outside of the economic entity. (Since the purchases of electricity by MGC from NEP and the purchases of gas by NEP from MGC did not occur outside of the economic entity they are also eliminated).

The consolidated balance sheet of NEP will report all of the cash, receivables, plant, etc. of the economic entity. It will also report all of the liabilities of the economic entity. (Amounts owed and receivable between NEP and MGC are eliminated in the consolidated balance sheet).

Presentation of Consolidated Financial Statements

A parent company presenting its consolidated financial statements must present these statements along with its standalone financial statements.

The users of financial statements of a parent company are typically concerned with and are required to be educated about, the results of operations and financial position of not only the company itself but also of that group together.

This requirement is served by offering the users of financial statements:

a. Standalone financial statements of a parent; and

b. Consolidated financial statements that provide financial information about the business group as that of a lone enterprise without respect to the legal restrictions of the distinct legal entities.

Scope of Consolidated Financial Statements

A parent company which presents its consolidated financial statements must consolidate all of its subsidiaries, foreign as well as domestic. Where a company doesn't have any subsidiary, however, has associates and/or joint ventures such company also needs to prepare consolidated financial statements as per Accounting Standard 23 – Accounting for Associates in Consolidated Financial Statements and Accounting Standard 27 – Financial Reporting of Interests in JVs respectively.

Exclusion of Subsidiaries

A Subsidiary must be excluded from the consolidation when:

- Control is planned to be temporary since the subsidiary was taken over and was held exclusively for disposal in the near future.
- The subsidiary is operating under severe long-standing restrictions that considerably impair the subsidiary's ability to transfer funds to its parent.

In a consolidated financial statement, investments in such subsidiaries must be accounted for as per AS 13 – Accounting for Investments. Reasons for which a subsidiary isn't included in the consolidation must be disclosed in such consolidated financial statements.

Consolidation Procedures

While preparing a consolidated financial statement, the parent company's financial statements and its subsidiaries must be combined line by line by totaling together similar items such as assets, liabilities, income, and expenses.

For consolidating financial statements in a way to present financial information about a group as that of a lone enterprise, the below-motioned steps must be taken:

- Eliminate the cost to the parent of its investment made in each of its subsidiaries and such parent's equity portion of each of its subsidiaries, at the date when the investment in such subsidiaries are made;

- Any additional cost to the parent company of the investment in the subsidiary over the parent company's share of the equity of subsidiary, at the date on which the investment in such subsidiary is done, must be shown as goodwill for recognizing as the asset in its consolidated financial statements.
- When the cost to the parent of the investment in the subsidiary is lower than the parent company's share of the equity of subsidiary, a date on which the investment in such subsidiary is done, the difference must be treated as the capital reserve in its consolidated financial statements.
- A portion of minority interests in net income of the consolidated subsidiary for reporting period must be recognized and adjusted against income of the group for arriving at the net income which is attributable to owners of such parent company.
- A portion of minority interests in net assets of the consolidated subsidiaries must be recognized and provided for in consolidated balance sheet distinctly from the equity and liabilities of the parent company. Minority interests in net assets comprise of:
    1. Amount of equity which is attributable to the minorities at the date on which such investment in the subsidiary is done.
    2. Minorities' share of the movements in equity from the date the relationship of parent-subsidiary came in to force.

Where carrying investment amount in a subsidiary is different from the cost, such carrying amount is to be considered for the above calculations.

Accounting for Investments in the Subsidiaries in Separate Financial Statement of the Parent

In a parent company's separate financial statements, the investments made in subsidiaries must be accounted for as per AS 13 – Accounting for Investments.

Disclosures in the Financial Statements

Following disclosures must be made w.r.t. AS 21 Consolidated Financial Statements:

a. In the consolidated financial statements the list of all the subsidiaries of the parent company which includes the name, country of residence or incorporation, the share of ownership interest and, in case different, the share of voting power held.

b. In case the consolidation of particular subsidiary hasn't been made according to the grounds permissible in the accounting standard, reasons for which such subsidiary isn't included in the consolidation must be disclosed in such consolidated financial statements.

c. In the consolidated financial statements, where valid:

1. Type of relationship between a parent and its subsidiary, whether direct control or indirect control through the subsidiaries.
2. Effect of acquisition and disposal of the subsidiaries on financial position at the date of reporting results for the reporting period and on corresponding amounts for preceding period.
3. Name of the subsidiary(s) of which reporting date(s) is different.

Income Statement

The income statement is one of a company's core financial statements that shows their profit and loss over a period of time. The profit or loss is determined by taking all revenues and subtracting all expenses from both operating and non-operating activities.

The income statement is one of three statements used in both corporate finance (including financial modeling) and accounting. The statement displays the company's revenue, costs, gross profit, selling and administrative expenses, other expenses and income, taxes paid, and net profit, in a coherent and logical manner.

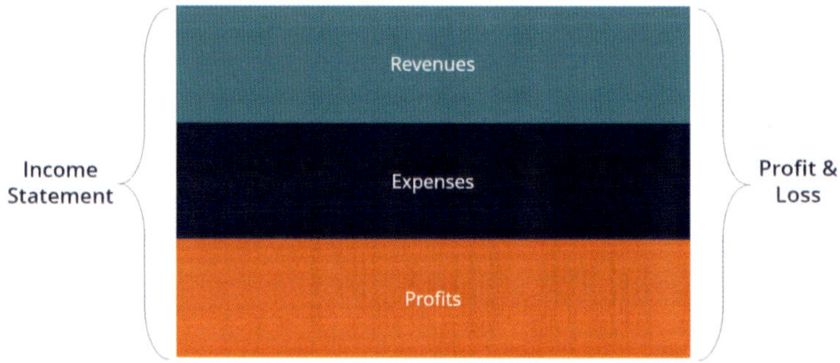

The statement is divided into time periods that logically follow the company's operations. The most common periodic division is monthly (for internal reporting), although certain companies may use a thirteen-period cycle. These periodic statements are aggregated into total values for quarterly and annual results.

This statement is a great place to begin the financial model, as it requires the least amount of information from the balance sheet and cash flow statement. Thus, in terms of information, the income statement is a predecessor to the other two core statements.

Balance Sheet

The balance sheet is one of the three fundamental financial statements and is key to both financial modeling and accounting. The balance sheet displays the company's total assets, and how these assets are financed, through either debt or equity. It can also sometimes be referred to as a statement of net worth, or a statement of financial position. The balance sheet is based on the fundamental equation: Assets = Liabilities + Equity.

A Simple Balance Sheet

CFI's Financial Analysis Course.

As such, the balance sheet is divided into two sides (or sections). The left side of the balance sheet outlines all a company's assets. On the right side, the balance sheet outlines the companies liabilities and shareholders' equity. On either side, the main line items are generally classified by liquidity. More liquid accounts like Inventory, Cash, and Trades Payables are placed before illiquid accounts such as Plant, Property, and Equipment (PP&E) and Long-Term Debt. The assets and liabilities are also separated into two categories: current asset/liabilities and non-current (long-term) assets/liabilities.

Example Balance Sheet

Below is an example of Amazon's 2017 balance sheet. As you will see, it starts with current assets, then non-current assets and total assets. Below that is liabilities and stockholders' equity which includes current liabilities, non-current liabilities, and finally shareholders' equity.

CONSOLIDATED BALANCE SHEETS
(in millions, except per share data)

	December 31, 2016	December 31, 2017
ASSETS		
Current assets:		
Cash and cash equivalents	$ 19,334	$ 20,522
Marketable securities	6,647	10,464
Inventories	11,461	16,047
Accounts receivable, net and other	8,339	13,164
Total current assets	45,781	60,197
Property and equipment, net	29,114	48,866
Goodwill	3,784	13,350
Other assets	4,723	8,897
Total assets	$ 83,402	$ 131,310
LIABILITIES AND STOCKHOLDERS' EQUITY		
Current liabilities:		
Accounts payable	$ 25,309	$ 34,616
Accrued expenses and other	13,739	18,170
Unearned revenue	4,768	5,097
Total current liabilities	43,816	57,883
Long-term debt	7,694	24,743
Other long-term liabilities	12,607	20,975
Commitments and contingencies (Note 7)		
Stockholders' equity:		
Preferred stock, $0.01 par value:		
Authorized shares — 500		
Issued and outstanding shares — none	—	—
Common stock, $0.01 par value:		
Authorized shares — 5,000		
Issued shares — 500 and 507		
Outstanding shares — 477 and 484	5	5
Treasury stock, at cost	(1,837)	(1,837)
Additional paid-in capital	17,186	21,389
Accumulated other comprehensive loss	(985)	(484)
Retained earnings	4,916	8,636
Total stockholders' equity	19,285	27,709
Total liabilities and stockholders' equity	$ 83,402	$ 131,310

See accompanying notes to consolidated financial statements.

Cash Flow Statement

The Cash flow statement is a very important financial statement, as it reveals how much cash the company is actually generating. Is this information not revealed in the profit and loss (P&L) statement you may think? Well, the answer is both a yes and a no.

Consider the Following Scenario

Assume a simple coffee shop selling coffee and short eats. All the sales the shop does is mostly on cash basis, meaning if a customer wants to have a cup of coffee and a snack, he needs to have enough money to buy what he wants. Going by that on a particular day, assume the shop manages to sell $ 2,500/- worth of coffee and $ 3,000/- worth of snacks. It is evident that the shop's income is $ 5,500/- for that day. $ 5,500/- is reported as revenues in P&L, and there is no ambiguity with this.

Now think about another business that sells laptops. For sake of simplicity, let us assume that the shop sells only 1 type of laptop at a standard fixed rate of $ 25,000/- per laptop. Assume on a certain day, the shop manages to sells 20 such laptops. Clearly the revenue for the shop would be $ 25,000 x 20 = $ 500,000/-. But what if 5 of the 20 laptops were sold on credit? A credit sale is when the customer takes the product today but pays the cash at a later point in time. In this situation here is how the numbers would look:

Cash sale: 15 * 25000 = $ 375,000/-

Credit sale: 5 * 25000 = $ 125,000/-

Total sales: $ 500,000/-

If this shop was to show its total revenue in its P&L statement, you would just see a revenue of $ 500,000/- which may seem good on the face of it. However, how much of this $ 500,000/- is actually present in the company's bank account is not clear. What if this company had a loan of $ 400,000/- that had to be repaid back urgently? Even though the company has a sale of $ 500,000 it has only $ 375,000/- in its account. This means the company has a cash crunch, as it cannot meet its debt obligations.

The cash flow statement captures this information. A statement of cash flows should be presented as an integral part of an entity's financial statements. Hence in this context evaluation of the cash flow statement is highly critical as it reveals amongst other things, the true cash position of the company.

To sum up, every company's financial performance is not so much dependent on the profits earned during a period, but more realistically on liquidity or cash flows.

Statement of Changes in Equity

The statement of changes in equity is a reconciliation of the beginning and ending balances in a company's equity during a reporting period. It is not considered an essential part of the monthly financial statements, and so is the most likely of all the financial statements not to be issued. However, it is a common part of the annual financial statements. The statement starts with the beginning equity balance, and then adds or subtracts such items as profits and dividend payments to arrive at the ending ending balance. The general calculation structure of the statement is:

Beginning equity + Net income – Dividends +/- Other changes

= Ending equity

The transactions most likely to appear on this statement are as follows:

- Net profit or loss
- Dividend payments
- Proceeds from the sale of stock
- Treasury stock purchases
- Gains and losses recognized directly in equity
- Effects of changes due to errors in prior periods
- Effects of changes in fair value for certain assets.

The statement of changes in equity is most commonly presented as a separate statement, but can also be added to another financial statement.

It is also possible to provide a greatly expanded version of the statement that discloses the various elements of equity. For example, it could separately identify the par value of common stock, additional paid-in capital, retained earnings, and treasury stock, with all of these elements then rolling up into the ending equity total.

To prepare the statement, follow these steps:

1. Create separate accounts in the general ledger for each type of equity. Thus, there are different accounts for the par value of stock, additional paid-in capital, and retained earnings. Each of these accounts is represented by a separate column in the statement.
2. Transfer every transaction within each equity account to a spreadsheet, and identify it in the spreadsheet.
3. Aggregate the transactions within the spreadsheet into similar types, and transfer them to separate line items in the statement of changes in equity.
4. Complete the statement, and verify that the beginning and ending balances in it match the general ledger, and that the aggregated line items within it add up to the ending balances for all columns.

Example

Following is an illustrative example of a Statement of Changes in Equity

	Share Capital	Retained Earnings	Revaluation Surplus	Total Equity
	USD	USD	USD	USD
Balance at 1 January 2011	100,000	30,000	-	130,000
Changes in accounting policy	-	-	-	-

Correction of prior period error	-	-	-	-
Restated balance	100,000	30,000	-	130,000
Changes in equity for the year 2011				
Issue of share capital	-	-	-	-
Income for the year	-	25,000	-	25,000
Revaluation gain	-	-	10,000	10,000
Dividends	-	(15,000)	-	(15,000)
Balance at 31 December 2011	100,000	40,000	10,000	150,000
Changes in equity for the year 2012				
Issue of share capital	-	-	-	-
Income for the year	-	30,000	-	30,000
Revaluation gain	-	-	5,000	5,000
Dividends	-	(20,000)	-	(20,000)
Balance at 31 December 2012	100,000	50,000	15,000	165,000

Components

Following are the main elements of statement of changes in equity:

Opening Balance

This represents the balance of shareholders' equity reserves at the start of the comparative reporting period as reflected in the prior period's statement of financial position. The opening balance is unadjusted in respect of the correction of prior period errors rectified in the current period and also the effect of changes in accounting policy implemented during the year as these are presented separately in the statement of changes in equity.

Effect of Changes in Accounting Policies

Since changes in accounting policies are applied retrospectively, an adjustment is required in stockholders' reserves at the start of the comparative reporting period to restate the opening equity to the amount that would be arrived if the new accounting policy had always been applied.

Effect of Correction of Prior Period Error

The effect of correction of prior period errors must be presented separately in the statement of changes in equity as an adjustment to opening reserves. The effect of the corrections may not be netted off against the opening balance of the equity reserves so that the amounts presented in current period statement might be easily reconciled and traced from prior period financial statements.

Restated Balance

This represents the equity attributable to stockholders at the start of the comparative period after the adjustments in respect of changes in accounting policies and correction of prior period errors as explained above.

Changes in Share Capital

Issue of further share capital during the period must be added in the statement of changes in equity whereas redemption of shares must be deducted therefrom. The effects of issue and redemption of shares must be presented separately for share capital reserve and share premium reserve.

Dividends

Dividend payments issued or announced during the period must be deducted from shareholder equity as they represent distribution of wealth attributable to stockholders.

Income / Loss for the Period

This represents the profit or loss attributable to shareholders during the period as reported in the income statement.

Changes in Revaluation Reserve

Revaluation gains and losses recognized during the period must be presented in the statement of changes in equity to the extent that they are recognized outside the income statement. Revaluation gains recognized in income statement due to reversal of previous impairment losses however shall not be presented separately in the statement of changes in equity as they would already be incorporated in the profit or loss for the period.

Other Gains & Losses

Any other gains and losses not recognized in the income statement may be presented in the statement of changes in equity such as actuarial gains and losses arising from the application of IAS 19 Employee Benefit.

Closing Balance

This represents the balance of shareholders' equity reserves at the end of the reporting period as reflected in the statement of financial position.

Purpose & Importance

Statement of changes in equity helps users of financial statement to identify the factors that cause a change in the owners' equity over the accounting periods. Whereas movement in shareholder reserves can be observed from the balance sheet, statement of changes in equity discloses significant information about equity reserves that is not presented separately elsewhere in the financial statements which may be useful in understanding the nature of change in equity reserves. Examples of such information include share capital issue and redemption during the period, the effects of changes in accounting policies and correction of prior period errors, gains and losses recognized outside income statement, dividends declared and bonus shares issued during the period.

References

- Financial-statements, encyclopedia: inc.com, Retrieved 09 March 2018
- Consolidated-financial-statements: accountingcoach.com, Retrieved 28 May 2018
- As-21-consolidated-financial-statements: cleartax.in, Retrieved 16 April 2018
- Balance-sheet, accounting: corporatefinanceinstitute.com, Retrieved 21 April 2018
- Statement-of-changes-in-equity: accountingtools.com, Retrieved 20 June 2018

3

Statement of Profit or Loss

A statement of profit or loss or an income statement is a financial statement, which reflects a company's revenues and expenses for a given period. This chapter has been carefully written to provide an introduction to the varied concepts of income statement such as profit and loss, income and expense, etc.

Income

Income is the revenue a business earns from selling its goods and services or the money an individual receives in compensation for his or her labor, services, or investments. Businesses report this figure on the income statement whereas individuals report theirs on the form 1040.

The accounting profession is similar to other professions where words have many different meanings depending on the context. Income is used in the accounting profession to mean several different things.

One meaning of income refers to revenue or sales. Revenue is the money that a company receives from selling goods or services throughout the course of business. Revenue is an equity account that has a credit balance. Throughout the year sales are recorded in the revenue accounts and posted to trial balance. The revenue is then reported on the first line of the income statement. This is often called gross income, total sales, or top line sales since it includes all the company income and sales before deducting expenses.

Another meaning of income refers to net income. Net income is completely different than gross income. Net income appears at the bottom of the income statement after all of the cost of goods sold and operating expenses have been subtracted out. Net income equals the total company revenues minus total company expenses. As you can see, the net income definition is much different than the revenue definition of income.

The generic term income is most commonly used to refer to net income instead of revenues. Be careful when you read examples or see problems that reference a company's income. You'll need to analyze the question and figure out what meaning of income the question is using. More often than not, the net income definition will be used.

Example

Ted's Pizzeria sells pizzas for $10 each. One of Ted's customers' orders 10 pizzas. Thus, Ted records the income by crediting the revenues account for $100 and debiting the cash account for $100.

Individuals receive income through earning wages by working and/or making investments into financial assets such as stocks, bonds and real estate. For instance, an investor's stock holding may pay income in the form of an annual 5% dividend. In most countries, earned income is taxed by the government before it is received. The revenue generated by income taxes finances government actions and programs as determined by federal and state budgets. The Internal Revenue Service (IRS) calls income from sources other than a job, such as investment income, "unearned income".

Taxable Income

Income from wages, salaries, interest, dividends, business income, capital gains and pensions received during a given tax year are considered taxable income in the United States. Other taxable income includes annuity payments, rental income, farming and fishing income, unemployment compensation, retirement plan distributions and stock options. Lesser known taxable income includes gambling income, bartending income and jury duty pay.

Tax-Exempt and Tax-Reduced Income

Types of income that may be tax-exempt include interest income from U.S. Treasury securities (which is exempt at the state and local levels), interest from municipal bonds (which is potentially exempt at the federal, state and local levels) and capital gains that are offset by capital losses. Types of income taxed at lower rates include qualified dividends and long-term capital gains. Social Security income is sometimes taxable, depending on how much other income the taxpayer receives during the year.

Disposable and Discretionary Income

Disposable income is money that's remaining after paying taxes. Individuals spend disposable income on necessities, such as housing, food and transportation. Discretionary income is money that's remaining after paying all necessary expenses. People spend discretionary income on items like vacations, restaurant meals, cable television and movies. In a recession, individuals tend to be more prudent with their discretionary income. For example, a family may use their discretionary income to make extra payments on their mortgage or save it for an unexpected expense.

Comprehensive Income

Comprehensive income is the change in equity during a period resulting from transactions and other events, other than those changes resulting from transactions with owners in their capacity as owners.

Comprehensive income is generally defined as a change in a company's net assets which can be accredited to the events which are not under the owners' control. Calculating comprehensive income can present a corporation with valuable info about the all-round financial stability of the business. Besides, using the basic formula of determining comprehensive income presents an easily understandable snapshot of how the company has performed since the previous analysis.

Comprehensive income is the total of net income and other items (other comprehensive income) which must find a way around the comprehensive income statement since they have not been realized, counting items like an unrealized holding profit or loss from on hand sale securities and foreign currency translation profits and losses. These items are, however, not a part of net income but are still important enough to be counted in comprehensive income, providing a user with a bigger and more comprehensive picture of the entity as a whole.

Financial Analysis of Comprehensive Income

The key attempt of comprehensive income is to evaluate the sum total of all financial and operating events which have changed the value of an owner's interest in a business. It is evaluated on a per-share basis to incarcerate the effects of dilution and options. Moreover, it cancels out the equity transactions' effects for which the owner would be uninterested, like share buy-backs, dividend payments, and share issues at market value.

It is estimated by the reconciliation of book-value per share from the commencement of the time period to the closing stages of that period. This is abstractly the same as measuring the growth of a child by finding the difference between his heights on every birthday. All other line items are estimated, and the equation is then solved for comprehensive income.

Other Comprehensive Income

Other comprehensive income is those revenues, expenses, gains, and losses under both Generally Accepted Accounting Principles and International Financial Reporting Standards that are excluded from net income on the income statement. This means that they are instead listed after net income on the income statement.

Revenues, expenses, gains and losses appear in other comprehensive income when they have not yet been realized. Something has been realized when the underlying transaction has been completed, such as when an investment is sold. Thus, if your company has invested in bonds and the value of those bonds changes, you recognize the difference as a gain or loss in other comprehensive income. Once you sell the bonds, you have then realized the gain or loss associated with the bonds, and can then shift the gain or loss out of other comprehensive income and into a line item higher in the income statement, so that it is a part of net income.

Examples of items that may be classified in other comprehensive income are:

- Unrealized holding gains or losses on investments that are classified as available for sale.
- Foreign currency translation gains or losses.
- Pension plan gains or losses.
- Pension prior service costs or credits.

It is acceptable to either report components of other comprehensive income net of related tax effects, or before related tax effects with a single aggregate income tax expense or benefit shown that relates to all of the other comprehensive income items.

Other comprehensive income is designed to give the reader of a company's financial statements a more comprehensive view of the financial status of the entity, though in practice it is possible that it introduces too much complexity to the income statement.

Total comprehensive income is the combination of profit or loss and other comprehensive income.

Deferred Income

Deferred Revenue (also called Unearned Revenue) is generated when a company receives payment for goods and/or services that it has not yet earned. In accrual accounting, revenue is only recognized when it is earned. If a customer pays for good/services in advance, the company does not record any revenue on its income statement and instead records a liability on its balance sheet.

Liabilities and stockholders' equity		
Current liabilities:		
Accounts payable, accrued expenses and other liabilities	$ 1,752,664	$ 1,349,338
Deferred revenue	5,505,689	4,267,667
Total current liabilities	7,258,353	5,617,005
Deferred revenue, noncurrent	37,113	23,886
Convertible 0.25% senior notes, net	1,116,360	1,088,097
Term loan	497,221	0
Loan assumed on 50 Fre[illegible]	[illegible]	197,998
Revolving credit facility	196,542	0
Other noncurrent liabilities	780,939	833,065
Total liabilities	10,084,796	7,760,051
Commitments and contingencies (Notes 13 and 15)		

Unearned Revenue

Example of Deferred Revenue

Let's look at a detailed example of the accounting entries a company would make when deferred revenue is created and then depleted.

On August 1, Cloud Storage Co received a $1,200 payment for a one-year contract from a new client. Since the services are to be expensed over a year, the company must take a year to earn the revenue and divide it into monthly amounts of $100.

On August 1, the company would record a revenue of $0 on the income statement. On the balance sheet, cash would increase by $1,200 and a liability called deferred revenue of $1,200 would be created.

On September 1, the company would record a revenue of $100 on the income statement. On the balance sheet, cash would be the unaffected and the deferred revenue liability would reduce to $1,100 while net income of $100 would be added to retained earnings in shareholders' equity.

The pattern would repeat each month until the end of 12 months when total revenue recognized over the period is $1,200, retained earnings are $1,200 and cash is $1,200. At that point, the deferred revenue from the transaction is now $0.

Benefits of Record Deferred Revenue

The simple answer is that they are required to, due to the accounting principles of revenue recognition. Just as expenses are accrued and smoothed out over time, so are revenues.

The timing of payments from customers can be volatile and unpredictable, so it makes sense to ignore the timing of the cash payment and recognize revenue when it is earned.

Cash From Operating Activities

We've seen what happens to the income statement and balance sheet. Now, let's look at the impact on the cash flow statement.

Referring to the example above, on August 1, when the company's net income is $0, it would see an increase in current liabilities of $1,200, which would result in cash from operating activities of $1,200.

In all subsequent months, cash from operations would be $0 as each $100 increment in net income would be offset by a corresponding $100 decrease in current liabilities (the deferred revenue account).

Recording Deferred Revenue

You will record deferred revenue on your balance sheet. What type of account is deferred revenue? You will record deferred revenue on your business balance sheet as a liability, not an asset.

Receiving a payment is normally considered an asset. But, prepayments are liabilities because it is not yet earned, and you still owe something to a customer. The deferred revenue turns into earned revenue (which is an asset) only after the customer receives the good or service.

Let's say you own a candy shop. A customer pays you $180 for a 12-month candy subscription. You need to make a deferred revenue journal entry. When you receive the money, you will debit it to your cash account because the amount of cash your business has increased. And, you will credit your deferred revenue account because the amount of deferred revenue is increasing

Date	Account	Notes	Debit	Credit
1/11	Cash	Payment for candy	180.00	180.00
	Deferred revenue	subscription		

Each month, one-twelfth of the deferred revenue will become earned revenue. In this case, $15 per month will become revenue. You must make an adjusting entry to decrease (debit) your deferred revenue account and increase (credit) your revenue account.

Date	Account	Notes	Debit	Credit
1/11	Deferred revenue	One month of candy	15.00	15.00
	Revenue	subscription		

Calculating Deferred Revenue

Deferred revenue is easy to calculate. When a customer gives you an advance payment, you will increase your deferred revenue account. As you deliver goods or services, your deferred revenue account will decrease.

Expense

An expense is the reduction in value of an asset as it is used to generate revenue. If the underlying asset is to be used over a long period of time, the expense takes the form of depreciation, and is charged ratably over the useful life of the asset. If the expense is for an immediately consumed item, such as a salary, then it is usually charged to expense as incurred. Common expenses are:

- Cost of goods sold
- Rent expense
- Wages expense
- Utilities expense

If an expenditure is for a minor amount that may not be consumed for a long period of time, it is usually charged to expense at once, to eliminate the accounting staff time that would otherwise be required to track it as an asset.

Under cash basis accounting, an expense is usually recorded only when a cash payment has been made to a supplier or an employee. Under the accrual basis of accounting, an expense is recorded, when there is a reduction in the value of an asset, irrespective of any related cash outflow.

The purchase of an asset may be recorded as an expense if the amount paid is less than the capitalization limit used by a company. If the amount paid had been higher than the capitalization limit, then it instead would have been recorded as an asset and charged to expense at a later date, when the asset was consumed.

The accounting for an expense usually involves one of the following transactions:

- Debit to expense, credit to cash. Reflects a cash payment.
- Debit to expense, credit to accounts payable. Reflects a purchase made on credit.
- Debit to expense, credit to asset account. Reflects the charging to expense of an asset, such as depreciation expense on a fixed asset.
- Debit to expense, credit to other liabilities account. Reflects a payment not involving trade payables, such as the interest payment on a loan, or an accrued expense.

Under the matching principle, expenses are typically recognized in the same period in which related revenues are recognized. For example, if goods are sold in January, then both the revenues and cost of goods sold related to the sale transaction should be recorded in January.

An expense is not the same as an expenditure. An expenditure is a payment or the incurrence of a liability, whereas an expense represents the consumption of an asset. Thus, a company could make a $10,000 expenditure of cash for a fixed asset, but the $10,000 asset would only be charged to expense over the term of its useful life. Thus, an expenditure generally occurs up front, while the recognition of an expense might be spread over an extended period of time.

Expense management is the concept of reviewing expenses to determine which ones can be safely reduced or eliminated without having an offsetting negative impact on revenues or on the development of future products or services. Budgets and historical trend analysis are expense management tools.

Recording an Expense

Expenses are recorded on the debit side of an expense account (which is an income statement account) and a credit is recorded to either a liability or an asset account in accordance with double-entry bookkeeping.

When the expense is recorded on the profit & loss report is dependent upon the accounting method chosen by a business. Under the accrual method of accounting, an expense is recorded when it is incurred by a business (which might differ from when cash actually changes hand).

For example: A business pays for internet service in their offices monthly but receives and pays the bill the following month. However, they will record the rent for the month the cost was incurred even though payment was made the following month under accrual accounting.

Registering an expense under the cash accounting method, on the other hand, means that each expense is recorded only when money actually changes hands.

For example: A business pays for electricity quarterly, and receives the bill at the end of each quarter. Although the period covers several months, the amount is only entered into the record at the end of each quarter when the bill is paid.

Expenses you can Claim

As a freelancer or small business owner, you can claim certain expenses against tax. As of 2016/17, the personal allowance in the UK is £11,000. This means that you can offset up to this amount to lower your tax payments.

Allowable expenses include but are not limited to the following:

- Cost of office supplies such as paper, pens, ink toner, etc.
- Travel costs such as mileage, as long as it is specifically for business operations.
- Costs of running your office, including electricity, internet, heating, etc.
- Marketing and advertising fees.
- Supplies purchased for resale, such as raw materials.

Profit

Profit is a financial benefit that is realized when the amount of revenue gained from a business activity exceeds the expenses, costs and taxes needed to sustain the activity. Any profit that is gained goes to the business's owners, who may or may not decide to spend it on the business. Profit is calculated as total revenue less total expenses.

Profit is the money a business makes after accounting for all expenses. Regardless of whether the business is a couple of kids running a lemonade stand or a publicly traded multinational company, consistently earning profit is every company's goal. As a result, much of business performance is based on profitability in its various forms. Some analysts are interested in top-line profitability, whereas others are interested in profitability before expenses, such as taxes and interest, and still others are only concerned with profitability after all expenses have been paid.

There are three major types of profit that analysts analyze: gross profit, operating profit and net profit. Each type gives the analyst more information about a company's performance, especially when compared against other time periods and industry competitors. All three levels of profitability can be found on the income statement.

Gross Profit Margin

One of the most commonly used ratios is the gross profit margin, which looks at gross profit as a percentage of turnover (sales). You will find both of these figures in the income statement.

The formula used is gross profit divided by turnover, multiplied by a hundred to turn it into a percentage.

For example: An organization's

Gross profit is $ 300,000

Sales/Revenue were $ 1,200,000

Its percentage gross profit margin would be ($ 300,000 ÷ $ 1,200,000) x 100 = 25%

This means that for every $ 1 of sales the organization achieves, profit (after taking off the costs of production) is 25 cents.

Many people are often confused by the terms 'gross profit margin' and 'mark-up.' The definition of each term shows how they differ and also shows that you use a different formula to arrive at a figure for each.

Gross profit margin - expresses gross profit as a percentage of total sales.

Mark-up - is the figure or percentage added by management to cover the cost of goods and the required profit margin for a product or service.

From these definitions you can see that the key difference is that management have control over and define what they require as a mark-up, whereas gross profit is dependent on how many sales are made and their value, which management can set targets for, but cannot control directly.

Industries often have what is considered an acceptable range for their mark-up, without which an organization would not be able to operate. You should investigate whether the sector you are interested in has such a range.

The formula for calculating mark-up is:

Mark-up = (total revenue - cost of sales) / cost of sales

This is then multiplied by 100 to give a percentage

For example: An organization's

Sales/Income was $ 1,200,000

Cost of Sales is $ 900,000

Its percentage mark-up would be ($ 1,200,000 - $ 900,000) ÷ $ 900,000 = 0.33 x 100 = 33%

This means that to maintain their profitability the organization needs to mark-up by a third.

Net Profit Margin

This ratio is similar to the gross profit margin but looks at net profit as a percentage of turnovers. Net profit is shown on the income statement and is defined as follows:

Net profit is the figure left after all operating and non-operating expenses have been deducted from total revenue or income.

To calculate the net profit margin of an organization as a percentage you would divide net profit by total revenue or income and multiply the answer by a hundred to turn it into a percentage.

For example: An organization's

Sales/Revenue was $ 1,200,000

Net Profit is $ 120,000

Its percentage net profit would be = ($ 120,000 ÷ $ 1,200,000) x 100 = 10%

You need to be mindful that your net profit is calculated after taking account of all costs and therefore can be affected by a variety of things, such as:

- Declining gross profit
- Increased selling
- Rising administration costs

If your net profit percentage is declining it is worth looking at your costs on an individual basis to see what you can do about those that have increased the most as a proportion of sales.

It is important to look at the trend that emerges over several accounting periods, as opposed to individual figures. The ratios can be used to measure periods other than a full year, as long as you have the relevant income statements.

Return on Assets

You can also measure the level of profit compared to the value of net assets invested in an organization. The assets are the major items that need to be in place for the organization to operate.

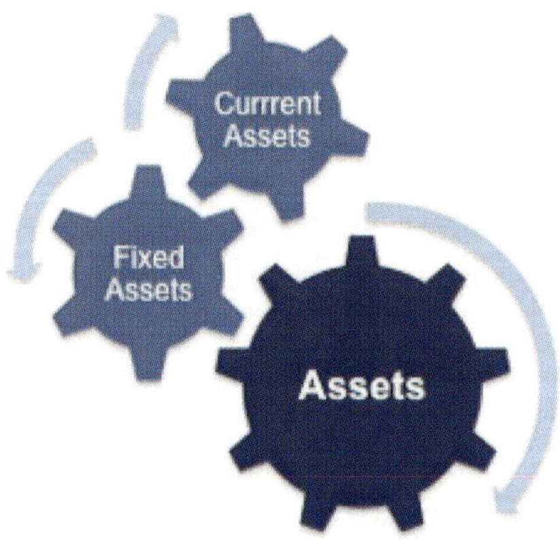

These include such items as:

- Fixed assets
- Buildings

- Plant
- Vehicles
- Computers, etc.
- Current assets
- Stock
- Debtors
- Cash

The organization's total net assets are calculated by taking total liabilities from total assets. This represents the amount of capital invested in the organization. Your net assets figure can be taken directly from the balance sheet. You can therefore look at the net profit as a percentage of capital employed.

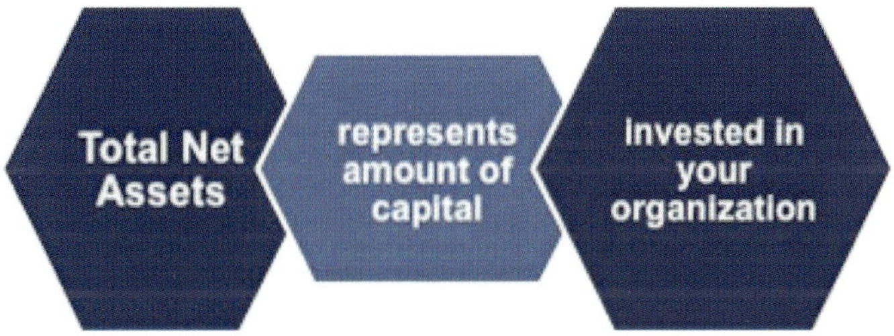

The return that an organization can expect depends on the industry sector and the economic cycle. However, it remains a good measure of operational efficiency for an organization.

The ratio is calculated by dividing net assets by net profit and then multiplying it by a hundred to turn it into a percentage, as this is the usual way it is expressed.

You would find the net profit figure on the income statement and the net assets would be shown on the corresponding balance sheet.

For example:

An organization's

- Net Profit is $ 120,000

- Net Assets are $ 60,000

Its return on assets would be $(\$60{,}000 \div \$120{,}000)\ x\ 100 = 50\%$

When calculating this ratio you can choose to express it using figures before or after tax.

Capital employed is the net amount invested in your organization by its investors or owners and is taken from the balance sheet. Many people consider this the most important ratio overall and it is useful to compare the results with a return that can be obtained outside of the organization - for example, a low-risk investment in government bonds. The organization's return on assets can be improved either by increasing profitability or decreasing the capital employed.

Loss

A loss isn't realized until it actually hits your pocketbook. Suppose your business holds stock in another company, and that stock drops $ 5,000 in value. If you still own the stock, the loss is only on paper – what accountants call an unrealized loss. If you sell the stock and eat the $ 5,000, it becomes realized. When you make out your financial statements, you treat realized and unrealized losses differently.

Unrealized Losses

Just because you haven't realized a loss yet doesn't mean you can ignore it in your financial statements. You report unrealized losses and gains on the balance sheet as "other comprehensive income." The balance sheet includes three sections: owners' equity, liabilities and assets. You enter other comprehensive income in the owners' equity section. Equity will increase or dwindle, depending whether you record a loss or a gain.

Your income statement is where you report your profits and losses for a given period – a month, a quarter, a year. It's the financial statement that measures your profitability. If you earned more than you spent, you have net income. If you lost more than you made, you have a net loss. It covers not only the money from your business operations but all income and all expenses, for every reason.

If you sell an asset at a loss – stock, a car, a building, a subsidiary – you report it as a realized loss on the income statement. Suppose you have a delivery truck with a book value of $ 10,000. You sell it, but only receive $ 7,500 – a $ 2,500 realized loss. You then make a negative $ 2,500 entry on the income statement.

The statement reports three types of losses. First are expenses associated with your primary operations. If you deliver flowers, that might include the cost of buying or growing them, plus gas and other expenses for your truck. Second come "nonoperating" expenses, such as interest on loans. Nonoperating losses are the third category. That's where you report realized losses on investments and assets.

Retained Earnings

When you realize a loss, that changes where you record it on the balance sheet. Suppose you have a $ 5,000 unrealized loss recorded as other comprehensive income. You sell the asset and realize the loss. Now you remove the loss from other comprehensive income and report it in retained earnings instead. Retained earnings are the profits your company made that weren't distributed to shareholders as a dividend.

Earnings may not be in the form of cash: If you spent $ 60,000 of your profits on new equipment, that still counts as $ 60,000 of new equipment. If you sell the equipment for $ 45,000 cash, that's $ 15,000 less in the retained earnings account.

Income Statement

The income statement also called a profit and loss statement is a report made by company management that shows the revenue, expenses, and net income or loss for a period. The income statement is one of the main four financial statements that are issued by companies: balance sheet, income statement, statement of owner's equity, and statement of cash flows.

The income statement shows income and expenses for a specific period of time. This could be monthly, quarterly, semi-annually, or annually. A January income statement for example would show all the income and expenses for the month. It would also show the net income or loss at the end of January. Income statements created for management are usually shorter in time frame. These weekly or monthly income statements help management evaluate the company's performance. Quarterly and annual income statements are more commonly used by investors and creditors to track the overall performance of the company.

Income statements usually include a heading with the name of the company, the title of the statement, and the time period. Depending on the company's size and complexity, the income statement can be large or small. A condensed income statement will have three main categories: revenues, expenses, and net income or loss. Revenues are listed and totaled first with expenses following. The expenses are usually sorted either alphabetically or by dollar amount. After the expenses are totaled, net income can be calculated by subtracting the total expenses from the total income.

Example

Jazz Music Shop, Inc. Income Statement For the Year Ended December 31, 2015		
Revenues		
Merchandise Sales	$ 5,000.00	
Music Lesson Income	1,400.00	
Total Revenues:		$ 6,400.00
Expenses		
Salaries	500	
Rent expense	100	
Depreciation expense	234	
Utilities expense	950	
Supplies expense	31	
Total Expenses:		1,815.00
Net Income		$ 4,585.00

Components of an Income Statement

The income statement may have minor variations between different companies, as expenses and income will be dependent on the type of operations or business conducted. However, there are several generic line items that are commonly seen in the income statement.

The most common income statement items include:

Revenue/Sales

Sales Revenue is the company's revenue from sales or services, displayed at the very top of the statement. This value will be gross of the costs associated with creating the goods sold or in providing services. Some companies have multiple revenue streams that add to a total revenue line.

Cost of Goods Sold (COGS)

Cost of Goods Sold (COGS) is a line-item that aggregates the direct costs associated with selling products to generate revenue. This line item can also be called Cost of Sales if the company is a service business. Direct costs can include labor, parts, materials, and an allocation of other expenses such as depreciation.

Gross Profit

Gross Profit Gross profit is calculated by subtracting Cost of Goods Sold (or Cost of Sales) from Sales Revenue.

Marketing, Advertising, and Promotion Expenses

Most businesses have some expenses related to selling goods and/or services. Marketing, advertising, and promotion expenses are often grouped together as they are similar expenses, all related to selling.

General and Administrative (G&A) Expenses

SG&A Expenses include the selling, general, and the administrative section that contains all other indirect costs associated with running the business. This includes salaries and wages, rent and office expenses, insurance, travel expenses, and sometimes depreciation and amortization, along with other operational expenses. Entities may, however, elect to separate out depreciation and amortization in its own section.

Other Expenses

Businesses often have other expenses that are unique to their industry. Other expenses may include things such as fulfillment, technology, and research and development (R&D) costs.

EBITDA

EBITDA, while not present in all income statements, stands for Earnings before Interest, Tax, Depreciation, and Amortization. It is calculated by subtracting SG&A expenses (excluding amortization and depreciation) from gross profit.

Depreciation & Amortization Expense

Depreciation and amortization are non-cash expenses that are created by accountants to spread out the cost of capital assets such as Property, Plant, and Equipment (PP&E).

Operating Income

Operating Income represents what's earned from regular business operations. In other words, it's the profit before any non-operating income, non-operating expenses, interest or taxes are subtracted from revenues. EBIT is a term commonly used in finance and stands for Earnings before Interest and Tax.

Interest

Interest expense: It is common for companies to split out interest expense and interest income as a separate line item in the income statement. This is done to be able to reconcile the difference between EBIT and EBT. Interest expense is determined by the debt schedule.

EBT (Pre-Tax Income)

EBT stands for Earnings before Tax, also known as pre-tax income, and is found by subtracting interest expense from Operating Income. This is the final subtotal before arriving at net income.

Income Taxes

Income Taxes refer to the relevant taxes charged on pre-tax income. The total tax expense can consist of both current taxes and future taxes.

Net Income

Net Income is calculated by deducting income taxes from pre-tax income. This is the amount that flows into retained earnings on the balance sheet, after deductions for any dividends.

A Real Example of an Income Statement

CONSOLIDATED STATEMENTS OF OPERATIONS
(in millions, except per share data)

	Year Ended December 31,		
	2015	2016	2017
Net product sales	$ 79,268	$ 94,665	$ 118,573
Net service sales	27,738	41,322	59,293
Total net sales	107,006	135,987	177,866
Operating expenses:			
Cost of sales	71,651	88,265	111,934
Fulfillment	13,410	17,619	25,249
Marketing	5,254	7,233	10,069
Technology and content	12,540	16,085	22,620
General and administrative	1,747	2,432	3,674
Other operating expense, net	171	167	214
Total operating expenses	104,773	131,801	173,760
Operating income	2,233	4,186	4,106
Interest income	50	100	202
Interest expense	(459)	(484)	(848)
Other income (expense), net	(256)	90	346
Total non-operating income (expense)	(665)	(294)	(300)
Income before income taxes	1,568	3,892	3,806
Provision for income taxes	(950)	(1,425)	(769)
Equity-method investment activity, net of tax	(22)	(96)	(4)
Net income	$ 596	$ 2,371	$ 3,033
Basic earnings per share	$ 1.28	$ 5.01	$ 6.32
Diluted earnings per share	$ 1.25	$ 4.90	$ 6.15
Weighted-average shares used in computation of earnings per share:			
Basic	467	474	480
Diluted	477	484	493

See accompanying notes to consolidated financial statements.

Above is an example of Amazon's consolidated statement of operations, or income statement, for the years ended December 31, 2015 – 2017. Take a look at the P&L and then read a breakdown of it below.

Starting at the top we see that Amazon has two different revenue streams – products and services – which combine to form total revenue.

There is no gross profit subtotal, as the cost of sales is grouped will all other expenses, which include fulfillment, marketing, technology, content, general and administration (G&A), and other expenses.

After deducting all the above expenses we finally arrive at the first subtotal on the income statement, Operating Income (also known as EBIT or Earnings before Interest and Taxes).

Everything below Operating Income is not related to the ongoing operation of the business – such as non-operating expenses, provision for income taxes (i.e., future taxes) and equity-method investment activity (profits or losses from minority investments), net of tax.

Finally, we arrive at the net income (or net loss) which is then divided by the weighted average shares outstanding to determine Earnings per Share (EPS).

Build an Income Statement in a Financial Model

After preparing the skeleton of an income statement as such, it can then be integrated into a proper financial model to forecast future performance.

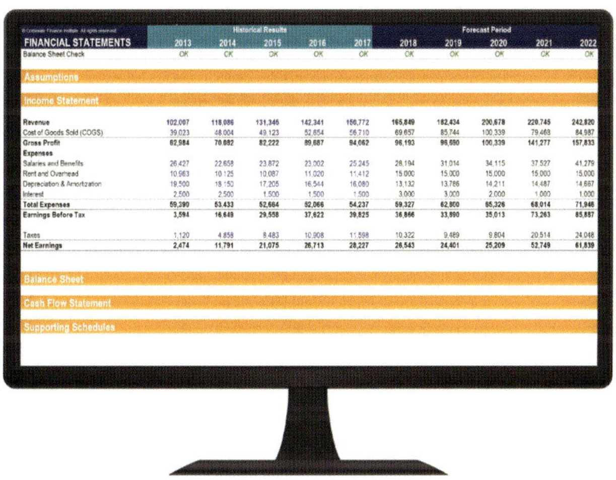

Step 1

First, input historical data for any available time periods into the income statement. Format historical data input using a specific format in order to be able to differentiate between hardcoded data and calculated data. As a reminder, a common method of formatting such data is to color any hardcoded input in blue, while coloring calculated data or linking data in black. Doing so enables the user and reader to know where changes in inputs can be made, and to know which cells contain formulae and, as such, should not be changed or tampered with. Regardless of the formatting method chosen, however, remember to remain consistent usage in order to avoid confusion.

Step 2

Next, analyze the trend in the available historical data to create drivers and assumptions for future forecasting. For example, analyze the trend in sales to forecast sales growth, analyzing the COGS as a percentage of sales to forecast future COGS.

Step 3

Finally, using the drivers and assumptions prepared in the previous step, forecast future values for all the line items within the income statement. Forecast specific line items, and use these to calculate subtotals. For example, for future gross profit, it is better to forecast COGS and sales and subtract them from each other, rather than to forecast future gross profit directly.

Income Statement Template

Income Statement Template	2014	2015	2016	2017	2018
Revenue	**102,007**	**118,086**	**131,345**	**142,341**	**150,772**
Cost of Goods Sold (COGS)	39,023	48,004	49,123	52,654	56,710
Gross Profit	**62,984**	**70,082**	**82,222**	**89,687**	**94,062**
Expenses					
Salaries and Benefits	26,427	22,658	23,872	23,002	25,245
Rent and Overhead	10,963	10,125	10,087	11,020	11,412
Depreciation & Amortization	19,500	18,150	17,205	16,544	16,080
Interest	2,500	2,500	1,500	1,500	1,500
Other	8,820	6,225	1,659	3,911	5,996
Total Expenses	**68,210**	**59,658**	**54,323**	**55,977**	**60,233**
Earnings Before Tax	**(5,226)**	**10,424**	**27,899**	**33,711**	**33,829**
Taxes	1,120	4,858	8,483	10,908	11,598
Net Earnings	**(6,346)**	**5,566**	**19,416**	**22,802**	**22,231**

What are Common Drivers for Each Income Statement Item

Line Item	Driver or Assumption
Sales Revenue	Selected growth percentage, pegged growth percentage based on index (such as GDP)
Cost of Goods Sold	Percentage of sales, Fixed dollar value

SG&A	Percentage of sales, fixed amount, trend, fixed dollar value
Depreciation and Amortization	Depreciation Schedule
Interest Expense	Debt Schedule
Income Tax	Percentage of pre-tax income (effective tax rate)

While these drivers are commonly used, they are just general guidelines. There are situations where intuition must be exercised to determine the proper driver or assumption to use. For example, a specific entity may have zero revenue. As such, the percentage of sales driver cannot be used for COGS. Instead, an analyst may have to rely on examining the past trend of COGS to determine assumptions for forecasting COGS into the future.

The core statements used in financial modeling are the same core statements used in accounting. There are three: the Income Statement, the Balance Sheet, and the Cash Flow Statement. In a financial model, each of these statements will impact the values of the other statements.

Purpose & Use

Income Statement provides the basis for measuring performance of an entity over the course of an accounting period.

Performance can be assessed from the income statement in terms of the following:

- Change in sales revenue over the period and in comparison to industry growth.
- Change in gross profit margin, operating profit margin and net profit margin over the period.
- Increase or decrease in net profit, operating profit and gross profit over the period.
- Comparison of the entity's profitability with other organizations operating in similar industries or sectors.

Income statement also forms the basis of important financial evaluation of an entity when it is analyzed in conjunction with information contained in other financial statements such as:

- Change in earnings per share over the period.
- Analysis of working capital in comparison to similar income statement elements (e.g. the ratio of receivables reported in the balance sheet to the credit sales reported in the income statement, i.e. debtor turnover ratio).
- Analysis of interest cover and dividend cover ratios.

References

- What-is-other-comprehensive-income: accountingtools.com, Retrieved 16 April 2018
- Deferred-revenue, accounting, resources: corporatefinanceinstitute.com, Retrieved 24 March 2018
- Deferred-revenue-record-calculate, accounting: patriotsoftware.com, Retrieved 11 July 2018
- Include-realized-loss-income-statement-39368: smallbusiness.chron.com, Retrieved 30 June 2018
- Income-statement, accounting-dictionary: myaccountingcourse.com, Retrieved 26 April 2018
- Income-statement-profit-and-loss, statements, financial: accounting-simplified.com, Retrieved 30 April 2018

4

Cash Flow Statement

A cash flow statement is a financial statement, which shows the way in which any change in balance sheet accounts and income has an impact on cash and cash equivalents. This chapter discusses in elaborate detail the significant aspects of cash flow statement such as cash flow and cash flow activities for an extensive understanding.

Cash Flow

Cash flow is the money that is moving (flowing) in and out of your business in a month. Although it does seem sometimes that cash flow only goes one way - out of the business - it does flow both ways:

- Cash is coming in from customers or clients who are buying your products or services. If customers don't pay at the time of purchase, some of your cash flow is coming from collections of accounts receivable.
- Cash is going out of your business in the form of payments for expenses, like rent or a mortgage, in monthly loan payments, and in payments for taxes and other accounts payable.

Think of 'cash flow' as a picture of your business checking account. If more money is coming in than is going out, you are in a "positive cash flow" situation and you have enough to pay your bills. If more cash is going out than coming in, you are in danger of being overdrawn, and you will need to find money to cover your overdrafts. This is why new businesses typically need working capital, in the form of a loan or line of credit, to cover shortages in cash flow.

Cash vs. Real Cash

For some businesses, like restaurants and some retailers, cash is really cash - currency and paper money. The business takes cash from customers and sometimes pays its bills in cash. Cash businesses have a special issue with keeping track of cash flow, especially since they may not track income unless there are invoices or other paperwork. Cash businesses are more at risk of being audited by the IRS.

Importants of Cash Flow

Lack of cash is one of the biggest reasons small businesses fail. The Small Business Administration says that “inadequate cash reserves” are a top reason startups don’t succeed. It’s called “running out of money,” and it will shut you down faster than anything else.

Cash Flow When Starting a Business

Dealing with cash flow issues is most difficult when you are starting a business. You have many expenses and money is going out fast. And you may have no sales or customers who are paying you. You will need some other temporary sources of cash, like through a temporary line of credit, to get you going and on to a positive cash flow situation.

Cash Flow in a Seasonal Business

Cash flow is particularly important for seasonal businesses - those that have a large fluctuation of business at different times of the year, like holiday businesses and summer businesses. Managing cash flow in this type of business is tricky, but it can be done, with diligence.

Cash Flow vs. Profit

It’s possible for your business to make a profit, but have no cash. How can that happen? The short answer is that profit is an accounting concept, while cash, is only the amount in the business checking account. You can have assets, like accounts receivable (money owed to you by customers) but if you can’t collect on what’s owed, you won’t have cash.

Your accounting system may also show a difference between cash and profits. If your business runs on accrual accounting, you recognize income when the invoice is sent, even though the customer hasn’t paid. In this case, you might show a profit but not have the cash.

Analyzing Cash Flow

The best way to keep track of cash flow in your business is to run a cash flow report.

A cash flow statement looks at the change to cash (in this case, your business checking account), from different business activities and increases or decreases in other accounts on the business balance sheet.

For example:

- What happens to cash if a customer pays a bill?

- What happens to cash if your business purchases supplies?
- What happens to cash if you buy a computer?
- What happens to cash if you pay an employee or independent contractor?

At times, you may need to keep track of cash flow on a weekly, maybe even a daily basis.

We suggest:

A quick and easy way to perform a cash flow analysis is to compare the total unpaid purchases to the total sales due at the end of each month. If the total unpaid purchases are greater than the total sales due, you'll need to spend more cash than you receive in the next month, indicating a potential cash flow problem.

To dig deeper into this statement:

1. At the end of this month, look at your total sales.
2. Add up the purchases you have made that still need to be paid for.
3. The difference is what you will need to bring in as income to stay even.

If this monthly cash shortage continues for several months, you'll get further and further behind.

Discounted Cash Flow

Discounted cash flow, or DCF, is one approach to valuing a business, by calculating the value of its future cash flow projections. The key to understanding this, however, is the concept that money in the future is not worth as much as that same money today. That's referred to as the time value of money.

To calculate what a certain amount of money is worth in the future, you have to discount it, or account for the fact that you lost the chance to invest it and earn money from it. Hence, why it is called the discounted cash flow method.

To illustrate the point, let's say that your company made $ 10,000 today. That $ 10,000 today is worth more than $ 10,000 a year from now, or five years from now. That's because you could invest today's $ 10,000 and earn interest that would increase the total amount after a year. At an interest rate of 5%, in a year that $ 10,000 would grow to be worth $ 10,500. Obviously, $ 10,500 are worth more than $ 10,000.

Calculating DCF

The elements of DCF are 1) The period of time to be used for evaluation, say a business life of 10 years, 2) the flows of cash that will occur every year in that business as best as you can guess, 3) your own internal discount rate or, put another way, what your money could earn if invested in something else of equivalent risk. The calculation itself is very easily done in a spreadsheet with a simple formula. What is really important in DCF is assessing the business and accurately predicting what flows of cash it will yield.

Obtaining the annual cash flow to be discounted is done as follows:

1. Start with net income after tax.

2. Add depreciation for the year (because depreciation is not a cash cost).

3. Deduct change in working capital from the previous year. This change may actually be negative, in which case this operation will add to cash. In a growing operation it will be positive and so will require cash.

4. Deduct capital expenditures.

Working capital is current assets less current liabilities. Unless the DCF is very detailed, the usual items included are the "biggies," receivables and inventories on the asset side and payables on the liabilities side, only changes being counted. If receivables were $ 100,000 at the beginning of the year and $ 130,000 at the end, $ 30,000 is the change. If inventories decreased from $ 40,000 to $ 35,000, the change is - $ 5,000—for a net change in assets of $ 25,000. Assume payables went from $ 80,000 to $ 110,000. The change in liabilities then is $ 30,000. Change in assets less liabilities is therefore - $ 5,000. This amount is deducted, from net income after tax, but deducting a negative causes it to be added. In effect the situation in this case means that the cash position of the business has improved. Finally capital expenditures, a flat drain on cash, are deducted.

These estimates of the cash flow are repeated for every year of the forecast period, in this case a ten-year cycle. To derive the crucial starting number, net income after tax, the analyst must, of course, project sales and costs assuming some reasonable growth rate for the operation—usually based on the target company's history. He or she must derive necessary inventory levels to support projected sales—and also calculate additions to capital based on capacity at the beginning of the period.

Most DCFs end by assuming that at the end of the cycle the company will be sold again at some conservative multiple of its after-tax earnings. This number is then plugged in as a "residual value" for the 11th year.

Next, and crucially, the analyst must determine what discount rate to use. Suppose the prospective buyer of the company enjoys a net return on its own, current investments in its own business of 16.7 percent. It may use that rate as a minimum or as an acceptable average return.

Now, with the annual cash flows neatly keyed into a spreadsheet down a column, each row representing a year—and the 11th year carrying the "resale residual," application of a discount formula can be applied. The formula for each row is quite simple:

$$PV = FV\ \tilde{A}\text{—}(1 + dr)?\text{-}n.$$

In this formula, PV stands for present value, namely right now, in the year of analysis. FV is the cash projected for one of the years in the future. dr is the discount rate. The 16.7 percent would be entered as .167. The caret symbol stands for exponentiation; n is the number of years; the negative n is the negative value of the year. Thus year 1 is -1, year 2 is -2 and so on.

Let us assume that the years begin with 2007 and that these years are in column A, beginning on row 5 of our spreadsheet. The cash flows are in column B, also beginning on row 5. Then, the formula in column C, row 5, will read:

$$= B5 * (1 + 0.167)?(-(A5 - 2006))$$

Replicating this formula down to the last row, row 15 (which will start with 2017 and will hold the residual), will automatically transform the projected cash flows into their discounted equivalents. Simply adding those up will result in the discounted cash flow value of the business. Assume that the cash flows in column B are (with 1,000s suppressed) 135, 137, 138, 142, 145, 150, 150, 170, 169, 175 and the last, the residual, is 675, the discounting formula will produce the values 116, 101, 87, 77, 67, 59, 51, 41, 42, 37, and, finally, 123. These values will add to 809. In actual cash, as projected, the business will generate \$ 2,186,000, the sum of the first set of numbers. But by discounting using the 16.7 rate, that value, today, is worth \$ 809,000. Thus if the asking price is at or below that value, the deal is good. If it is higher, the prospective buyer should probably pass.

Other Issues

Discounted cash flow analysis is almost always applied when a company is thinking of purchasing another. The technique is ultimately simple enough if applied with care. An ordinary spreadsheet is enough to do the job. But the real job is not really the application of a math formula.

"The simplicity of a DCF valuation is probably what contributes most to underestimating the time required for valuation jobs in the first place. Think about it—it isn't the DCF calculations that require any time; they run in an instant. But the DCF is only as good as its inputs, so that old adage, 'you are what you eat;' couldn't be truer with respect to DCF. Good estimates yield good valuations; bad estimates yield bad valuations. How do we get a reasonable range of estimates for our discounted cash flow? Therein lies the problem—the gremlin that eats away our time, drives us crazy, and makes us feel like plodding amateurs."

DCF, in other words, greatly depends on many much fuzzier issues, the most uncertain of which is how the future will treat the business we are thinking of buying. Here, as always, a thorough knowledge of the industry, conservative assumptions, due diligence in looking at the business in detail, especially visits with its clients and suppliers, and also a certain humility on the buyer's part are of crucial importance. Many owners have great confidence in their own abilities and a low estimate of the seller's. That should be a much bigger red flag than a lackluster DCF number.

Free Cash Flow

Free cash flow is the cash a company produces through its operations, less the cost of expenditures on assets. In other words, free cash flow or FCF is the cash left over after a company pays for its operating expenses and capital expenditures or CAPEX.

Free cash flow is an important measurement since it shows how efficient a company is at generating cash. Investors use free cash flow to measure whether a company might have enough cash, after funding operations and capital expenditures, to pay investors through dividends and share buybacks.

Calculating Free Cash Flow

To calculate FCF, from the cash flow statement, we'll find the item cash flow from operations (also referred to as "operating cash" or "net cash from operating activities") and subtract capital expenditure required for current operations from it.

The Free Cash Flow formula is:

Free Cash Flow = Operating cash flow - Capital expenditures

Example of Free Cash Flow

Macy's Inc. (M)

Below is Macy's cash flow statement for the fiscal year ending 2017 according to the company's 10K statement.

Macy's recorded the following:

- Cash flow from operating activities = $ 1.944 billion
- Capital expenditures - $ 760 million
- Macy's FCF = $ 1,944 - $ 760 = $ 1.184 billion

Macy's, Inc.

Consolidated Statements of Cash Flows (Unaudited)

(millions)

	53 Weeks Ended February 3, 2018	
Cash flows from operating activities:		
Net income	$ 1,536	
Adjustments to reconcile net income to net cash provided by operating activities:		
Restructuring, impairment, store closing and other costs	186	
Settlement charges	105	
Depreciation and amortization	991	
Stock-based compensation expense	58	
Gains on sale of real estate	(544)	
Amortization of financing costs and premium on acquired debt	(45)	
Changes in assets and liabilities:		
(Increase) decrease in receivables	120	
Decrease in merchandise inventories	221	
Increase in prepaid expenses and other current assets	(14)	
Increase (decrease) in merchandise accounts payable	162	
Decrease in accounts payable, accrued liabilities and other items not separately identified	(179)	
Increase (decrease) in current income taxes	(114)	
Decrease in deferred income taxes	(412)	
Change in other assets and liabilities not separately identified	(127)	
Net cash provided by operating activities	1,944	
Cash flows from investing activities:		
Purchase of property and equipment	(487)	($760 million)
Capitalized software	(273)	
Disposition of property and equipment	411	
Other, net	(24)	
Net cash used by investing activities	(373)	

Interpreting Free Cash Flow

We can see that Macy's had a large amount of free cash flow, which can be used to pay dividends, expand operations, and deleverage its balance sheet, i.e. reduce debt.

Please note the $411 million credit from the sale of property and equipment listed under Cash Flows from Investing Activities was not included since it's a one-time event and not part of everyday cash flow activities.

Growing free cash flows are frequently a prelude to increased earnings. Companies that experience surging FCF – due to revenue growth, efficiency improvements, cost reductions, share buy backs, dividend distributions or debt elimination – can reward investors tomorrow. That is why many in the investment community cherish FCF as a measure of value. When a firm's share price is low and free cash flow is on the rise, the odds are good that earnings and share value will soon be heading up.

By contrast, shrinking FCF might signal that companies are unable to sustain earnings growth. An insufficient FCF for earnings growth can force a company to boost its debt levels or not have the liquidity to stay in business.

To calculate free cash flow another way, you'll need the income statement and balance sheet. Start with net income and add back charges for depreciation and amortization. Make an additional adjustment for changes in working capital, which is done by subtracting current liabilities from current assets. Then subtract capital expenditure (or spending on plants and equipment):

Net income

+ Depreciation/Amortization

- Change in Working Capital

- Capital Expenditure

= Free Cash Flow

It might seem odd to add back depreciation/amortization since it accounts for capital spending. The reasoning behind the adjustment is that free cash flow is meant to measure money being spent right now, not transactions that happened in the past. This makes FCF a useful instrument for identifying growing companies with high up-front costs, which may eat into earnings now but have the potential to pay off later.

One drawback to using the free cash flow method is that capital expenditures can vary dramatically from year to year and between different industries. That's why it's critical to measure FCF over multiple periods and against the backdrop of the company's industry.

It's important to note that an exceedingly high FCF might be an indication that the company is not investing in their business properly such as updating their plant and equipment. Conversely, negative FCF might not necessarily mean a company is in financial trouble, but rather, investing heavily in expanding their market share which would likely lead to future growth.

Value investors often look for companies with high or improving cash flows but with undervalued share prices. Rising cash flow is often seen as an indicator that future growth is likely.

Free Cash Flow to Equity

Free cash flow to equity (FCFE) is a measure of how much cash is available to the equity shareholders of a company after all expenses, reinvestment, and debt are paid. FCFE is a measure of equity capital usage. It is calculated as:

FCFE = Net Income Net Capital Expenditure Change in Net Working Capital + New Debt - Debt Repayment.

Free cash flow to equity (FCFE) is often used by analysts in an attempt to determine the value of a company. This method of valuation gained popularity as an alternative to the dividend discount model (DDM), especially if a company does not pay a dividend.

Although FCFE may calculate the amount available to shareholders, it does not necessarily equate to the amount paid out to shareholders.

Components of the FCFE

Specifically, free cash flow to equity is composed of net income, capital expenditures, working capital, and debt. Net income is located on the company income statement. Capital expenditures can be found within the cash flows from investing section on the cash flow statement. Working capital is also found on the cash flow statement; however, it is in the cash flows from operations section. In general, working capital represents the difference between the company's most current assets and liabilities. These are short-term capital requirements related to immediate operations. Net borrowings can also be found on the cash flow statement in the cash flows from financing section. It is important to remember that interest expense is already included in net income so you do not need to add back interest expense.

Valuation using FCFE

Using the Gordon Growth Model, the FCFE is used to calculate the value of equity using this formula:

$$V_{equity} = FCFE/\left(r - g\right)$$

where V_{equity} = value of the stock today

FCFE = expected FCFE for next year

r = cost of equity of the firm

g = growth rate in FCFE for the firm

This model is used to find the value of the equity claim of a company, and is only appropriate to use if capital expenditure is not significantly greater than depreciation and if the beta of the company's stock is close to 1 or below 1.

Interpret the FCFE

Analysts also use FCFE to determine if dividend payments and stock repurchases are paid for with free cash flow to equity or some other form of financing. Investors want to see a dividend payment and share repurchase that is fully paid by FCFE. If FCFE is less than the dividend payment and the cost to buy back shares, the company is funding with either debt or existing capital, or issuing new securities. Existing capital includes retained earnings made in previous periods. This is not what investors want to see in a current or prospective investment, even if interest rates are low. Some analysts argue that borrowing to pay for share repurchases when shares are trading at a discount and rates are historically low is a good investment. However, this is only the case if the company's share price goes up in the future.

If the company's dividend payment fund is significantly less than the FCFE, then the firm is using the excess to increase its cash level or to invest in marketable securities.

Finally, if the funds spent to buy back shares or pay dividends is approximately equal to the FCFE, then the firm is paying it all to its investors.

Cash Flow Statement

A Cash Flow Statement (also called the Statement of Cash Flows) shows how much cash is generated and used during a given time period. It is one of the main financial statements analysts use in building a three statement model. The main categories found in a cash flow statement are the (1) operating activities, (2) investing activities, and (3) financing activities of a company and are organized respectively. The total cash provided from or used by each of the three activities is summed to arrive at the total change in cash for the period, which is then added to the opening cash balance to arrive at the cash flow statement's bottom line, the closing cash balance.

One of the primary reasons cash inflows and outflows are observed is to compare the cash from operations to net income. This comparison helps company management, analysts, and investors to gauge how well a company is running its operations. The cash flow statement reflects the actual amount of money the company receives from its operations. The reason for the difference between cash and profit is because the income statement is prepared under the accrual basis of accounting, where it matches revenues and expenses for the accounting period, even though revenues may actually not have yet been collected and expenses may not have yet been paid.

	A B C	E	F	G	H	I	J	K	L
1	© Corporate Finance Institute. All rights reserved.		Historical Results				Forecast Period		
2	**Brick 'n' Mortar Co Model**	**2014**	**2015**	**2016**	**2017**	**2018**	**2019**	**2020**	**2021**
103									
104	**Cash Flow Statement**								
105									
106	**Cash from Operating Activities**								
107	Net Earnings	4,466	8,071	10,161	10,706	19,201	23,910	28,510	32,118
108	Plus: Depreciation & Amortization	10,165	9,635	9,265	9,006	4,203	4,512	4,760	4,958
109	Less: Changes in Working Capital	953	434	506	463	2,477	147	1,079	1,077
110	**Cash from Operations**	**13,677**	**17,272**	**18,921**	**19,248**	**20,926**	**28,274**	**32,190**	**35,998**
111									
112	**Cash from Investing Activities**								
113	Investments in Property & Equipment	(8,401)	(8,401)	(8,401)	(8,401)	(5,750)	(5,750)	(5,750)	(5,750)
114	Investments in Businesses	-	(150,000)	-	-	(370,000)	-	-	-
115	**Cash from Investing**	**(8,401)**	**(158,401)**	**(8,401)**	**(8,401)**	**(375,750)**	**(5,750)**	**(5,750)**	**(5,750)**
116									
117	**Cash from Financing Activities**								
118	Issuance (repayment) of debt	-	(11,201)	-	-	-	-	-	-
119	Issuance (repayment) of equity	-	200,000	-	-	500,000	-	-	-
120	Payment of Dividends	-	-	-	-	-	-	-	-
121	**Cash from Financing**	**-**	**188,799**	**-**	**-**	**500,000**	**-**	**-**	**-**
122									
123	Net Increase (decrease) in Cash	5,277	47,671	10,520	10,847	145,176	22,524	26,440	30,248
124	Opening Cash Balance	37,573	42,850	90,521	101,041	111,889	257,065	279,589	306,030
125	**Closing Cash Balance**	**42,850**	**90,521**	**101,041**	**111,889**	**257,065**	**279,589**	**306,030**	**336,278**
126									

Drafting of Cash Flow Statement

Below is a breakdown of each section in a statement of cash flows. While each company will have its own unique line items, the general setup is usually the same.

Cash Flow Activities

Cash Flow from Operating Activities

The cash flow statement is commonly presented using the indirect method. It starts with net income or loss, followed by additions to or subtractions from that amount to adjust the net income to a total cash flow figure. What is added or subtracted are changes in the account balances of items found in current assets and current liabilities on the balance sheet, as well as non-cash accounts (e.g., stock-based compensation). We then arrive at the cash version of a company's net income.

Net Earnings

This amount is the bottom line of an income statement. Net income or earnings shows the profitability of a company over a period of time. It is calculated by taking the revenues and subtracting from it COGS and total expenses, which includes SG&A, Depreciation and Amortization, interest, etc.

Plus: Depreciation and Amortization (D&A)

The value of various assets declines over time when used in a business. As a result, D&A are expenses that allocate the cost of an asset over its useful life. Depreciation involves tangible assets such as buildings, machinery, and equipment, whereas amortization involves intangible assets such as patents, copyrights, goodwill, and software.

D&A reduces net income in the income statement. However, we add this back into the cash flow statement to adjust net income because these are non-cash expenses. In other words, no cash transactions are involved.

Less: Changes in Working Capital

Working capital represents the difference between a company's current assets and current liabilities. Any changes in current assets (other than cash) and current liabilities affect the cash balance in operating activities.

For instance, when a company buys more inventory, current assets increase. This positive change in inventory is subtracted from net income because it is seen as a cash outflow. It's the same case for accounts receivable. When it increases, it means the company sold their goods on credit. There was no cash transaction, so accounts receivable is also subtracted from net income.

On the other hand, if a current liability item such as accounts payable increases, this is considered a cash inflow, because the company has more cash to keep in its business. This is then added to net income.

Cash from Operations

When all the adjustments have been made, we arrive at the net cash provided by the company's operating activities. This is not a replacement for net income, but rather a summary of how much cash is generated from the company's core business.

Cash Flow from Investing Activities

This category on the statement of cash flows is referred to as investing activities and reports changes in capital expenditures (capex) and long-term investments. Capex can refer to the purchase of property, plant, or equipment assets. Long-term investments may include debt and equity instruments of other companies. Another important item found here is acquisitions of other businesses. A key to remember is that a change in the long-term assets in the balance sheet is reported in the investing activities of the cash flow statement.

Investments in Property and Equipment

These investments might mean purchases of new office equipment such as computers and printers for a growing number of employees, or the purchase of new land and a building to house business operations and logistics of the company. These items are necessary to keep the company running. These investments are a cash outflow, and therefore will have a negative impact when we calculate the net increase in cash from all activities.

Cash from Investing

This is the total amount of cash provided by (used in) investing activities. In our example, we have a net outflow for each and every year.

Cash Flow from Financing Activities

This category is also called financing activities and reports any issuance or repurchases of stocks and bonds of the company, as well as any dividend payments it makes. The changes in long-term liabilities and stockholders' equity in the balance sheet are reported in financing activities.

Issuance (Repayment) of Debt

A company issues debt as a way to finance its operations. The more cash it has, the better, as it will be able to expand rapidly. Unlike equity, issuing debt doesn't grant any ownership interest in the company, so it doesn't dilute the ownership of existing shareholders. The issuance of debt is a cash inflow, because a company finds investors willing to act as lenders. However, when these investors are paid back, then the debt repayment is a cash outflow.

Issuance (Repayment) of Equity

This is another way of financing a company's operations. Unlike debt, equity holders have some ownership stake in the business in exchange for money given to the company for use. Future earnings must be shared with these equity holders or investors. Issuance of equity is an additional source of cash, so it's a cash inflow. Conversely, an equity repayment is a cash outflow. This is buying back, through cash payment, the equity from its investors and thereby increasing the stake held by the company itself.

Cash from Financing

This is also called the net cash provided by (used in) financing activities. The cash from financing is calculated by summing up all the cash inflows and outflows related to changes in long-term liabilities and shareholders' equity accounts.

The last section on the statement of cash flows is a reconciliation of the total cash position, which connects to the balance sheet. This is the final piece of the puzzle when linking the three financial statements.

Net Increase (Decrease) in Cash and Closing Cash Balance

Once we have all net cash balances for each of the three sections of the cash flow statement, we sum them all up to find the net cash increase or decrease for the given time period. We then take this amount and add it to the opening cash balance to eventually arrive at the closing cash balance. This amount will be reported in the balance sheet statement under the current asset section.

Opening Cash Balance

The opening cash balance is last year's closing cash balance. We can find this amount from last year's cash flow statement and balance sheet statement.

Real-life Example of a Cash Flow Statement

Below is an example of Amazon's 2016 statement of cash flows. As you can see by the orange rectangles, there are three clear sections that add to the total change and end of period cash position. For a closer look, you can download Amazon's financial statements.

CONSOLIDATED STATEMENTS OF CASH FLOWS
(in millions)

	Year Ended December 31,		
	2014	2015	2016
CASH AND CASH EQUIVALENTS, BEGINNING OF PERIOD	$ 8,658	$ 14,557	$ 15,890
OPERATING ACTIVITIES:			
Net income (loss)	(241)	596	2,371
Adjustments to reconcile net income (loss) to net cash from operating activities:			
Depreciation of property and equipment, including internal-use software and website development, and other amortization, including capitalized content costs	4,746	6,281	8,116
Stock-based compensation	1,497	2,119	2,975
Other operating expense, net	129	155	160
Other expense (income), net	59	250	(20)
Deferred income taxes	(316)	81	(246)
Excess tax benefits from stock-based compensation	(6)	(119)	(829)
Changes in operating assets and liabilities:			
Inventories	(1,193)	(2,187)	(1,426)
Accounts receivable, net and other	(1,039)	(1,755)	(3,367)
Accounts payable	1,759	4,294	5,030
Accrued expenses and other	706	913	1,724
Additions to unearned revenue	4,433	7,401	11,931
Amortization of previously unearned revenue	(3,692)	(6,109)	(9,976)
Net cash provided by (used in) operating activities	6,842	11,920	16,443
INVESTING ACTIVITIES:			
Purchases of property and equipment, including internal-use software and website development, net	(4,893)	(4,589)	(6,737)
Acquisitions, net of cash acquired, and other	(979)	(795)	(116)
Sales and maturities of marketable securities	3,349	3,025	4,733
Purchases of marketable securities	(2,542)	(4,091)	(7,756)
Net cash provided by (used in) investing activities	(5,065)	(6,450)	(9,876)
FINANCING ACTIVITIES:			
Excess tax benefits from stock-based compensation	6	119	829
Proceeds from long-term debt and other	6,359	353	621
Repayments of long-term debt and other	(513)	(1,652)	(354)
Principal repayments of capital lease obligations	(1,285)	(2,462)	(3,860)
Principal repayments of finance lease obligations	(135)	(121)	(147)
Net cash provided by (used in) financing activities	4,432	(3,763)	(2,911)
Foreign currency effect on cash and cash equivalents	(310)	(374)	(212)
Net increase (decrease) in cash and cash equivalents	5,899	1,333	3,444
CASH AND CASH EQUIVALENTS, END OF PERIOD	$ 14,557	$ 15,890	$ 19,334

Build a Statement of Cash Flows in a Financial Model

A cash flow statement model in Excel displays both historical and projected data. Before this model can be created, we first need to have the income statement and balance sheet statement models built in Excel, since their data will ultimately drive the cash flow statement model.

	A B C	E	F	G	H	I	J	K	L
1	© Corporate Finance Institute. All rights reserved.	Historical Results				Forecast Period			
2	**Brick 'n' Mortar Co Model**	2014	2015	2016	2017	2018	2019	2020	2021
103									
104	**Cash Flow Statement**								
105									
106	**Cash from Operating Activities**								
107	Net Earnings	4,466	8,071	10,161	10,706	19,201	23,910	28,510	32,118
108	Plus: Depreciation & Amortization	10,165	9,635	9,265	9,006	4,203	4,512	4,760	4,958
109	Less: Changes in Working Capital	953	434	506	463	2,477	147	1,079	1,077
110	**Cash from Operations**	**13,677**	**17,272**	**18,921**	**19,248**	**20,926**	**28,274**	**32,190**	**35,998**
111									
112	**Cash from Investing Activities**								
113	Investments in Property & Equipment	(8,401)	(8,401)	(8,401)	(8,401)	(5,750)	(5,750)	(5,750)	(5,750)
114	Investments in Businesses	-	(150,000)	-	-	(370,000)	-	-	-
115	**Cash from Investing**	**(8,401)**	**(158,401)**	**(8,401)**	**(8,401)**	**(375,750)**	**(5,750)**	**(5,750)**	**(5,750)**
116									
117	**Cash from Financing Activities**								
118	Issuance (repayment) of debt	-	(11,201)	-	-	-	-	-	-
119	Issuance (repayment) of equity	-	200,000	-	-	500,000	-	-	-
120	Payment of Dividends	-	-	-	-	-	-	-	-
121	**Cash from Financing**	-	**188,799**	-	-	**500,000**	-	-	-
122									
123	Net Increase (decrease) in Cash	5,277	47,671	10,520	10,847	145,176	22,524	26,440	30,248
124	Opening Cash Balance	37,573	42,850	90,521	101,041	111,889	257,065	279,589	306,030
125	**Closing Cash Balance**	**42,850**	**90,521**	**101,041**	**111,889**	**257,065**	**279,589**	**306,030**	**336,278**
126									

As we have seen from our financial model example, it shows all the historical data in a blue font, while the forecasted data appears in a black font. The figure below just serves as a general guideline as to where to find historical data to hardcode for the line items. Additionally, it shows where we find, in the financial model, the calculated or reference data to fill up the forecast period section. When all three statements are built in Excel, we now have what we call a "three statement model". Below is a summary of how to build a statement of cash flows in Excel.

References

- Cash-flow-how-it-works-to-keep-your-business-afloat-398180: thebalancesmb.com, Retrieved 13 April 2018
- Discounted-cash-flow-dcf, encyclopedia: shopify.com, Retrieved 10 May 2018
- What-formula-calculating-free-cash-flow.asp-033015: investopedia.com, Retrieved 25 March 2018
- Free cash flow to equity.asp: investopedia.com, Retrieved 09 April 2018
- Cash-flow-statement, accounting, knowledge, resources: corporatefinanceinstitute.com, Retrieved 11 July 2018

5

Statement of Financial Position

A statement of financial position or a balance sheet is reflective of the financial position of a business. It is a summary of the balances of an organization or an individual and consists of consolidated information of assets and liabilities and ownership equity. These aspects of the balance sheet have been carefully analyzed in this chapter.

The balance sheet is a financial report that lists a company's assets (what it owns), liabilities (what it owes to others), and equity.

The first section of the balance sheet gives a detailed list of a company's assets, including long-term assets (such as real estate and machinery), current assets (anything that can easily be converted to cash in less than a year), and cash.

The second section goes over the company's liabilities, or what it owes others. This is always an important section for investors to read because even the most stable of companies will face problems if it has an unusually high amount of debt on its books (especially if it has to pay it back sooner rather than later).

The third section outlines stockholders' equity, and provides information on common and preferred stock, retained earnings, and capital surplus.

Importance of Balance Sheet

A balance sheet can help both business owners and investors understand the financial health of a company. And because companies generally include the corresponding balance sheet figures from previous quarters, balance sheets can be a useful way for investors to track trends in the way a business pays off its debts, builds its assets, or improves its financial standing.

Assets

An asset is a resource that has some economic value to a company and can be used in a current or future period to generate revenues.

These resources take many forms from cash to buildings and are recorded on the balance sheet until they are used. Once these resources are used or spent, they are transferred from the balance sheet to the income statement and called expenditures.

Example

Tom and Bob are starting a machine shop that will do general fabrication. When a company is first started, it doesn't have any resources. Thus, the Tom and Bob must invest their own money or equipment to get the company started. This initial investment is considered owner's equity. Both Tom and Bob contribute a piece of machinery to the new company.

Once the business receives the equipment, it can start using that resource to generate income. When the company sells its parts, it receives cash. As the business brings in more jobs, Tom and Bob start to use their profits to purchases more equipment to fulfill additional orders.

Tom and Bob work throughout the year growing the business until they run out of room at their current location. They need to look for a new building, but they don't have enough money to purchase it with the cash they have in the bank, so they get a loan. The bank lends the enough capital to purchase a building where they can keep their operations going.

In our short example, we saw three ways three different assets were acquired. First, the company acquired equipment by a contribution from its owners. Second, the company used its own assets to purchases more assets when it bought additional equipment with its cash. Third, the company took out a loan to purchase a building.

It's important to note that nowhere in the assets definition have we said that the company must own these resources. Remember the asset definition, it's simply a resource that the company has control of and can use to generate revenues. Many businesses have loans, notes, and leases on equipment that either directly or indirectly eliminates their true ownership of the resources, but they still have control of it.

Types of Asset Classes

When assets are presented on the balance sheet, they are typically divided into different classes or categories based on when they will be used. Resources that are expected to be consumed within the current period are classified as current assets while resources that expected to be used in future periods are called non-current assets. Another class of resources is intangible assets. There resources typically consist of intellectual property. Resources that don't fit into any of these three classes are simply called other assets.

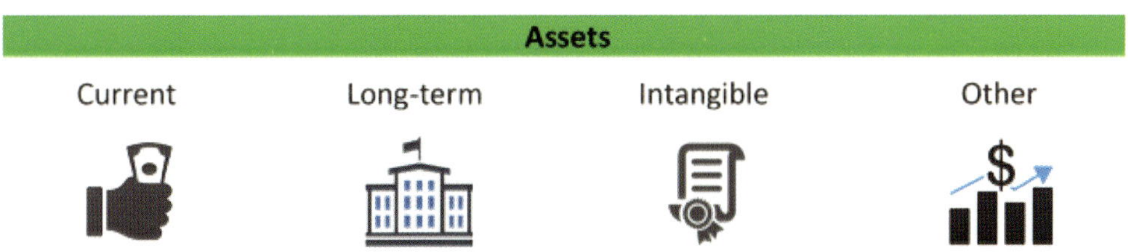

Current Assets

- Cash and equivalents: Cash is any currency in the possession of the business. This could be cash in a register, money in the bank, or treasure bills in a safe deposit box. These liquid assets can be used to purchase any other resource, settle debts, or pay investors.
- Accounts Receivable: Accounts receivable is an IOU from a customer. Many businesses allow customers to purchase goods on account and pay for them at a future date. Accounts receivable is the acknowledgement that the customer owes the company money for the goods.
- Inventory: Inventory is merchandise that the company intends to sell for a profit. This merchandise could be purchased or manufactured by the company.
- Investments: Investments that management intends to sell in the current period are considered current resources. These investments typically consist of stocks and bonds.

Long-term Assets

- Land: Property is a resource that is considered long-term in nature because it will be used over time and will not be consumed in the current period.
- Buildings: A building is obviously a resourced used over time. Many companies stay in the same building for decades. Thus, it is considered a long-term resource.
- Equipment: Equipment like machinery, vehicles, and furniture all has a useful life of more than one year.

Intangible Assets

- Patents/Trademarks/Copyrights: These are all examples of intellectual property that a company can own or control to generate revenues over time. In fact, some of the most value assets in the world are intangible in nature. Think about Walt Disney's Mickey Mouse or Apple's iPhone designs.

Other Assets

- Investments: Investments like stocks, bonds, and property that are intended to be held for more than one year are typically listed separately from the investments that management believes will sell in the current period.

Short-term vs. Long-term

Short term assets, also called current assets, are resources that are expected to be used or could be used in the current period. These resources include examples like cash and accounts receivable. Keep in mind that a company might doesn't always use all of its cash every period, but it could. That's what makes it short-term.

Long term assets, on the other hand, are resources that are expected to last more than one accounting period. Some examples include fixed assets, equipment, and buildings. All of these resources have longer useful lives than one period.

Tangible vs. Intangible

Tangible assets include any resources with a physical presence. Some examples include cash, fixed assets, and equipment. Some of these resources are depreciated while others are not.

Intangible assets are resources that don't have a physical presence. You can think of these like ideas. You can't touch an idea, but it is real and it's a thing. Some examples include patents, copyrights, and trademarks. Most of these resources are amortized over their useful lives or periodically checked for impairment losses.

Assets Valued and Recorded in Accounting

According to the historical cost principle, assets are recorded on the books at the price the company paid for them. This is true for all assets except for a few different types of investments that are adjusted to fair market value and some intangible assets that are purchased indirectly like goodwill.

Since a company depends on its resources to generate revenues, many businesses are often valued by their level of asset ownership. In other words, an investor could calculate a rough value of a business by subtracting the outstanding loans from the assets of the company to see what resources the company actually owns.

A company with more resources is generally deemed to be worth more than one with fewer resources. This isn't always the case, however. Most investors predict return rates on assets. If the company doesn't perform well, the company valuation could go down simply because it isn't using its resources effectively.

Assets and Depreciation

In accrual accounting, if a resource can be used for more than one period, it shouldn't be expensed immediately. Instead, it is capitalized and the cost of the asset is recognized over the life of the assets. Depreciation is a way to assign the cost of an asset over its useful lives. It's also a way to recognize the use of the asset and record the devaluation of it over time.

Fixed assets and other long-term assets like buildings are depreciated while land is not. Other assets, like intangibles, are amortized.

Current Asset

A current asset is cash and any other company asset that will be turning to cash within one year from the date shown in the heading of the company's balance sheet. (If a company has an operating cycle that is longer than one year, an asset that will turn to cash within the length of its operating cycle is considered to be a current asset).

Current assets are generally listed first on a company's balance sheet and will be presented in the order of liquidity. That means they will appear in the following order: cash (which includes currency, checking accounts, petty cash), temporary investments, accounts receivable, inventory, supplies, and prepaid expenses. (Supplies and prepaid expenses will not literally be converted to cash. They are included because they will allow the company to avoid paying cash for these items during the upcoming year).

It is important that the amount of each current asset not be overstated. For example, accounts receivable, inventories, and temporary investments should have valuation accounts so that the amounts reported will not be greater than the amounts that will be received when the assets turn to cash. This is important because the amount of company's working capital and its current ratio are computed using the current assets' reported amounts.

Current assets are also referred to as short term assets.

Current Assets Formula

It's easy to calculate the current assets of your company. However, it's important to make sure that all assets classified as "current" are included in the calculation, since there are many.

The current assets formula is:

Current Assets = (Cash & Cash Equivalents) + (Accounts Receivables) + (Inventory) + (Marketable Securities) + (Prepaid Expenses) + (Other Liquid Assets)

Cash and Cash Equivalents

Cash includes bills, currency notes, coins, checks received but not yet deposited, and petty cash. Cash equivalents typically include money in bank accounts, money market accounts, and short-term investments with a maturity of 90 days or less (like U.S. Treasury bills and commercial paper). Cash and cash equivalents are typically reported on the balance sheet as the first current asset.

Accounts Receivables

Accounts receivables represent the value of a company's outstanding invoices owed by customers for products and/or services delivered. Accounts receivables should ideally be collected within 90 days or less with a 90% collection rate. They are considered current assets because they can be converted to cash when collected and typically have repayment terms between 30-90 days.

Inventory

Inventory refers to any raw materials, in-process products, and/or finished goods that are ready or soon to be ready for sale. Inventory is considered a current asset because it is converted to cash when sold. Ideally, inventory should be sold within one year or less to risk overstocking.

Marketable Securities

Marketable securities represent a company's short-term investments or unrestricted financial instrument available for sale. Marketable securities are considered current assets because their maturities are typically less than one year. They are usually traded on an open market – such as a public stock exchange or public bond exchange – at a set price to readily available buyers.

Prepaid Expenses

Prepaid expenses are expenditures paid for in advance. They are reported on a balance sheet as current assets until the bill actually becomes due. Prepaid expenses are short-term assets because they typically come due within a few months of being recorded. One example of a prepaid expense is prepaid rent.

For example, if your rent is 1,000 per month and you choose to pay for the next 3 months at once, your prepaid rent asset account will increase to 3,000. At the start of each month when rent is due, you'll reduce your prepaid rent account by 1,000 and recognize an equal rent expense of 1,000.

Other Liquid Assets

Other liquid assets include any other assets that can be converted to cash within one year. This can include previous long-term investments that are maturing within a year or a property or piece of equipment that is set to be sold within a year.

Current Assets Example

To calculate current assets, all you have to do is add your short-term balance sheet assets together that can be converted into cash within one year.

Let's say that your company's short-term assets include the following on your balance sheet:

- Cash & Cash Equivalents: $90,000
- Accounts Receivable: $30,000
- Marketable Securities: $120,000
- Inventory: $50,000
- Prepaid Expenses: $18,000

Based on the above data, your short-term assets are calculated as follows:

$90,000 + $30,000 + $120,000 + $50,000 + $18,000 = $308,000.

Importance of Current Assets

Current assets are important because they are used to pay for operational expenses and other short-term financial obligations. The value of your short-term assets to your current liabilities gives you insights into your short-term liquidity, also known as your net working capital. Typically, more short-term assets than liabilities is good, while fewer short-term assets than liabilities results in financial insolvency.

However, the ideal ratio of your short-term assets to your current liabilities is between 1.2 to 2. Anything lower than 1 means your short-term assets are not enough to cover your current financial obligations. Although, if your current ratio is higher than 2, it may indicate that your company isn't efficiently using its short-term assets to generate revenue.

Calculation of Average Current Assets

The average current assets of a company is the average value of a company's short-term assets from one period to another. Average current assets are typically calculated as average annual assets. This gives business owners an idea of the average monthly short-term assets they should expect, which helps them manage, plan, and budget for the future.

For example, to calculate average total assets for the year, add the total current assets from the end of the previous year to the total short-term assets from the end of the present year, and then divide by two. The formula for the average current assets is as follows:

Average Current Assets = (Total current assets for previous period + Total current assets for current period) / 2

For example, if on Dec 31st, 2017, your current assets are $97,000, and then on Dec

31st, 2018, your current assets are $73,000, your average short-term assets for the period would be:

($97,000 + $73,000) / 2 = $85,000

In conclusion, current assets are key to a company's short-term liquidity. Assets are classified and reported as short-term assets on a company's balance sheet if they can be converted to cash within one year or less. Typically, a company that has more short-term assets than current liabilities is considered financially stable.

Long Term Investments

Trading securities are investments that were made with the intent of reselling them in the very near future, hopefully at a profit. Such investments are considered highly liquid and are classified on the balance sheet as current assets. They are carried at fair market value, and the changes in value are measured and included in the operating income of each period.

However, not all investments are made with the goal of turning a quick profit. Many investments are acquired with the intent of holding them for an extended period of time. The appropriate accounting methodology depends on obtaining a deeper understanding of the nature/intent of the particular investment. But, many investments are acquired with longer-term goals in mind.

For example, one company may acquire a majority (more than 50%) of the stock of another. In this case, the acquirer (known as the parent) must consolidate the accounts of the subsidiary.

Sometimes, one company may acquire a substantial amount of the stock of another without obtaining control. This situation generally arises when the ownership level rises above 20%, but stays below the 50% level that will trigger consolidation. In these cases, the investor is deemed to have the ability to significantly influence the investee company. Accounting rules specify the "equity method" of accounting for such investments.

Not all investments are in stock. Sometimes a company may invest in a "bond" (you have no doubt heard the term "stocks and bonds"). A bond payable is a mere "promise" (i.e., bond) to "pay" (i.e., payable). Thus, the issuer of a bond payable receives money today from an investor in exchange for the issuer's promise to repay the money in the future.

By default, the final category for an investment is known as the "available for sale" category. When an investment is not trading, not held-to-maturity, not involving consolidation, and not involving the equity method, by default, it is considered to be an "available for sale" investment. Even though this is a default category, do not assume it to be unimportant. Massive amounts of investments are so classified within typical corporate accounting records. We will begin our look at long-term investments by examining this important category of investments.

The Fair Value Measurement Option

Available for Sale Securities

The accounting for "available for sale" securities will look quite similar to the accounting for trading securities. In both cases, the investment asset account will be reflected at fair value.

To be sure, there is one big difference between the accounting for trading securities and available-for-sale securities. This difference pertains to the recognition of the changes in value. For trading securities, the changes in value were recorded in operating income. However, such is not the case for available-for-sale securities. Here, the changes in value go into a special account. We will call this account Unrealized Gain/Loss- OCI, where "OCI" will represent "Other Comprehensive Income."

Other comprehensive income: This notion of other comprehensive income is somewhat unique and requires special discussion at this time. There is a long history of accounting evolution that explains how the accounting rule makers eventually came to develop the concept of OCI. To make a long story short, most transactions and events make their way through the income statement. As a result, it can be said that the income statement is "all-inclusive." Once upon a time, this was not the case; only operational items were included in the income statement. Nonrecurring or non-operating related transactions and events were charged or credited directly to equity, bypassing the income statement entirely (a "current operating" concept of income).

Importantly, you must take note that the accounting profession now embraces the all-inclusive approach to measuring income. In fact, a deeper study of accounting will reveal that the income statement structure can grow in complexity to capture various types of unique transactions and events (e.g., extraordinary gains and losses, etc.) -- but, the income statement does capture those transactions and events, however odd they may appear.

There are a few areas where accounting rules have evolved to provide for special circumstances/"exceptions." And, OCI is intended to capture those exceptions. One exception is the Unrealized Gain/Loss - OCI on available-for-sale securities. As you will soon see, the changes in value on such securities are recognized, not in operating income as with trading securities, but instead in this unique account. The OCI gain/loss is generally charged or credited directly to an equity account (Accumulated OCI), thereby bypassing the income statement.

Illustration: Let us amend the Trading Securities illustration -- such that the investments were more appropriately classified as available for sale securities:

Assume that Webster Company acquired an investment in Merriam Corporation. The intent was not for trading purposes, control, or to exert significant influence. The following entry was needed on March 3, 20X6, the day Webster bought stock of Merriam:

3-3-X6	Available for Sale Securities	50,000	
	Cash		50,000
	To record the purchase of 5,000 shares of Merriam stock at $10 per share		

Next, assume that financial statements were being prepared on March 31. By that date, Merriam's stock declined to $9 per share. Accounting rules require that the investment "be written down" to current value, with a corresponding charge against OCI. The charge is recorded as follows:

3-31-X6	Unrealized Gain/Loss - OCI	5,000	
	Available for Sale Securities		5,000
	To record a $1 per share decrease in the value of 5,000 shares of Merriam stock		

This charge against OCI will reduce stockholders' equity (the balance sheet remains in balance with both assets and equity being decreased by like amounts). But, net income is not reduced, as there is no charge to a "normal" income statement account. The rationale here, whether you agree or disagree, is that the net income is not affected by temporary fluctuations in market value -- since the intent is to hold the investment for a longer term period.

During April, the stock of Merriam bounced up $3 per share to $12. Webster now needs to prepare this adjustment:

4-30-X6	Available for Sale Securities	15,000	
	Unrealized Gain/Loss - OCI		15,000
	To record a $3 per share increase in the value of 5,000 shares of Merriam stock		

Notice that the three journal entries now have the available for sale securities valued at $60,000 ($50,000 - $5,000 + $15,000). This is equal to their market value ($12 X 5,000 = $60,000). The OCI has been adjusted for a total of $10,000 credit ($5,000 debit and $15,000 credit). This cumulative credit corresponds to the total increase in value of the original $50,000 investment.

The preceding illustration assumed a single investment. However, the treatment would be the same even if the available for sale securities consisted of a portfolio of many investments. That is, each and every investment would be adjusted to fair value.

Alternative -- A valuation adjustments account: As an alternative to directly adjusting the Available for Sale Securities account, some companies may maintain a separate Valuation Adjustments account that is added to or subtracted from the Available for Sale Securities account. The results are the same; the reasons for using the alternative approach is to provide additional information that may be needed for more complex accounting and tax purposes. This coverage is best reserved for more advanced courses.

Dividends and interest: Dividends or interest received on available for sale securities is reported as income and included in the income statement:

9-15-X5	Cash	75	
	Dividend Income		75
	To record receipt of dividend on available for sale security investment		

The balance sheet appearance: The above discussion would produce the following balance sheet presentation of available for sale securities at March 31 and April 30. To aid the illustration, all accounts are held constant during the month of April, with the exception of those that change because of the fluctuation in value of Merriam's stock.

WEBSTER COMPANY
Balance Sheet
March 31, 20X6

ASSETS				LIABILITIES		
Current assets				**Current Liabilities**		
Cash		$ 100,000		Accounts payable	$ 80,000	
Trading securities		50,000		Salaries payable	10,000	
Accounts receivable		75,000		Interest payable	15,000	
Inventories		200,000		Taxes payable	5,000	
Prepaid insurance		25,000	$ 450,000	Current portion of note	40,000	$ 150,000
Long-term Investments						
Available for sale securities		$ 45,000		**Long-term Liabilities**		
Cash value of insurance		10,000	55,000	Note payable	$ 190,000	
Property, Plant & Equip.				Mortgage liability	110,000	300,000
Land		$ 25,000		**Total liabilities**		$ 450,000
Building and equipment	$ 150,000					
Less: Accumulated depreciation	(50,000)	100,000	125,000	STOCKHOLDERS' EQUITY		
Intangible Assets				Capital stock	$ 300,000	
Goodwill			275,000	Retained earnings	170,000	
Other Assets				Accumulated other comprehensive income/loss	(5,000)	
Receivable from employee			10,000	**Total stockholders' equity**		465,000
Total assets			$ 915,000	**Total Liabilities and equity**		$ 915,000

In reviewing this illustration, note that Available for Sale Securities are customarily classified in the Long-term Investments section of the balance sheet. And, take note the OCI adjustment is merely appended to stockholders' equity.

WEBSTER COMPANY
Balance Sheet
April 30, 20X6

ASSETS				LIABILITIES		
Current assets				**Current Liabilities**		
Cash		$ 100,000		Accounts payable	$ 80,000	
Trading securities		50,000		Salaries payable	10,000	
Accounts receivable		75,000		Interest payable	15,000	
Inventories		200,000		Taxes payable	5,000	
Prepaid insurance		25,000	$ 450,000	Current portion of note	40,000	$ 150,000
Long-term Investments						
Available for sale securities		$ 60,000		**Long-term Liabilities**		
Cash value of insurance		10,000	70,000	Note payable	$ 190,000	
Property, Plant & Equip.				Mortgage liability	110,000	300,000
Land		$ 25,000		**Total liabilities**		$ 450,000
Building and equipment	$ 150,000					
Less: Accumulated depreciation	(50,000)	100,000	125,000	STOCKHOLDERS' EQUITY		
Intangible Assets				Capital stock	$ 300,000	
Goodwill			275,000	Retained earnings	170,000	
Other Assets				Accumulated other comprehensive income/gain	10,000	
Receivable from employee			10,000	**Total stockholders' equity**		480,000
Total assets			$ 930,000	**Total Liabilities and equity**		$ 930,000

Held to Maturity Securities

Investments in bonds: It was noted earlier that certain types of financial instruments have a fixed maturity date; the most typical of such instruments are "bonds." The held to maturity securities are to be accounted for by the amortized cost method.

To elaborate, if we wish to borrow money we would typically approach a bank or other lender and they would likely be able to accommodate our request. But, a corporate giant's credit needs may exceed the lending capacity of any single bank or lender. Therefore, the large corporate borrower may instead issue "bonds," thereby splitting a large loan into many small units. For example, a bond issuer may borrow $500,000,000 by issuing 500,000 individual bonds with a face amount of $1,000 each (500,000 X $1,000 = $500,000,000). If we wished to loan some money to that corporate giant, we could do so by simply buying ("investing in") one or more of their bonds.

The specifics of bonds will be covered in much greater detail in a subsequent chapter, where we will look at a full range of issues from the perspective of the issuer (i.e., borrower). However, for now we are only going to consider bonds from the investor perspective. You need to understand just a few basics:

1. Each bond will have an associated "face value" (e.g., $1,000) that corresponds to the amount of principal to be paid at maturity,

2. Each bond will have a contract or stated interest rate (e.g., 5% -- meaning that the bond pays interest each year equal to 5% of the face amount), and

3. Each bond will have a term (e.g., 10 years -- meaning the bonds mature 10 years from the designated issue date).

In other words, a $1,000, 5%, 10-year bond would pay $50 per year for 10 years (as interest), and then pay $1,000 at the stated maturity date 10 years after the original date of the bond.

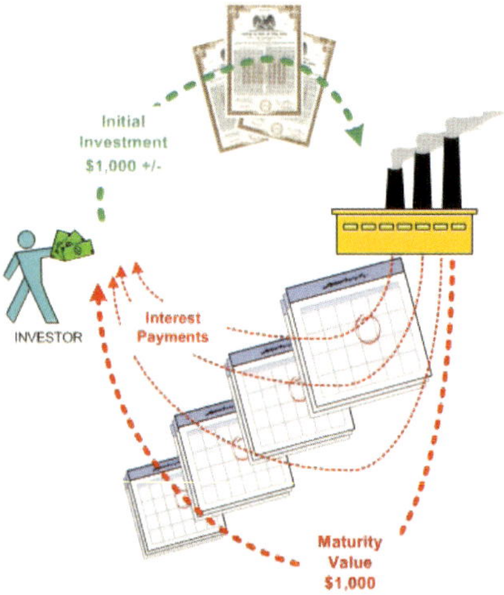

The issue price: How much would you pay for the above 5%, 10-year bond: Exactly $1,000, more than $1,000, or less than $1,000? The answer to this question depends on many factors, including the credit-worthiness of the issuer, the remaining time to maturity, and the overall market conditions. If the "going rate" of interest for other bonds was 8%, you would likely avoid this 5% bond (or, only buy it if it were issued at a deep discount). On the other hand, the 5% rate might look pretty good if the "going rate" was 3% for other similar bonds (in which case you might actually pay a premium to get the bond). So, bonds might have an issue price that is at their face value (also known as "par"), or above (at a premium) or below (at a discount) face. The price of a bond is typically stated as percentage of face; for example 103 would mean 103% of face, or $1,030.

Recording the initial investment: An Investment in Bonds account (at the purchase price plus brokerage fees and other incidental acquisition costs) is established at the time of purchase. Importantly, premiums and discounts are not recorded in separate accounts:

Illustration of bonds purchased at par:

1-1-X3	Investment in Bonds	5,000	
	Cash		5,000
	To record the purchase of five $1,000, 5%, 3-year bonds at par -- interest payable semi-annually		

The above entry reflects a bond purchase as described, while the following entry reflects the correct accounting for the receipt of the first interest payment after 6 months.

6-30-X3	Cash	125	
	Interest Income		125
	To record the receipt of an interest payment ($5,000 par X .05 interest X 6/12 months)		

Now, the entry that is recorded on June 30 would be repeated with each subsequent interest payment -- continuing through the final interest payment on December 31, 20X5. In addition, at maturity, when the bond principal is repaid, the investor would make this final accounting entry:

12-31-X5	Cash	5,000	
	Investment in Bonds		5,000
	To record the redemption of bond investment at maturity		

Illustration of bonds purchased at a premium: When bonds are purchased at a premium, the investor pays more than the face value up front. However, the bond's maturity value is unchanged; thus, the amount due at maturity is less than the initial issue price. This may seem unfair, but consider that the investor is likely generating higher annual interest receipts than on other available bonds -- that is why the premium was paid to begin with. So, it all sort of comes out even in the end. Assume the same facts as for the above bond illustration, but this time imagine that the market rate of interest was something less than 5%. Now, the 5% bonds would be very attractive, and entice investors to pay a premium:

1-1-X3	Investment in Bonds	5,300	
	Cash		5,300
	To record the purchase of five $1,000, 5%, 3-year bonds at 106 -- interest payable semi-annually		

The above entry assumes the investor paid 106% of par ($5,000 X 106% = $5,300). However, remember that only $5,000 will be repaid at maturity. Thus, the investor will be "out" $300 over the life of the bond. Thus, accrual accounting dictates that this $300 "cost" be amortized ("recognized over the life of the bond") as a reduction of the interest income:

6-30-X3	Cash	125	
	Interest Income		75
	Investment in Bonds		50
	To record the receipt of an interest payment ($5,000 par X .05 interest X 6/12 months = $125; $300 premium X 6 months/36 months = $50 amortization)		

The preceding entry is undoubtedly one of the more confusing entries in accounting, and bears additional explanation. Even though $125 was received, only $75 is being recorded as interest income. The other $50 is treated as a return of the initial investment; it corresponds to the premium amortization ($300 premium allocated evenly over the life of the bond -- $300 X (6 months/36 months)) and is credited against the Investment in Bonds account. This process of premium amortization (and the above entry) would be repeated with each interest payment date. Therefore, after three years, the Investment in Bonds account would be reduced to $5,000 ($5,300 - ($50 amortization X 6 semiannual interest recordings)). This method of tracking amortized cost is called the straight-line method. There is another conceptually superior approach to amortization, called the effective-interest method. However, it is a bit more complex and the straight-line method presented here is acceptable so long as its results are not materially different than would result under the effective-interest method.

In addition, at maturity, when the bond principal is repaid, the investor would make this final accounting entry:

12-31-X5	Cash	5,000	
	Investment in Bonds		5,000
	To record the redemption of bond investment at maturity		

In an attempt to make sense of the above, perhaps it is helpful to reflect on just the "cash out" and the "cash in." How much cash did the investor pay out? It was $5,300; the amount of the initial investment. How much cash did the investor get back? It was $5,750; $125 every 6 months for 3 years and $5,000 at maturity. What is the difference? It is $450 ($5,750 - $5,300) -- which is equal to the income recognized above ($75 every 6 months, for 3 years). At its very essence, accounting measures the change in money as income.

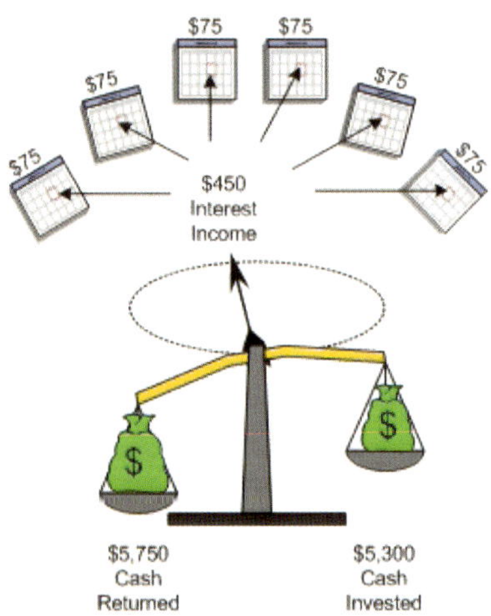

Bond accounting is no exception, although it is sometimes illusive to see. The following "amortization" table reveals certain facts about the bond investment accounting, and is worth studying to be sure you understand each amount in the table. Be sure to "tie" the amounts in the table to the entries above:

Date	Cash Received	Interest Income	Premium Amortization	Investment in Bonds
1-1-X3	$ (5,300) cr			$ 5,300
6-30-X3	125 dr	$ 75 cr	$ 50 cr	5,250
12-31-X3	125 dr	75 cr	50 cr	5,200
6-30-X4	125 dr	75 cr	50 cr	5,150
12-31-X4	125 dr	75 cr	50 cr	5,100
6-30-X5	125 dr	75 cr	50 cr	5,050
12-31-X5	125 dr	75 cr	50 cr	5,000
12-31-X5	5,000 dr	-	-	-
	$ 450	$ 450	$ 300	

Sometimes, complex topics like this are easier to understand when you think about the balance sheet impact of a transaction. For example, on 12-31-X4, Cash is increased $125, but the Investment in Bond account is decreased by $50 (dropping from $5,150 to $5,100). Thus, total assets increased by a net of $75. The balance sheet remains in balance because the corresponding $75 of interest income causes a corresponding increase in retained earnings.

Illustration of bonds purchased at a discount: The discount scenario is very similar to the premium scenario, but "in reverse." When bonds are purchased at a discount, the investor pays less than the face value up front. However, the bond's maturity value is unchanged; thus, the amount due at maturity is more than the initial issue price. This may seem like a bargain, but consider that the investor is likely getting lower annual interest receipts than is available on other bonds -- that is why the discount existed in the first place. Assume the same facts as for the previous bond illustration, except imagine that the market rate of interest was something more than 5%. Now, the 5% bonds would not be very attractive, and investors would only be willing to buy them at a discount:

1-1-X3	Investment in Bonds	4,850	
	Cash		4,850
	To record the purchase of five $1,000, 5%, 3-year bonds at 97 -- interest payable semiannually		

The above entry assumes the investor paid 97% of par ($5,000 X 97% = $4,850). However, remember that a full $5,000 will be repaid at maturity. Thus, the investor will get an additional $150 over the life of the bond. Accrual accounting dictates that this $150 "benefit" be recognized over the life of the bond as an increase in interest income:

6-30-X3	Cash	125	
	Investment in Bonds	25	
	Interest Income		150
	To record the receipt of an interest payment ($5,000 par X .05 interest X 6/12 months = $125; $150 discount X 6 months/36 months = $25 amortization)		

The preceding entry would be repeated at each interest payment date. Again, further explanation may prove helpful. In addition to the $125 received, another $25 of interest income is recorded. The other $25 is added to the Investment in Bonds account; as it corresponds to the discount amortization ($150 discount allocated evenly over the life of the bond -- $150 X (6 months/36 months)). This process of discount amortization would be repeated with each interest payment. Therefore, after three years, the Investment in Bonds account would be increased to $5,000 ($4,850 + ($25 amortization X 6 semiannual interest recordings)). This is another example of the straight-line method of amortization since the amount of interest is the same each period.

When the bond principal is repaid at maturity, the investor would also make this final accounting entry:

12-31-X5	Cash	5,000	
	Investment in Bonds		5,000
	To record the redemption of bond investment at maturity		

Let's consider the "cash out" and the "cash in." How much cash did the investor pay out? It was $4,850; the amount of the initial investment. How much cash did the investor get back? It is the same as it was in the preceding illustration -- $5,750; $125 every 6 months for 3 years and $5,000 at maturity. What is the difference? It is $900 ($5,750 - $4,850) -- which is equal to the income recognized above ($150 every 6 months, for 3 years).

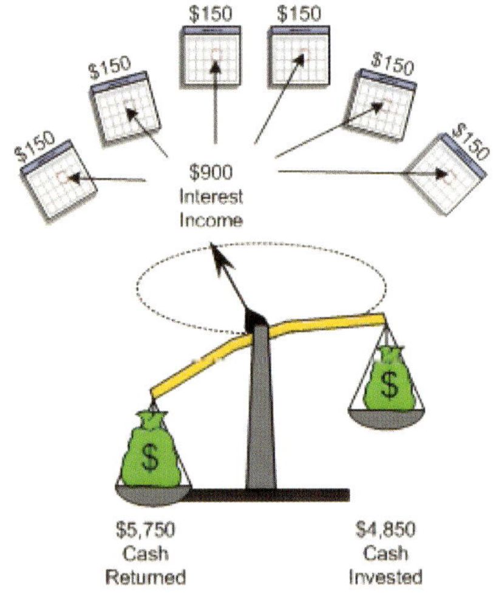

Be sure to "tie" the amounts in the following amortization table to the related entries:

Date	Cash Received	Interest Income	Discount Amortization	Investment in Bonds
1-1-X3	$ (4,850) cr			$ 4,850
6-30-X3	125 dr	$ 150 cr	$ 25 dr	4,875
12-31-X3	125 dr	150 cr	$ 25 dr	4,900
6-30-X4	125 dr	150 cr	$ 25 dr	4,925
12-31-X4	125 dr	150 cr	$ 25 dr	4,950
6-30-X5	125 dr	150 cr	$ 25 dr	4,975
12-31-X5	125 dr	150 cr	$ 25 dr	5,000
12-31-X5	5,000 dr	-	-	-
	$ 900	$ 900	$ 150	

Can you picture the balance sheet impact on 6-30-X5? Cash increased by $125, and the Investment in Bond account increased $25. Thus, total assets increased by $150. The balance sheet remains in balance because the corresponding $150 of interest income causes a corresponding increase in retained earnings.

The Equity Method of Accounting

The equity method: On occasion, an investor may acquire enough ownership in the stock of another company to permit the exercise of "significant influence" over the investee company. For example, the investor has some direction over corporate policy, and can sway the election of the board of directors and other matters of corporate governance and decision making. Generally, this is deemed to occur when one company owns more than 20% of the stock of the other -- although the ultimate decision about the existence of "significant influence" remains a matter of judgment based on an assessment of all facts and circumstances. Once significant influence is present, generally accepted accounting principles require that the investment be accounted for under the "equity method".

With the equity method, the accounting for an investment is set to track the "equity" of the investee. That is, when the investee makes money (and experiences a corresponding increase in equity), the investor will similarly record its share of that profit (and vice-versa for a loss). The initial accounting commences by recording the investment at cost:

4-1-X3	Investment	50,000	
	Cash		50,000
	To record the purchase of 5,000 shares of Legg stock at $10 per share. Legg has 20,000 shares outstanding, and the investment in 25% of Legg (5,000/20,000 = 25%) is sufficient to give the investor significant influence		

Next, assume that Legg reports income for the three-month period ending June 30, 20X3, in the amount of $10,000. The investor would simultaneously record its "share" of this reported income as follows:

6-30-X3	Investment	2,500	
	Investment Income		2,500
	To record investor's share of Legg's reported income (25% X $10,000)		

Importantly, this entry causes the Investment account to increase by the investor's share of the investee's increase in its own equity (i.e., Legg's equity increased $10,000, and the entry causes the investor's Investment account to increase by $2,500), thus the name "equity method." Notice, too, that the credit causes the investor to recognize income of $2,500, again corresponding to its share of Legg's reported income for the period. Of course, a loss would be reported in just the opposite fashion.

When Legg pays out dividends (and decreases its equity), the investor will need to reduce its Investment account:

7-01-X3	Cash	1,000	
	Investment		1,000
	To record the receipt of $1,000 in dividends from Legg — Legg declared and paid a total of $4,000 ($4,000 X 25% = $1,000)		

The above entry is based on the assumption that Legg declared and paid a $4,000 dividend on July 1. This treats dividends as a return of the investment (not income, because the income is recorded as it is earned rather than when distributed). In the case of dividends, notice that the investee's equity reduction is met with a corresponding proportionate reduction of the Investment account on the books of the investor.

Note that market-value adjustments are usually not utilized when the equity method is employed. Essentially, the Investment account tracks the equity of the investee, increasing as the investee reports income and decreasing as the investee distributes dividends.

Fixed Asset

A fixed asset is a long-term part of a property that a company possesses and utilizes in the generation of its revenue and is not anticipated that would be devoured or consumed into cash in coming next one year. A typical case of fixed asset is a producer's plant resources, for example, its structures and hardware. The word "fix" indicates that these assets won't be sold in the current bookkeeping year.

Let's consider that ABC firm plans to purchase an office worth 20 lakhs rupees. The building has a physical shape, will last longer than a year and creates income, making it a fixed asset. Thus ABC firm will now have a place from where they can maintain their business operation and are solely responsible for the building as well.

Fixed assets additionally incorporate any property that organization doesn't sell directly to the customer. This can be furniture, engine vehicles, PCs and much more. Let's assume it cost around five lakhs. Thus, ABC firm acquired a fixed asset worth Rs. 25 lakhs, and this will also reflect in their balance sheet. This fixed asset is useful in calculating overall revenue of the company.

Importance of Fixed Assets

Detailed documentation of an organization's capital adds to the understanding of the financial wellbeing and estimation of that business. Data including fixed assets and depreciation is additionally utilized by potential financial specialists when they are thinking about whether an organization is a profitable or non-profitable firm. While deciding the estimation of a fixed asset, the strategy for depreciation must be considered.

Since the value of the assets depreciates as it is utilized, as it ages, or as latest models are presented, it is critical for a firm to enlist and track depreciation from the time of procurement. Fixed assets are incorporated into the asset report at their initial expense, and after that depreciation all through their life until they are sold, supplanted on the accounting report at their residual esteem.

Accounting For Fixed Asset

If your business has a fixed assets, sound accounting standards can fill in as a manual for properly represent these long haul goods on your bookkeeping records. Particular exchanges that influence capital to incorporate the buy, revaluation, devaluation and sale of the asset. This trade is vital to the exactness of your business' financial records and reports.

Fixed Asset Turnover Ratio

Fixed assets turnover proportion is an activity proportion that measures how effectively an organization is using its fixed resources in producing income. Financial specialists utilize this equation to see how well the organization is using their devices and equipment to produce sales. This idea is imperative to financial specialists since they need to have the capacity to gauge an exact profit for their venture.

Fixed Assets Turnover Ratio = Net Revenue / Aggregate Fixed Assets

Where, Net Revenue = Gross Revenue – Sales Return

Aggregate Fixed Assets = Fixed Assets – Total Depreciation

For example, consider the above example of ABC firm with a fixed asset worth 25 lakhs and the depreciating cost is five lakhs yearly. Consider their net revenue is 50 lakhs. If we calculate the fixed assets turnover ratio for ABC firm, it comes out to be 2.5. This ratio is considered as a critical factor for investors.

Types of Fixed Asset

Fixed assets are classified into two main types: Tangible and Intangible Assets.

Tangible Assets

These incorporate things, for example, buildings, land, hardware, various equipment, vehicles, furniture and much more. Think about your tangible resources as things you need to maintain your business. To value them, you begin with what you obtained or rented them for and after that apply the fitting depreciation strategies to diminish their value.

Some fixed assets, for example, land or structures may appreciate and not depreciate in long tenure. You need to consider this factor as well in your balance sheet.

Intangible Assets

These can incorporate goodwill, licenses, registered or trademarked names, and even phone numbers, any innovation, and websites if you ever plan to sell. For assets such as phone numbers and trademarked or patented things, it's somewhat harder to decide value.

Goodwill is an elusive resource, and this kind of asset is simpler to calculate by finding the difference between organizations actual cost and cost at which it is sold or purchased for. Most of the other intangible resources are hard to estimate.

Intangible Asset

An intangible asset is an asset that is not physical in nature. Goodwill, brand recognition and intellectual property, such as patents, trademarks and copyrights, are all intangible assets. Intangible assets exist in opposition to tangible assets, which include land, vehicles, equipment and inventory. Additionally, financial assets such as stocks and bonds, which derive their value from contractual claims, are considered tangible assets.

An intangible asset can be classified as either indefinite or definite. A company's brand name is considered an indefinite intangible asset because it stays with the company for as long as it continues operations. An example of a definite intangible asset would be a legal agreement to operate under another company's patent, with no plans of extending the agreement. Therefore, the agreement has a limited life and is classified as a definite asset.

While intangible assets don't have the obvious physical value of a factory or equipment, they can prove valuable for a firm and be critical to its long-term success or failure. For example, a business such as Coca-Cola wouldn't be nearly as successful if it not for the money made through brand-name recognition. Although brand recognition is not a physical asset that can be seen or touched, it can have a meaningful impact on generating sales.

Valuing Intangible Assets

Businesses can create or acquire intangible assets. For example, a business may create a mailing list of clients or establish a patent. A business could also choose to acquire intangibles. If a business creates an intangible asset, it can write off the expenses from the process, such as filing the patent application, hiring a lawyer and other related costs. In addition, all the expenses along the way of creating the intangible asset are expensed. However, intangible assets created by a company do not show up on the balance sheet and have no recorded book value. Because of this, when a company is purchased, often the purchase price is above the book value of assets on the balance sheet. The purchasing company records the premium paid as an intangible asset, goodwill, on its balance sheet.

Intangible assets only show up on the balance sheet if they have been acquired. If Company ABC purchases a patent from Company XYZ for an agreed-upon amount of $1 billion, then Company ABC would record a transaction for $1 billion in intangible assets that would show up under long-term assets. The $1 billion asset would then be written off over a number of years via amortization. Indefinite life intangible assets, such as goodwill, are not amortized. Rather, these assets are assessed each year for impairment, which is when the carrying value exceeds the asset's fair value.

Examples of Intangible Assets

- Marketing-related intangible assets
    - Trademarks
    - Newspaper mastheads
    - Internet domain names
    - Noncompetition agreements
- Customer-related intangible assets

  - Customer lists
  - Order backlog
  - Customer relationships
- Artistic-related intangible assets
  - Performance events
  - Literary works
  - Musical works
  - Pictures
  - Motion pictures and television programs
- Contract-based intangible assets
  - Licensing agreements
  - Service contracts
  - Lease agreements
  - Franchise agreements
  - Broadcast rights
  - Employment contracts
  - Use rights (such as drilling rights or water rights)
- Technology-based intangible assets
  - Patented technology
  - Computer software
  - Trade secrets (such as secret formulas and recipes)

Patents

A patent is considered an intangible asset; this is because a patent does not have physical substance, and provides long-term value to the owning entity. As such, the accounting for a patent is the same as for any other intangible fixed asset, which is:

- Initial recordation: Record the cost to acquire the patent as the initial asset cost. If a company files for a patent application, this cost will include the registration, documentation, and other legal fees associated with the application. If the company instead bought a patent from another party, the purchase price is the initial asset cost.

- Amortization: The owner of the patent gradually charges the cost of the patent to expense over the useful life of the patent, usually using the straight-line amortization method.
- Impairment: If a patent no longer provides value, or a reduced level of value, recognize an impairment to reduce or eliminate the carrying amount of the asset.
- Derecognition: Once the company is no longer making use of the patented idea, the asset can be derecognized by crediting the balance in the patent asset account and debiting the balance in the accumulated amortization account. If the asset has not been fully amortized at the time of derecognition, then any remaining unamortized balance must be recorded as a loss.

Consider the following additional points when accounting for patents:

- R&D expenditures: Note that the research and development (R&D) costs required to develop the idea being patented cannot be included in the capitalized cost of a patent. These R&D costs are instead charged to expense as incurred; the basis for this treatment is that R&D is inherently risky, without assurance of future benefits, so it should not be considered an asset.
- Useful life: A patent asset should not be amortized for longer than the lifespan of the protection afforded by the patent. If the expected useful life of the patent is even shorter, use the useful life for amortization purposes. Thus, the shorter of a patent's useful life and its legal life should be used for the amortization period.
- Capitalization limit: In practice, the costs of obtaining a patent may be so small that they do not meet or exceed a company's capitalization limit. If so, charge these costs to expense as incurred. In many larger companies with higher capitalization limits, this means that patents are rarely recorded as assets unless they have been purchased from other entities.

Copyrights

Copyright refers to the legal right of the owner of intellectual property. In simpler terms, copyright is the right to copy. This means that the original creator of a product and anyone he gives authorization to are the only ones with the exclusive right to reproduce the work. Copyright law gives creators of original material, the exclusive right to further develop them for a given amount of time, at which point the copyrighted item becomes public domain.

When someone creates a product that is viewed as original and that required significant mental activity to create, this product becomes intellectual property that must be protected from unauthorized duplication. Examples of unique creations include computer software, art, poetry, graphic designs, musical lyrics and compositions, novels, film, original architectural designs, website content, etc. One safeguard that can be used to protect an original creation is copyright.

Under copyright law, a work is considered original if the author created it from independent thinking void of duplication. This type of work is known as Original Work of Authorship (OWA). Anyone with an original work of authorship automatically has the copyright to that work, preventing anyone else from using or replicating it. The copyright can be registered voluntarily by the original owner if he or she would like to get an upper hand in the legal system if the need arises.

Not all types of work can be copyrighted though. A copyright does not protect ideas, discoveries, concepts and theories. Brand names, logos, slogans, domain names and titles also cannot be protected under copyright law. For an original work to fall under creation, it has to be in tangible form. This means that any speech, discoveries, musical scores or ideas have to be written down in physical form in order to be protected by copyright.

While copyright law is not all-encompassing, other laws, such as patent and trademark laws, may impose additional sanctions. Although copyrights, trademarks, and patents are frequently used interchangeably, they are different forms of protection for intellectual property. Trademark laws protect material that is used to distinguish an individual's or corporation's work from another entity. These materials include words, phrases, or symbols, such as logos, slogans and brand names which copyright laws do not cover. Patents cover inventions for a limited period of time. Patented materials include products like industrial processes, machines and chemical positions.

Duration of Copyright

In the U.S., an original owner is protected by copyright laws all his life until 70 years after his death. But copyright protection varies from country to country, and can stand for 50 to 100 years after the individual's death, depending on the country. If the original author of the copyrighted material is a corporation, the copyright protection period will be shorter.

U.S. copyright law has experienced a number of amendments and changes that have altered the duration of copyright protection. The life of the author plus 70 years protection can be attributed to the 1998 Copyright Term Extension Act, (also known as the Mickey Mouse Protection Act or Sonny Bono Act) which generally increased copyright protections by 20 years.

Trademark

Trademarks are logos, symbols and designs registered with the federal government and used by a business to identify its brands or the entity itself. Trademarks are assets that are included on a small business' balance sheet as "intangible assets," since they lack material substance like machinery and equipment that occupy physical space. The cost of a trademark is "capitalized" or recorded as an asset on a company's books with the use of a standard journal entry.

Asset Account Numbers

Capitalization of a trademark requires that you record a journal entry to the company's general ledger. Since accounts are assigned to a general ledger based on a numbering system, the capitalization of an asset requires that you gather the general ledger account number for two asset accounts: "cash" and "trademark." The account numbers may be found on a report known as the "chart of accounts," which includes the individual account numbers for all accounts included on a company's books.

Account Balance of Trademarks Entry

The balance of asset accounts is always increased with a debit on the general ledger. To increase the trademark asset account, enter the general ledger account number for "trademarks" you found on the chart of accounts on the first line of the journal entry in the column labeled "account number." Enter the total dollar amount of the trademark in the column labeled "debit."

Account Balance of Cash Entry

After you book the "trademarks" asset account increase, the asset account "cash" is reduced by a credit on the general ledger. To reduce the company's cash balance for the payment to obtain the trademark, enter the account number for cash as found on the chart of accounts on the second line, and enter the dollar amount of the cash payment in the column labeled "credit."

Example of Journal Entry

To illustrate the journal entries that capitalize trademark costs, assume your small business incurred $1,500 in trademark costs. The journal entries to capitalize the trademark costs appear as follows:

Debit intangible assets/trademark $1,500 Credit cash $1,500

Record the Journal Entry

Lastly, you need to make a permanent record of the entry on the company's general ledger by posting the entry to the company's books. To make sure the entry posted accurately, print and check a copy of the trial balance, a report that shows the debit and credit balances of a company's general ledger accounts. The trademark has now been capitalized to the corporation's books.

Goodwill

Goodwill may be described as the aggregate of those intangible attributes of a business which contributes to its superior earning capacity over a normal return on investment. It may arise from such attributes as favorable locations, the ability and skill of its employees and management, quality of its products and services, customer satisfaction etc.

Features of Goodwill

1. Goodwill is an intangible asset: It is non-visible but it is not a fictitious asset.
2. It cannot be separated from the business and therefore cannot be sold like other identifiable and separable assets, without disposing off the business as a whole.
3. The value of goodwill has no relation to the amount invested or cost incurred in order to build it.
4. Valuation of goodwill is subjective and is highly dependent on the judgment of the valuer.
5. Goodwill is subject to fluctuations. The value of goodwill may fluctuate widely according to internal and external factors of business.

Types of Goodwill

Goodwill is generally of two types:

a. Purchased goodwill; and
b. Non-Purchased or Inherent goodwill.

Purchased Goodwill

Purchased goodwill arises when a business concern is purchased and the purchase consideration paid exceeds the fair value of the separable net assets acquired. The purchased goodwill is shown on the assets side of the Balance sheet. 'Accounting for fixed assets' states that only purchased goodwill should be recognized in the books of accounts.

Non-Purchased Goodwill/Inherent Goodwill

Inherent goodwill is the value of business in excess of the fair value of its separable net assets. It is referred to as internally generated goodwill and it arises over a period of time due to good reputation of a business. The value of goodwill may be positive or negative. Positive goodwill arises when the value of business as a whole is more than the fair value of its net assets. It is negative when the value of the business is less than the value of its net assets.

Factors Affecting Goodwill

The important factors that give rise to goodwill are as follows:

1. Outstanding quality of products/services.
2. Locational factors: If a business is located at a favorable place; it enhances the value of goodwill.
3. The period for which the business has been in business.
4. Special advantages: A company that enjoys special advantages such as favorable contracts, assured supply of raw material at low rates, possession of trademarks, patents, copyrights, technical knowhow and research and development, well known collaborators etc. contribute to higher value of goodwill.
5. Nature of Business: A business having stable continuous demand for its products such as consumer goods is able to earn more profits and hence has more goodwill. If the business is risky, profits will be uncertain. The monopoly condition or limited competition enables the enterprise to earn higher profits which leads to higher value of goodwill.
6. Good relations with customers, suppliers, labor and government.
7. Efficiency of Management: A firm having efficient management enjoys advantages of high productivity and cost of efficiency. This leads to higher profits which in turn increases the value of goodwill.
8. Capital Required: If two businesses have same rate of profit, the business which requires lesser amount of capital tends to enjoy more goodwill.

Accounting for Goodwill

The various ways in which goodwill can be accounted for are as follows:

1. Carry it as an asset and write it off over a period of years through the profit and loss account.
2. Write it off against profits or accumulated reserves immediately.
3. Retain it as an asset with no write-off unless a permanent diminution in value becomes evident.
4. Show it as a deduction from shareholders' funds which may be authorized carried forward indefinitely.

In this connection, it is important to state that goodwill should be recognized and recorded in business only when some consideration in money or money's worth has been paid for it.

Impairment

Accounts commonly recognize and record the values of all of a company's assets. The value of these assets is usually determined by the current market.

But often, the value of an asset changes as time passes. Impairment relflects the reduction in the quality, durability, quantity or market value of an asset.

Conversely, appreciation is when the value of an asset increases.

A Reduction of Value

The value of fixed assets (e.g. buildings, machinery, land) can be prone to impairment. Numerous factors could lead to their reduction in value.

For example, wear and tear, poor management, new competition, technological innovations, etc. could all result in an asset becoming less valuable.

Regular use can often result in the reduced value of an asset. For instance, this is often the case with assets such as machinery. However, an asset can also simply depreciate in value over time. This depreciation is usually distributed throughout the asset's lifetime.

Impairment is usually subjective. It can be problematic to determine the fair value of an asset, and therefore various conclusions about this value can be found.

The Profit and Loss Account

The impairment losses are accounted in the profit-and-loss account.

In order to measure the impairment value of an asset, a comparison of the value of the asset with its recoverable amount (the highest value that can be retrieved by selling the fixed asset) must be made.

Tangible Assets

Tangible assets are physical, measurable resources; like property, plant, and equipment, used in a company's operations to produce a profit. These assets include anything with a physical nature that is used within a company.

These resources can be divided into two main categories: current and fixed. Current assets are resources that will be consumed in the current period like inventory. Fixed assets are long-term resources that will provide value for future periods to come. Some examples include machinery, vehicles, and buildings.

These resources can be damaged, repaired, stolen, and purchased because they are real items that get used in the normal course of business. Management must ensure these resources are guarded and maintained properly in order to preserve their usefulness. Tangibles can also use as collateral for loans.

All tangibles are reported on the balance sheet at their historical cost, but some have special reporting requirements. Long-term fixed assets must be depreciated over their useful lives with the accumulated depreciation reported on the front of the balance sheet.

List of Tangible Assets Examples

Property, Plant, and Equipment (PP&E) are long-lived tangible assets used in the production or sale of other assets. Cost of PP&E includes all expenditure (transportation, insurance, installation, broker cost, search cost, legal cost) that are necessary to acquire and ready them for use. If the plant is constructed, all the material, labor cost, overheads, interest cost during construction included in the Cost of PP&E.

Below is the list of Tangible assets examples:

1. Property: Property includes the land, building, office furniture etc.
2. Plant: Plant is the physical space where the workers work or provide services.
3. Equipment: This refers to the machinery, vehicles and other tools & equipment used to produce.
4. Inventory: This includes all types of inventory like the finished goods as well as WIP and raw material inventory.

Recording PP&E on the Balance Sheet

You record PP&E (Tangible assets) on the balance sheet at their original cost. You add to this all the costs involved in getting the asset ready for its intended use, such as legal fees, transportation to the current location, necessary testing and non-recoverable taxes. You do not record PP&E at its market value.

Tangible Assets Examples in Companies

Depending on the type of the company these assets may or may not make the largest asset amounts. Here are the two tangible asset examples:

- High capex companies like Oil and Gas companies, Real Estate Companies, Car Manufacturers have a large percentage of total assets tied up in Plant, Equipment, and Machinery. Therefore, you will find a large amount of tangible assets on the balance sheet.

- Services companies like Microsoft or Infosys will have far fewer assets. Such companies own a large number of intangible assets like patents, copyrights etc.

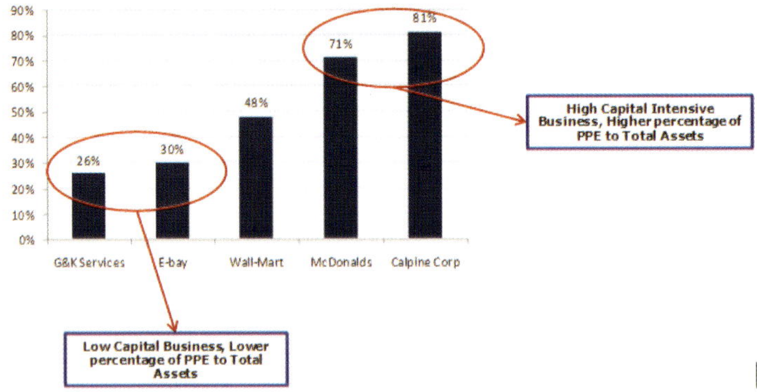

Value of Tangible Current Assets

The potential total cost of tangible current assets usually includes not only the amount for which it is purchased, as recorded in the relevant invoice as part of the inventory bought, but also includes any additional costs incurred due to transportation, for its installation and for insurance purposes as well.

Value of Tangible Fixed Assets

As already discussed, tangible fixed assets have their value spread over its expected lifespan instead of being accounted for only in the year when they might be purchased. A part of their value is being accounted for every year in the accounts of a firm, known as depreciation, which also stands for the monetary worth reduced after a certain period of use.

In conclusion, tangible assets form an integral and important part of assets owned by a business and play a critical role in carrying out business operations effectively. The way their worth might be calculated might be a matter of consideration, however, as fixed assets are depreciated over time and depending on the method of depreciation adopted, the figure could vary from one business to another. Then again, such assets have to be separated from intangible ones to be able to evaluate and measure their worth with any amount of accuracy and this is exactly what net tangible assets is all about.

Having said that, the relevance of measures associated with tangible assets obviously have their limitations due to the difference in levels of intangible and tangible assets for different industries. Certain industries tend to have greater intangible assets goodwill and hence a lower number associated with net tangible assets would not represent the real picture while assessing a company from an asset-based perspective. Keeping all the possible uses and limitations in mind, tangible assets and related measures can be employed with good effect.

Liabilities

In small business accounting, liabilities are existing debts that your business owes to another business, organization, vendor, employee, or government agency. You incur debts through regular business operations.

Liabilities can fluctuate daily as you add new debt and make payments. The more debts you have, the higher your liabilities are. And, the more debts you pay off, the lower your liabilities are.

Liabilities can make buying items for your business easier. With liabilities, you don't have to pay immediately after you receive a good or service. Instead, the vendor sends you an invoice. You pay the amount due at a later date. Until you pay the invoice, the money you owe is a liability.

Liabilities also help you finance your company. For example, a small business loan is a liability that can help you grow your business. You owe the loan amount to the bank. But as you pay off the loan, you can use the borrowed money to improve and expand your business.

Here are some common examples of liabilities:

- Loans
- Accounts payable
- Mortgages
- Deferred revenues (advances paid by your customers)
- Accrued expenses (expenses recognized in your books before they're paid)

All the above examples are debts that your company owes. To record debts in your books, you need to know the different kinds of liabilities.

Short-term vs. Long-term Liabilities

Liabilities are separated into two types: short-term and long-term. Both types of liabilities affect your finances differently.

Short-term liabilities are also called current liabilities. You pay short-term liabilities within one year of incurring them.

Examples of short-term liabilities include:

- Employee wages
- Accounts payable

- Utilities
- Supplies
- Invoices

Long-term liabilities are also called noncurrent liabilities. You pay long-term liabilities over a period that is longer than one year.

Examples of long-term liabilities include:

- Accrued expenses
- Loans lasting more than one year
- Mortgages
- Deferred taxes

Recording Liabilities on the Balance Sheet

Record your business's liabilities on your small business balance sheet. The balance sheet is a financial statement that shows your assets, liabilities, and equity. The balance sheet reveals a snapshot of your finances that compares what your business owns to what it owes.

Liabilities play a major role in understanding your business's profitability. To keep track of debts, record liabilities on the right side of the balance sheet. You should continually make records as you incur new debt and pay existing debt.

Short-term liabilities appear first on the right side of your balance sheet. List long-term liabilities after the total short-term liabilities.

The balance sheet is at the core of accounting for business owners, and is a great tool for understanding your finances. Here is an example of recording liabilities on the balance sheet:

Assets		Liabilities	
Cash	$17,500	Accounts Payable	$735
Accounts Receivable	$12,432	Notes Payable	$1,500
Inventory	$8,230	Total Short-term Liabilities	$2,235
Total Short-term Assets	$38,162	Paid in Capital	$500
Office Furniture	$3,510	Total Long-term Liabilities	$500
Office Equipment	$6,107		
Total Long-term Assets	$9,617	Total Liabilities	$2,735

		Equity	
		Owner's Equity	$20,000
		Retained Earnings	$25,044
Total Assets	$47,779	Total Liabilities and Equity	$47,779

The balance sheet doesn't just help you see how much your company owes. It also helps you secure financing from a bank, lender, or investor. A creditor might ask to review your balance sheet to determine the level of risk involved in working with you. The higher your liabilities, the bigger risk you are to the creditor.

Liabilities and Assets

On the balance sheet, you record both liabilities and assets. Your business's liabilities and assets directly correlate with each other.

Assets are the items your business owns that add value to your company. For example, buildings, equipment, accounts receivable, cash, and intellectual property are all assets. By comparing assets to liabilities from your balance sheet equation, you can find your net ownership within the company.

Your ownership in the business is called owner's equity. If you are a sole proprietor, you can find your owner's equity by subtracting the liabilities from assets.

Assets – Liabilities = Owner's Equity

If you have more assets than liabilities, you have positive equity. That means you can pay your debts and have money left over.

If you have more liabilities than assets, you have negative equity. Negative equity means you owe more to debtors than you own.

Difference between Expenses and Liabilities

As you complete your books, know the difference between business expenses and liabilities. Liabilities are the debts your business owes. Expenses include the costs you incur to generate revenue. For example, the cost of the materials you use to make goods is an expense, not a liability.

Expenses are directly related to revenue. By subtracting your expenses from revenue, you can find your business's net income. Liabilities are not related to revenue. You cannot find net income with liabilities.

Record expenses and liabilities on different financial statements. Liabilities are found on the balance sheet. Expenses are found on the income statement.

Current Liabilities

Current liabilities on balance sheet refer to the debts or obligations that a company owes and is required to settle within one fiscal year or its normal operating cycle, whichever is longer. Such obligations will require the use of current assets like cash, the creation of new current liability or providing of service for settlement. These liabilities are recorded on the Balance Sheet in the order of shortest term to longest term. The definition does not include amounts that are yet to be incurred as per the accrual basis of accounting. For example, salary to be paid to employees for services in the next fiscal year is not yet due since the services have not yet been incurred.

List of Current Liabilities Examples

A list of current liabilities examples are as follows:

Accounts Payable

Accounts payable is usually the major component of current liability representing payment due to suppliers within one year for raw materials bought as evidenced by supply invoices. Here is current liabilities example

Current Liabilities				
Notes and loans payable	$	13	$	4
Current portion of long-term debt		—		298
Accounts payable		1,124		1,110
Accrued income taxes		441		277
Other accruals		1,727		1,845
Total current liabilities		3,305		3,534

We note from above that Accounts Payable of Colgate is $1,124 million in 2016 and $1,110 million in 2015.

Notes Payable (Short-term)

Notes payable is short-term financial obligations evidenced by negotiable instruments like bank borrowings or obligations for equipment purchases. Maybe interest bearing or non-interest bearing

Current Liabilities				
Notes and loans payable	$	13	$	4
Current portion of long-term debt		—		298
Accounts payable		1,124		1,110
Accrued income taxes		441		277
Other accruals		1,727		1,845
Total current liabilities		3,305		3,534

Notes and loans payable for Colgate is $13 million and $4 million in 2016 and 2015, respectively.

Bank Account Overdrafts

Short term advances made by the banks to offset account overdrafts due to excess funding above the available limit. Also, have a look at revolving credit facility

Current Portion of Long-term Debt

Current Portion of long-term debt is a part of the long-term debt due within the next one year

Current Liabilities		
Notes and loans payable	$ 13	$ 4
Current portion of long-term debt	—	298
Accounts payable	1,124	1,110
Accrued income taxes	441	277
Other accruals	1,727	1,845
Total current liabilities	3,305	3,534

Current Lease Payable

Lease obligations due to the lessor in the short-term

Current liabilities:		
Accounts payable	$ 43	$ 63
Platform partners payable	153	171
Accrued expenses and other current liabilities	441	296
Deferred revenue and deposits	85	90
Current portion of capital lease obligations	312	279
Total current liabilities	1,034	899
Capital lease obligations, less current portion	394	398
Other liabilities	191	135
Total liabilities	1,619	1,432

Income Taxes or Current Tax Payable

Income Tax owed to the government but not yet paid

Current Liabilities		
Notes and loans payable	$ 13	$ 4
Current portion of long-term debt	—	298
Accounts payable	1,124	1,110
Accrued income taxes	441	277
Other accruals	1,727	1,845
Total current liabilities	3,305	3,534

We note from above that Colgate's accrued income tax was $441 million and $277 million, respectively.

Expenses (Liabilities)

Expenses not yet payable to the third party, but already incurred like interest and salary payable. These are accumulated with the passage of time, however, they will get paid when they become due. For example, salaries that the employees have earned but not been paid is reported as accrued salaries.

Current liabilities:		
Accounts payable	$ 43	$ 63
Platform partners payable	153	171
Accrued expenses and other current liabilities	441	296
Deferred revenue and deposits	85	90
Current portion of capital lease obligations	312	279
Total current liabilities	1,034	899
Capital lease obligations, less current portion	394	398
Other liabilities	191	135
Total liabilities	1,619	1,432

Dividend Payable

Dividends payables are Dividend declared, but yet to be paid to shareholders. Therefore they are recorded as current liabilities on balance sheet.

Unearned Revenue

Unearned revenues are advance payments made by customers for future work to be completed in the short term like an advance magazine subscription.

The below example details of unearned subscription revenues for a Media (magazine company)

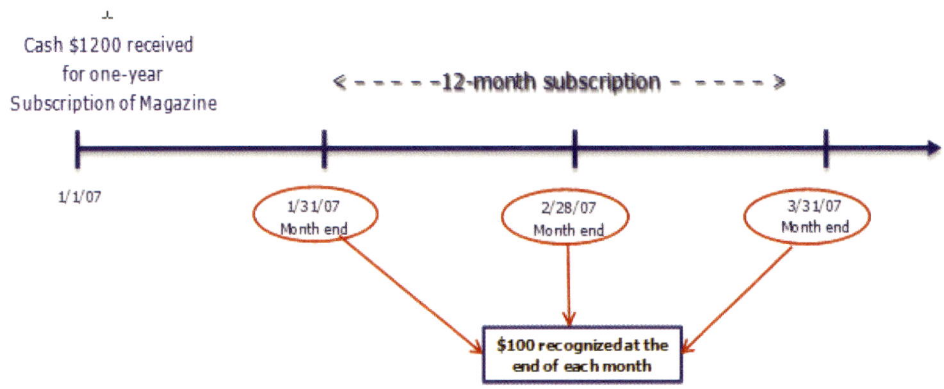

Analyze Current Liabilities on Balance Sheet

Current liabilities on balance sheet impose restrictions on the cash flow of a company and have to be managed prudently to ensure that the company has enough current assets to maintain short-term liquidity. In most cases, companies are required to maintain liabilities for recording payments which are not yet due. Again, companies may want to have liabilities because it lowers their long-term interest obligation.

Some of the important ways you can analyze current liabilities on balance sheet:

1. Working Capital and
2. Current Ratios (& Quick Ratio)

Working Capital

Working capital is the capital which makes fixed assets work in an organization. Working capital can be calculated as follows:

Working Capital formula = Current Assets – Current Liabilities

- A company's liquidity position can be gauged by analyzing its working capital. Excessive working capital means that level of current assets is much higher as compared to current liabilities on balance sheet. This excess capital blocked up in the assets has an opportunity cost for the firm since it can be invested in other areas for generating higher profits instead of staying idle within working capital.
- On the other extreme, inadequate working capital may pose short-term liquidity issues if the company maintains current assets which are not sufficient enough to meet the liabilities. Consistent liquidity issues may pose problems in the smooth functioning of the firm and affect the credibility of the company in the market.

Current Ratio and Quick Ratio

Current Liabilities on balance sheet are also used to calculate liquidity ratios like current ratio and quick ratio. These ratios are calculated as follows:

Current Ratio = Current Assets/Current Liabilities, and

Quick Ratio = (Current Assets- Inventories)/Current Liabilities

- While working capital is an absolute measure, current ratio or working capital ratio can be used to compare companies against peers. The ratio varies across industries and a ratio of 1.5 is usually an acceptable standard. A ratio above 2 or below 1 gives an indication of inadequate working capital management.
- Current Ratio is used in the financial analysis along with quick ratio which is a measure of company's ability to meet its liabilities using its more liquid assets. A company may boast of a high current ratio. However, it may so happen that most of its current assets are in the form of inventories which are difficult to convert into cash and hence, are less liquid. In case of immediate requirement of funds for meeting liabilities, these less liquid assets would be of no help to the company.
- A quick ratio of less than 1 would signify that the company would be unable to pay back its current liabilities on balance sheet. Thus a quick ratio is also referred to as acid test ratio which speaks of a company's financial strength.

Reasons for Current Liabilities being greater in Retail Industry

For the retail industry, the current ratio is usually less than 1 meaning that current liabilities on balance sheet are more than current assets.

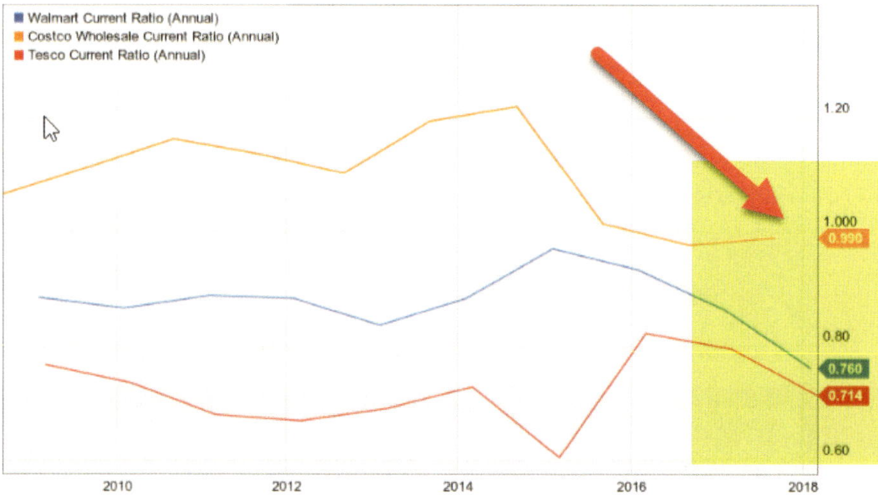

Costco Current Ratio is 0.99, Walmart Current ratio is 0.76 and that of Tesco is 0.714.

- Retailers like Walmart, Costco, and Tesco maintain minimal working capital since they are able to negotiate longer credit period with suppliers but can afford to offer little credit to customers.
- Thus they have much higher accounts payable compared to accounts receivable.
- Such retailers also maintain minimal inventory through efficient supply chain management.

In conclusion, Most Balance sheets separate current liabilities from long-term liabilities. This gives an idea of the short-term dues and is an important information for lenders, financial analysts, owners, and executives of the firm to analyze liquidity, working capital management and compare across firms in the industry. Being a part of the working capital, this is also significant for computing free cash flow of a firm.

Although it is more prudent to maintain current ratio and quick ratio of at least 1, the current ratio greater than one provides additional cushion to deal with unforeseen contingencies. Traditional manufacturing facilities maintain current assets at levels double that of current liabilities on balance sheet. However, the increased usage of just in time manufacturing technique in modern manufacturing companies like automobile sector has reduced the current ratio requirement.

Non-Current Liabilities

Noncurrent liabilities, also called long-term liabilities, are long-term financial obligations listed on a company's balance sheet that are not due for settlement within one year as opposed to current liabilities which are short-term debts.

Noncurrent liabilities are compared to a cash flow, to see if a company will be able to meet its financial obligations. While lenders are primarily concerned with short-term liquidity and the amount of current liabilities, long-term investors use noncurrent liabilities to gauge whether a company is using excessive leverage. The more stable a company's cash flows, the more debt it can support without increasing default risk.

Investors and creditors use numerous financial ratios to assess liquidity risk and leverage. The debt ratio compares a company's total debt to total assets, to provide a general idea of how leveraged it is. The lower the percentage, the less leverage a company is using and the stronger its equity position. The higher the ratio, the more financial risk a company is taking on. Other variants are the long term debt to total assets ratio and the long-term debt to capitalization ratio, which divides noncurrent liabilities by the amount of capital available.

Analysts also use coverage ratios to assess a company's financial health, including the cash flow-to-debt and the interest coverage ratio. The cash flow-to-debt ratio determines how long it would take a company to repay its debt if it devoted all of its cash flow to debt repayment. The interest coverage ratio, which is calculated by dividing a company's earnings before interest and taxes (EBIT) by its periodic debt interest payments, gauges whether enough income being generated to cover interest payments.

To assess short-term liquidity risk, analysts look at liquidity ratios like the current ratio, the quick ratio and the acid test ratio.

Noncurrent liabilities include debentures, long-term loans, bonds payable, deferred tax liabilities, long-term lease obligations and pension benefit obligations. The portion of a bond liability that will not be paid within the upcoming year is classified as a noncurrent liability. Mortgages, car payments or other loans for machinery, equipment or land are all long-term debts, except for the payments to be made in the subsequent 12 months.

When reporting a capital lease as an asset on the balance sheet, payments due after one year are noncurrent liabilities. Warranties covering more than a one-year period are also recorded as noncurrent liabilities. Other examples include deferred compensation, deferred revenue, derivatives and certain health care liabilities.

Debt that is due within 12 months may also be reported as a noncurrent liability, if there is intent to refinance this debt with a financial arrangement in the process to restructure the obligation to a noncurrent nature. Because current liabilities are broken down, noncurrent liabilities can be calculated by subtracting current liabilities from total debt.

Contingent Liability

A contingent liability is a potential loss that may occur at some point in the future, once various uncertainties have been resolved. This liability is not yet an actual, confirmed obligation. The exact status of a contingent liability is important when determining which liabilities to present in the balance sheet or in the attached disclosures. It is of interest to a financial analyst, who wants to understand the probability of such an issue becoming a full liability of a business, which could impact its status as a going concern.

When to Recognize a Contingent Liability

There are three scenarios for contingent liabilities, all involving different accounting treatments. They are:

- High probability: Record a contingent liability when it is probable that the loss will occur, and you can reasonably estimate the amount of the loss. If you can only estimate a range of possible amounts, then record that amount in the range that appears to be a better estimate than any other amount; if no amount is better, then record the lowest amount in the range. "Probable" means that the future event is likely to occur. You should also describe the liability in the footnotes that accompany the financial statements.
- Medium probability: Disclose the existence of the contingent liability in the notes accompanying the financial statements if the liability is reasonably possible but not probable, or if the liability is probable, but you cannot estimate the amount. "Reasonably possible" means that the chance of the event occurring is more than remote but less than likely.
- Low probability: Do not record or disclose the contingent liability if the probability of its occurrence is remote.

Examples of contingent liabilities are the outcome of a lawsuit, a government investigation, or the threat of expropriation. A warranty can also be considered a contingent liability, since there is uncertainty about the exact number of units that will be returned by customers for repair or replacement.

Example of a Contingent Liability

For example, ABC Company files a lawsuit against Unlucky Company for $500,000. Unlucky attorney feels that the suit is without merit, so Unlucky merely discloses the existence of the lawsuit in the notes accompanying its financial statements. Several months later, Unlucky attorney recommends that the company should settle out of court for $75,000; at this point, the liability is both probable and can be estimated, so Unlucky records a $75,000 liability. A possible entry for this transaction might be:

	Debit	Credit
Legal expense	75,000	
Accrued liabilities		75,000

When Unlucky later pays ABC company in the out-of-court settlement, the final entry is:

	Debit	Credit
Accrued liabilities	75,000	
Cash		75,000

Other Contingent Liability Issues

The accounting rules for the treatment of a contingent liability are quite liberal - there is no need to record a liability unless the risk of loss is quite high. Thus, you should review the disclosures accompanying a company's financial statements to see if there are additional risks that have not yet been recognized. These disclosures should be considered advance warning of amounts that may later appear as formal liabilities in the financial statements.

Accrued Liabilities

An accrued liability is an expense that a business has incurred but has not yet paid. A company can accrue liabilities for any number of obligations, and the accruals can be recorded as either short-term or long-term liabilities on a company's balance sheet. Payroll taxes, including Social Security, Medicare and federal unemployment taxes are liabilities that can be accrued periodically in preparation for payment before the taxes are due.

An accrued liability is a financial obligation a company incurs during a given period but has not yet paid for in that period. Although the cash flow has yet to occur, the company must still pay for the benefit received. Accrued liabilities only exist when using an accrual method of accounting. The other alternative the cash method does not accrue liabilities. Accrued liabilities are entered into the financial records during one period and are typically reversed in the next when paid. This will allow for the actual expense to be recorded at the accurate dollar amount when payment is made in full.

Purpose of Accrued Liability

The concept of an accrued liability relates to timing and the matching principle. Under accrual accounting, all expenses are to be recorded in financial statements in the period in which they are incurred, which may differ from the period in which they are paid. Expenses are recorded in the same period when related revenues are reported to provide financial statement users with accurate information regarding the costs required to generate revenue.

Situations Causing Accrued Liabilities

Accrued liabilities arise due to events that occur during the normal course of business. A company that purchased goods or services on a deferred payment plan will accrue liabilities, because the obligation to pay in the future exists. Employees may have performed work but have not yet received wages. Interest on loans may be accrued if interest fees have been incurred since the previous loan payment. Taxes owed to governments may be accrued because they may not be due until the next tax reporting period.

Example of Accrued Liability

At the end of a calendar year, salary and benefits must be recorded in the appropriate year, regardless of when the pay period ends and when paychecks are distributed. For example, a two-week pay period may extend from December 25 to January 7. Although the salaries and benefits will not be distributed until January, there is still one full week of expenses relating to December. Therefore, the salaries, benefits and taxes incurred from December 25 to December 31 are accrued liabilities. In the financial records, expenses will be debited to reflect an increase in the expenses. Meanwhile, various liabilities will be credited to report the increase in obligations at the end of the year.

Steps to Record Accrued Expenses

To record accrued expenses, use debit and credit journal entries. In accrual accounting, you must use a double-entry bookkeeping system. This method requires you to make two opposite but equal entries for each transaction.

Entries are debits and credits. Some accounts are increased by debits and decreased by credits. Other accounts are increased by credits and decreased by debits.

To make accrued expense entries, you need to know:

- Liabilities are increased by credits and decreased by debits.
- Expenses are increased by debits and decreased by credits.
- Assets (cash) are increased by debits and decreased by credits.

Remember, accrued liabilities are reversing entries. They are temporary entries used to adjust your books between accounting periods. So, you will make your initial journal entry for accrued expenses. Then, you will flip the original record with another entry when you pay the amount due.

Step 1: You Incur the Expense

You incur an expense at the end of the accounting period. You owe a debt but have not yet been billed. You need to make an accrued liability entry in your books.

Usually, an accrued expense journal entry is a debit to an expense account. The debit entry increases your expenses.

You also apply a credit to an accrued liabilities account. The credit increases your liabilities.

Account	Debit	Credit
Expense Account	X	
Accrued Liability Account		X

What happens when you make these entries? Your expenses increase on the income statement. And, your liabilities increase on the balance sheet.

Step 2: You Pay the Expense

At the beginning of the next accounting period, you pay the expense. You need to reverse the original entry in your books.

To reverse the transaction, debit the accrued liability account. The debit will decrease your liabilities. When you pay a debt, you have fewer liabilities.

You also credit an asset account. In this case, you credit the cash account because you paid the expense with cash. A credit decreases the amount of cash you have.

Account	Debit	Credit
Cash Account		X
Accrued Liability Account	X	

When the original entry is reversed (showing you paid the expense), it's removed from the balance sheet. This decreases liabilities. Your income statement also shows a decrease in cash.

If you don't adjust entries after paying expenses, you will have some issues in your books. Here are a few things that will likely happen:

- Liabilities will be understated on the balance sheet.
- Expenses will be understated on the income statement.
- Net income will be overstated.

Bottom line: Your financial reports will make it look like you have more money than you do. Make sure you keep your entries up-to-date each time you pay a liability.

Accrued Expenses vs. Accounts Payable

If by now, you're thinking accrued expenses sound a whole lot like accounts payable, you're right. Accrued expenses and accounts payable are similar, but not quite the same.

- What are accrued expenses and accounts payable?

Both accrued expenses and accounts payable are current liabilities, meaning they are short-term debts to be paid within a year. But, the nature of the entries differ.

Accounts payable includes amounts you need to pay for items or services bought on credit. These debts are usually owed to suppliers and vendors. You receive an invoice and owe the supplier money. The entry is an accounts payable.

Accrued liabilities recognize any unrecorded expenses incurred but not billed. Accrued liabilities occur from regular, periodic expenses.

- When are accrued expenses and accounts payable recorded?

Accounts payable is recorded based on invoices during the normal course of business. You recognize accounts payable every day as you receive bills.

Accrued liabilities are usually recorded at the end of an accounting period. You recognize them before receiving a bill.

- Why are accrued expenses and accounts payable recorded?

Accounts payable entries are made to track unpaid invoices. Use accounts payable entries to record bills your business needs to pay.

Accrued liabilities show goods and services that were delivered but not billed. For example, you use utilities. The utility company doesn't invoice you until after the period. To close your books, you must make an accrued expense journal entry. Accrued expenses can reveal how debts affect the business bottom line before receiving bills.

Long Term Liabilities

Long-term liabilities (also called non-current liabilities) are financial obligations of a company that are due after a year or more. Long-term liabilities are presented on a balance sheet of a company together with current liabilities which represent payments due within one year.

Classification of liabilities into current and non-current is important because it helps users of the financial statements in assessing the financial strength of a business in both short-term and long-term. While information about current liabilities of a company (together with its current assets) provide vital information about liquidity of a company, long-term liabilities (together with non-current assets) are critical for assessment of its long-term solvency.

IAS 1 Presentation of Financial Statements provides a more technical definition of long-term liabilities. It defines non-current liabilities as liabilities other than current liabilities. Current liabilities are defined as liabilities that are expected to be settled within normal operating cycle, held for the purpose of trading, expected to be settled within 12 months OR for which the company does not have any unconditional right to defer payment.

Long-term liabilities = liabilities - current liabilities.

Following is a list of some typical long-term liabilities:

1. Bonds payable
2. Loans payable
3. Deferred tax liability
4. Pensions payable
5. Post-retirement healthcare obligation
6. Finance lease payable

Not all bonds payable or bank loans payable are long-term in nature. Bond and loan repayments that are due within a year are classified as current liabilities and the rest are reported as long-term.

Bonds Payable

Companies raise money either (a) through issue of shares, which represent ownership stake in the company or (b) through issue of debt instruments, which represent a fixed amount to be repaid (together with interest) over a specified period of time in future. Bonds payable represent the later scenario i.e. financial obligations of a company which have a specified return and repayment date.

Loans Payable

While bonds payable represent financial obligations towards general investors (both individual and institutional), loans represent amount obtained typically from a bank or another company (such as sister concern or associate). Loans carry either a fixed or variable interest rate which the borrowing company pays over the term of the loan. The principal amount of the loan is either repaid at the end of the loan term or over the term of the loan.

Deferred Tax Liability

Deferred tax liability represents income tax payment a company saved today but which it shall be required to pay in future due to difference between financial accounting recognition criteria and tax laws.

Pension Payable

Pension payable liability arises when a company has a defined benefit plan. It is the present value of the amount the company shall pay the employees in future as compensation for their employment to date.

Post-retirement healthcare obligation is a liability similar to pensions payable in that it represents the expense the company is expected to incur in future to provide healthcare facilities to its employees after their retirement as compensation for their employment so far.

Leases Payable

Leases payable represent the present value of the lease payments a company shall make in future in return for use of an asset. Lease payable is recognized only where a lease is classified as finance lease.

Ratios Involving Long-term Liabilities

Following ratios have a long-term liabilities component:

- Debt ratio
- Equity multiplier (i.e. financial leverage ratio)
- Return on capital employed
- Debt coverage ratio

Example

Long-term Liabilities vs. Current Liabilities: Company A has the following liabilities as at 31 December 2014:

- Lease payable of $10 million (of which $1 million is payable each quarter).
- Net pension liability of $20 million (of which $2 million is payable by 31 December 2015).
- Bonds payable of $30 million (of which $10 million are due for payment on 30 June 2015). Interest accrued on the bonds as at 31 December 2014: $1 million.
- Bank loan of $10 million which originally due in 2017, but the company has defaulted on a covenant which has entitled the bank to demand repayment right now.

Find the amount that should be classified as non-current on the company's balance sheet as at 31 December 2011.

Long-term lease payable amounts to $6 million ($10 million minus $4 million paid over the next year i.e. $1 million in each quarter).

Long-term net pension liability is $18 million ($20 million minus $2 million).

Bonds payable of $20 million ($30 million minus $10 million on 30 June 2015). The whole amount of interest payable is current in nature because it is due immediately.

Though bank loan was originally a long-term liability, the default on a covenant has rendered it current because the company no longer has unconditional right to defer payment. Hence, the bank loan amount of $10 million is a current liability.

Total long-term liabilities that should appear on Company's A balance sheet as at 31 December 2015 amount to $47 million ($6 million plus $18 million plus $20 million).

Accounts Receivable

Accounts Receivable (AR) is the proceeds or payment which the company will receive from its customers who have purchased its goods & services on credit. Usually the credit period is short ranging from few days to months or in some cases maybe a year.

The word receivable refers to the payment not being realised. This means that the company must have extended a credit line to its customers. Usually, the company sells its goods and services both in cash as well as on credit.

When a company extends credit to the customer, the sale is realised when the invoice is generated, but the company extends a time period to the customers to pay the amount after some time. The time period could vary from 30-days to a few months.

Account Receivables (AR) are treated as current assets on the balance sheet. Let's understand AR with the help of an example. Suppose you are a manufacturer M/S XYZ Pvt. Ltd. and you manufacture tyres.

A customer gives you an order of Rs 1,00,000 for 100 tyres. Now, when the invoice is generated for that amount, sale is recorded, but to make the payment the company extends the credit period of 30-days to the customer.

Till that time the amount of Rs 1,00,000 becomes your account receivable because the customer will pay that amount before the period expires. If not, the company can charge a late fee or hand over the account to a collections department.

Once the payment is made, the cash segment in the balance sheet will increase by Rs 1,00,000, and the account receivable will be decreased by the same amount, because the customer has made the payment.

The amount of account receivable depends on the line of credit which the customer enjoys from the company. Usually, this is offered to customers who are frequent buyers.

Payment Terms of Accounts Receivables

The usual payment terms of accounts receivables include NET 30 which is usually a due date of around 30 days or such. The debtor is applicable to payment options within the due period, during which he may be offered substantial discounts for early payment options. Once the due date is successfully obtained, the creditor may impose the necessary fines for late fees as such. Other common payment terms include NET 45, NET 60 which involve the payment period of 45 and 60 respectively.

Any account receivable can be successfully initiated through a simple transaction. However, the whole strategic planning of maintaining and collecting the payments pertaining to the receivables can be whole complex processes. Such critical decisions are necessarily implemented using certain fiscal and financial policies established by the corresponding corporate agencies and business organizations respectively.

There is also a provision for outstanding amounts considering the pending customer debts which are then documented on the balance sheets under the term of 'contra account' that offsets total receivables. The inability of the payment collection even after this process is then negotiated by third party agencies via various payment plans, settlement offers and other legal actions.

Accounts Receivables Age Analysis

Also termed as the Debtor's book-keeping, the accounts receivables age analysis is duly divided into current, a period of 30 days, 60 days, 90 days or longer. The analysis reports thus generated are termed as the Aged Trial balance and contain the records of the customers certainly arranged according to established record keeping criteria.

Essential Terms of Accounts Receivables

The Accounts receivables process also known as the AR process is the complete cash flow from the payable organization to the receivable organization. This merely includes the following steps, the details of which are listed below accordingly:

1. Credit decisions: the supplier of the goods and services verifies the credibility of the customer in terms of the credit worthiness to facilitate the supply of products.
2. Bill distribution: This basically occurs once the goods or services are successfully delivered by the corresponding organization and the payments for the same are completed from the customer end.
3. Receipting, Allocation and Reconciliation: This particular process is undertaken by the AR officer who identifies the payment deposit into the supplier bank account, receipts the same into the AR system, and performs invoice allocation and reconciliation to verify the validity of the payment.
4. Collections: The collections officer identifies all the invoices that are short paid or unpaid in terms of the applicable due date.
5. Disputes Management: This is typically done when any issue arises on the customer end with reference to the bill payment.
6. Bad debt: Once the bill achieves the due date and remains pending either due to unresolved issue or non-payment, it is considered to be as bad debt.

Process Flow of Accounts Receivables

The general process flow of accounts receivables can be established accordingly into four major categories namely – the setup, creation of transactions, processing of cash and credit management accordingly. The details of this process flow are listed below accordingly for further clarification purposes.

Account Setup

As discussed above, prior to the setup, the company or the corresponding business organization analyzes the credit decision outcomes for best applicability. Once done, the setup of accounts receivables are cashed accordingly. This involves in-depth understanding of the structure of the company, the processing of the payments and subsequent reporting of the corresponding requirements.

The setup will include defining customers, the terms of implementation, financial charges incurred, the process levels and the default codes of the same. These criteria are essential to establish the payments processing and maintaining of customer balances and reporting accordingly.

Creation of Transaction

This particular stage of the account receivables process flow primarily defines the creation of invoices, debit memos and credit memos, etc. Once the invoices are created and the transactions are defined successfully, it is time for effective maintenance process of the existing invoices accordingly.

Processing of Cash

The basic concept of the accounts receivables process is defined in the cash processing stage wherein the cash payment details are mapped to the corresponding transactions. This is either done via manual or automatic processing and interfacing from fund transfer processes, different applications, etc. These processes are then maintained through the successful settlement of disputes, creation of chargebacks and reversing the application processes respectively. Once the whole requirements of the above mentioned processes are achieved, the corresponding bills of exchange are generated and stored in the database.

Credit Management

Credit management is achieved through review of customer balance sheets and processing of aging reports. Depending on the applicability of certain parameters, every transaction is tracked and submitted for data analysis and he reports for the same are generated over a particular period of time. Once these reports are generated, they are submitted to the reviewing department which then maps the data obtained to the corresponding interface for critical analysis of the financial segments of the given business organization. The accounts receivables data is also stored for further future references and maintained accordingly for best practices.

Accounts Receivable Turnover Ratio

The purpose of the ratio is to measure the amount of time it takes for a company to collect their accounts receivable on an average basis. It's a measurement that allows insight into the efficiency of the company in terms of asset use. It is usually performed annually.

To Calculate:

Turnover Ratio = Net Credit Sales / Average Net Receivables

Meaning of the Ratio

The length of the collection period is an important indication of when a company can expect to receive cash and therefore provides an idea of the current liquidity situation.

For example: John's Company has a turnover ratio of 8, which means that the accounts receivable typically turn over 8 times each year, so John's Company collects its receivables every 45.6 days.

To determine the average number of days it takes for a company to collect accounts receivable, divide 365 (number of days in a year) by the ratio (8) to calculate the answer: in this case, 45.6 days

Factoring

AR is also important because it can be sold by a company to a "factor," such as a bank or other financier.

Factoring, or the sale of accounts receivable, raises money for a company and boosts the seller's cash flow, but it also involves paying a fee to the factoring company in return for the faster payment of accounts receivable. The factor pays the original company for its AR and then collects the money due from customers.

Accounts Receivable Management

Accounts receivable management is the process of ensuring that customers pay their dues on time. It helps the businesses to prevent themselves from running out of working capital at any point of time. It also prevents overdue payment or non-payment of the pending amounts of the customers. It builds the businesses financial and liquidity position. A good receivable management contributes to the profitability by reducing the risk of any bad debts. Management is not only about reminding the customers and collecting the money on time. It also involves identifying the reasons for such delays and finding a solution to those issues.

Process Involved in the Accounts Receivable Management

An account receivable management process involves the following:

- Credit rating i.e. the paying ability of the customers shall be reviewed before agreeing to any terms and conditions.
- Continuously monitoring any risk of non-payment or delay in receiving the payments.
- Customer relations should be maintained and thus to reduce the bad debts.
- Addressing the complaints of the customers.
- After receiving the payments, the balances in the particular account receivable should be reduced.
- Preventing any bad debts of the receivables outstanding during a particular period.

Account Payable

When a company purchases goods on credit which needs to be paid back in a short period of time, it is known as Accounts Payable. It is treated as a liability and comes under the head 'current liabilities'. Accounts Payable is a short-term debt payment which needs to be paid to avoid default.

Accounts payable is a liability due to a particular creditor when it order goods or services without paying in cash up front, which means that you bought goods on credit. Accounts Payable as a term is not limited to companies. Even individuals like you and me have accounts payable.

We consume electricity, telephone, broadband and cable TV network. The bills get generated towards the end of the month or a particular billing period. It means that the service provider gave you some service and sends the bill which needs to be paid by a certain date or else you will default. This becomes accounts payable.

Let's also understand from a company's point of view. You are a company A, who purchases goods from company B on credit. The amount raised needs to be paid back in 30 days.

Company B will record the same sale as accounts receivable and company A will record the purchase as accounts payable. This is because company A has to pay company B.

Under the accounting (Accrual) methodology, this will be treated as a sale even though money has not exchanged hands yet. The accounts department needs to be extremely careful while processing transactions relating to Accounts Payable.

Here, time is the essence considering it is a short term debt which needs to be paid within a specific period of time. Along with that accuracy is the key, which involves the amount that needs to be paid along with the name of the supplier. Accuracy is important because it will impact the company's cash position.

Accounts Payable Process

The accounts payable process or function is immensely important since it involves nearly all of a company's payments outside of payroll. The accounts payable process might be carried out by an accounts payable department in a large corporation, by a small staff in a medium-sized company, or by a bookkeeper or perhaps the owner in a small business.

Regardless of the company's size, the mission of accounts payable is to pay only the company's bills and invoices that are legitimate and accurate. This means that before a vendor's invoice is entered into the accounting records and scheduled for payment, the invoice must reflect:

- What the company had ordered
- What the company has received
- The proper unit costs, calculations, totals, terms, etc.

To safeguard a company's cash and other assets, the accounts payable process should have internal controls. A few reasons for internal controls are to:

- Prevent paying a fraudulent invoice.
- Prevent paying an inaccurate invoice.
- Prevent paying a vendor invoice twice.
- Be certain that all vendor invoices are accounted for.

Periodically companies should seek professional assistance to improve its internal controls.

The accounts payable process must also be efficient and accurate in order for the company's financial statements to be accurate and complete. Because of double-entry accounting an omission of a vendor invoice will actually cause two accounts to report incorrect amounts. For example, if a repair expense is not recorded in a timely manner:

1. The liability will be omitted from the balance sheet, and
2. The repair expense will be omitted from the income statement.

If the vendor invoice for a repair is recorded twice, there will be two problems as well:

1. The liabilities will be overstated, and
2. Repairs expense will be overstated.

In other words, without the accounts payable process being up-to-date and well run, the company's management and other users of the financial statements will be receiving inaccurate feedback on the company's performance and financial position.

A poorly run accounts payable process can also mean missing a discount for paying some bills early. If vendor invoices are not paid when they become due, supplier relationships could be strained. This may lead to some vendors demanding cash on delivery. If that were to occur it could have extreme consequences for a cash-strapped company.

Just as delays in paying bills can cause problems, so could paying bills too soon. If vendor invoices are paid earlier than necessary, there may not be cash available to pay some other bills by their due dates.

Purchase Order

A purchase order or PO is prepared by a company to communicate and document precisely what the company is ordering from a vendor. The paper version of a purchase order is a multi-copy form with copies distributed to several people. The people or departments receiving a copy of the PO include:

- The person requesting that a PO be issued for the goods or services.
- The accounts payable department.
- The receiving department.
- The vendor.
- The person preparing the purchase order.

The purchase order will indicate a PO number, date prepared, company name, vendor name, name and phone number of a contact person, a description of the items being purchased, the quantity, unit prices, shipping method, date needed, and other pertinent information.

Receiving Report

A receiving report is a company's documentation of the goods it has received. The receiving report may be a paper form or it may be a computer entry. The quantity and description of the goods shown on the receiving report should be compared to the information on the company's purchase order.

After the receiving report and purchase order information are reconciled, they need to be compared to the vendor invoice. Hence, the receiving report is the second of the three documents in the three-way match.

Vendor Invoice

The supplier or vendor will send an invoice to the company that had received the goods and/or services on credit. When the invoice or bill is received, the customer will refer to it as a vendor invoice. Each vendor invoice is routed to accounts payable for processing. After the invoice is verified and approved, the amount will be credited to the company's Accounts Payable account and will also be debited to another account (often as an expense or asset).

A common technique for verifying a vendor invoice is the three-way match.

Three-way Match

The accounts payable process often uses a technique known as the three-way match to assure that only valid and accurate vendor invoices are recorded and paid. The three-way match involves the following:

Document	What it shows
Company purchase order	What the company had ordered and at what cost.
Company receiving report	What the company has received.
Vendor invoice	What the vendor billed the company.

Only when the details in the three documents are in agreement will a vendor's invoice be entered into the Accounts Payable account and scheduled for payment.

Good internal control of a company's resources is enhanced when the company assigns a separate employee with a specific, limited responsibility. The following chart illustrates the concept of the separation (or segregation) of duties involving accounts payable:

Person #1	Prepares the company's purchase orders (POs)
Person #2	Prepares the company's receiving reports
Person #3	Compares each PO, receiving report and vendor invoice
Person #4	Pays the vendors

When the duties are separated, it will require more than one dishonest person to steal from the company. Hence, small companies without sufficient staff to separate employees' responsibilities will have a greater risk of theft.

To illustrate the three-way match, let's assume that BuyerCo needs 10 cartridges of toner for its printers. BuyerCo issues a purchase order to SupplierCorp for 10 cartridges at $60 per cartridge that are to be delivered in 10 days. One copy of the PO is sent to SupplierCorp, one copy goes to the person requisitioning the cartridges, one copy goes to the receiving department, one copy goes to accounts payable, and one copy is retained by the person preparing the PO. When BuyerCo receives the cartridges, a receiving report is prepared.

The three-way match involves comparing the following information:

1. The description, quantity, cost and terms on the company's purchase order.
2. The description and quantity of goods shown on the receiving report.
3. The description, quantity, cost, terms, and math on the vendor invoice.

After determining that the information reconciles, the vendor invoice can be entered into the liability account Accounts Payable. The information entered into the accounting software will include invoice reference information (vendor name or code, invoice number and date, etc.), the amount to be credited to Accounts Payable, the amount(s) and account(s) to be debited and the date that the payment is to be made. The payment date is based on the terms shown on the invoice and the company's policy for making payments.

Lastly, the documents should be stamped or perforated to indicate they have been entered into the accounting system thus avoiding a duplicate payment.

Vouchers

Some companies use a voucher in order to document or "vouch for" the completeness of the approval process. You can visualize a voucher as a cover sheet for attaching the supporting documents (purchase order, receiving report, vendor's invoice, etc.) and for noting the approvals, account numbers, and other information for each vendor invoice or bill.

When the vendor invoice is paid, the voucher and its attachments (including a copy of the check that was issued) will be stored in a paid voucher/invoice file. If paper documents are involved, an office machine could perforate the word "PAID" through the voucher and its attachments. This is done to assure that a duplicate payment will not occur.

The unpaid invoices and vouchers will be held in an open file.

Vendor Invoices without Purchase Orders or Receiving Reports

Not all vendor invoices will have purchase orders or receiving reports. Hence, the three-way match is not always possible. For example, a company does not issue a purchase order to its electric utility for a pre-established amount of electricity for the following month. The same is true for the telephone, natural gas, sewer and water, freight-in, and so on.

There are also payments that are required every month in order to fulfill lease agreements or other contracts. Examples include the monthly rent for a storage facility, office rent, automobile payments, equipment leases, maintenance agreements, etc. Even though these obligations will not have purchase orders, the responsibility is unchanged: pay only the amounts that are legitimate and accurate.

Statements from Vendors

Vendors often send statements to their customers to indicate the amounts (listed by invoice number) that remain unpaid. When a vendor statement is received the details on the statement should be compared to the company's records.

The fact that a company can be receiving both invoices and statements from a vendor means there is the potential of a duplicate payment. In order to avoid making a duplicate payment, companies often establish the following rule: Pay only from vendor invoices; never pay from vendor statements.

Automated Accounting Process

As accounts payable process is vital for every organization, it requires a lot of employee time to be spent on successful implementation of this process. In order to set efficient accounts payable process automation becomes necessary. This will minimize the time and cost of invoice processing, employee headcount and much more. Automation will also help to reduce a lot of human errors and increase the efficiency of the employees.

There are many good accounting softwares available in the market which can streamline the accounts payable process. Such accounting softwares will eliminate all paperwork. Using electronic invoices, scanned copies of reports, email approvals, etc. will not only reduce the time involved in managing the payables but also will help in streamlining the business as a whole. They integrate with the organizations ERP usually. There are a lot of other value added services which can be utilized from these accounting softwares which will ultimately improve the business efficiency.

In simple words, most of the accounting software for payables will allow you to gather reports on outstanding payables, payment history, vendor balance tracking, forecasting outflows and much more.

Benefits of Automating your Accounts Payable

Accuracy

Anytime you type or write by hand, there is a possibility you will get a number wrong. One of the main job responsibilities of an accountant is to check and then double-check for simple math errors. Everyone knows that 1+1 = 2, but in a stack of hundreds of invoices, mistakes happen. Even a simple addition error can cost money and time as you untangle the mess. By automating accounts payable, you know that the invoice you enter will be the same invoice others see and respond to. If there is an error in the initial invoice, the system can be set up to easily recognize inconsistencies or errors.

Efficiency

By automating your accounts payable process, you relieve workers from monotonous tasks and free them to use their skills in more productive ways. In most cases, invoice processing is primarily focused on reading and entering figures, then checking them for accuracy. As this portion of the AP process is automation, accounts payable professionals can use their skills to maximum effect by shifting to a more analytics-focused role, looking for opportunities to improve cash flow and secure discounts from vendors.

Oversight

Even though it might seem that automating accounts payable could make you less aware of the day-to-day operations, the opposite is true. By pulling only relevant data and presenting it only to relevant parties, automated accounts payable gives you more oversight possibilities. By putting everything online in a transparent process, you can collate data into usable reports or drill down into specific clients and specific workers.

Streamlined Processes

Even the best manual approval process hit snags where some supplier invoices or payments may fall through the cracks. Accounts payable automation lets you automate the approval and entire workflow process, including checking to make sure that billed amounts are correct and that all relevant parties are notified and approve the expense at appropriate intervals. By automating this process, there is no need to chase down missing information. If there's a hitch at some point in the approval process, you know exactly where that is and how to fix it. If everything's going well and you simply want to check on the status of an invoice, you can do so with a few clicks.

Record Keeping

By automating your accounts payable and using a transparent, digital process for this critical business function, you're also creating a digital trail that anyone can follow. If you have stacks of paper forms in a file cabinet somewhere, you know that sometimes paper gets lost, along with critical signatures. Moving your accounts payable to an automated platform gives you the ability to track every step of your operations and then hold those records in keeping with a standardized retention schedule. If you ever need to present records to someone, such as a prospective partner, think how much simpler it will be for all involved to share digital versions complete with transaction histories, all automatically created as part of doing business.

Notes Receivable

The notes receivable is an account on the balance sheet usually under the current assets section if its life is less than a year. Specifically, a note receivable is a written promise to receive money at a future date. The money is usually made up of interest and principal.

A note receivable is often formed when a business, usually a bank, makes a loan to another business. A note will often be for less than a year, but some can be well in excess of this time frame. Recognize notes receivable income as interest income on the income statement. Thus, when payment is made the amounts affect the balance sheet as well as the income statement.

Money Bank is extending a $100,000 90 day note to Toys Inc. so that they can fund some of its short term needs for financing during the year. The note has an interest rate of 5% and is recorded by the bank as a note receivable on Money's balance sheet under the current assets section. At the end of the term, Toys inc. will pay the $100,000 in principal back to Money Bank, and approximately $1,233 (100,000 * 90/365 * .05) worth of interest. Record the amount as interest income on the incomes statement at the end of the year.

Components of a Note Receivable

Principle-the principle is the face value of the note. The principle equals the initial amount of credit provided.

- Maker: The maker of a note is the party who receives the credit and promises to pay the note's holder. The maker classifies the note as a note payable.
- Payee: The payee is the party that holds the note and receives payment from the maker when the note is due. The payee classifies the note as a note receivable.
- Interest: Notes generally specify an interest rate, which is used to determine how much interest the maker of the note must pay in addition to the principal.

Calculating interest-interest on short-term notes is calculated according to the following formula:

principle x annual interest rate x time period in years = interest

Example: interest on a four-month, 9%, $1,000 note equals $30.

Recognizing Notes Receivable

In accounting, notes receivables are accounts to keep track of accrued assets that have been earned but not yet received.

Accrued Assets

Accrued assets are assets, such as interest receivable or accounts receivable, that have not been recorded by the end of an accounting period. These assets represent rights to receive future payments that are not due at the balance sheet date. To present an accurate picture of the affairs of the business on the balance sheet, firms recognize these rights at the end of an accounting period by preparing an adjusting entry to correct the account balances. To indicate the dual nature of these adjustments, they record a related revenue in addition to the asset. We also call these adjustments 'accrued revenues' because the revenues must be recorded.

Recognizing and Reporting Notes Receivable

To record a journal entry for a sale on account, one must debit a receivable and credit a revenue account. When the customer pays off their accounts, one debits cash and credits the receivable in the journal entry. For example, a sale on account would be recorded similarly to the following interest receivable journal entry:

Adjustment 6—Interest revenue accrued	2010 Dec.	31	Interest Receivable	600	
			Interest Revenue		600
			To record one month's interest revenue.		

Notes Receivable Example: Recording an interest receivable journal entry

The ending balance on the trial balance sheet for accounts receivable is usually a debit. Business organizations which have become too large to perform such tasks by hand (or small ones that could but prefer not to) will generally use accounting software on a computer to perform this task. Companies have two methods available to them for measuring the net value of accounts receivable, which is generally computed by subtracting the balance of an allowance account from the accounts receivable account.

Allowance Method

The first method is the allowance method, which establishes a contra-asset account, allowance for doubtful accounts, or bad debt provision, that has the effect of reducing the balance for accounts receivable.

The amount of the bad debt provision can be computed in two ways, either (1) by reviewing each individual debt and deciding whether it is doubtful (a specific provision); or (2) by providing for a fixed percentage (e.g. 2%) of total debtors (a general provision). The change in the bad debt provision from year to year is posted to the bad debt expense account in the income statement.

Direct Write-off Method

This second method is simpler than the allowance method in that it allows for one simple entry to reduce accounts receivable to its net realizable value. The entry would consist of debiting a bad debt expense account and crediting the respective accounts receivable in the sales ledger.

The two methods are not mutually exclusive, and some businesses will have a provision for doubtful debts, writing off specific debts that they know to be bad (for example, if the debtor has gone into liquidation).

Valuing Notes Receivable

Companies have two methods available to them for measuring the net value of accounts receivable: the allowance method and the direct write-off method.

Notes Receivable

Notes Receivable represents claims for which formal instruments of credit are issued as evidence of debt, such as a promissory note. The credit instrument normally requires the debtor to pay interest and extends for time periods of 30 days or longer. Notes receivable are considered current assets if they are to be paid within 1 year and non-current if they are expected to be paid after one year.

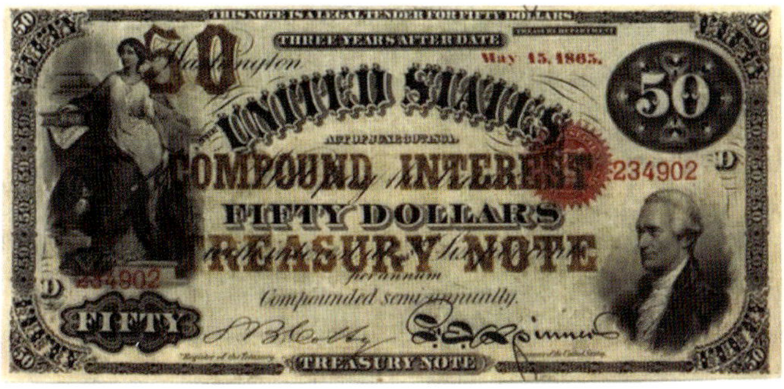

Compound Interest Treasury Note: Notes are short-term investment vehicles.

Reporting of Cash and Receivables

Accrued revenue (or accrued assets) is an asset such as proceeds from a delivery of goods or services, at which such income item is earned and the related revenue item is recognized, while cash for them is to be received in a latter accounting period. At that point its amount is deducted from accrued revenues.

Valuing Notes/Accounts Receivable

Companies have two methods available to them for measuring the net value of accounts receivable–the allowance method and the direct write-off method.

The Allowance Method

The first method is the allowance method, which establishes a contra-asset account, allowance for doubtful accounts, or bad debt provision, that has the effect of reducing the balance for accounts receivable. The amount of the bad debt provision can be computed in two ways:

1. By reviewing each individual debt and deciding whether it is doubtful (a specific provision).
2. By providing for a fixed percentage (e.g. 2%) of total debtors (a general provision).

The Direct Write Off Method

The second method is the direct write off method. It is simpler than the allowance method in that it allows for one simple entry to reduce accounts receivable to its net realizable value. The entry would consist of debiting a bad debt expense account and crediting the respective accounts receivable in the sales ledger.

Write-Offs

Companies use two methods for handling uncollectible accounts: the allowance method and the direct write-off method.

An accounting perspective:

Business insight

According to the Fair Debt Collection Practices Act, collection agencies can call persons only between 8 am and 9 pm, and cannot use foul language. Agencies can call employers only if the employers allow such calls. And, they can threaten to sue only if they really intend to do so.

Uncollectibles: Interesting Facts About Collection Agencies.

Because customers do not always keep their promises to pay, companies must provide for these uncollectible accounts in their records. This phenomenon is known, in the realm of accounting, as bad debt.

Companies use two methods for handling uncollectible accounts: the direct write-off method and the allowance method. The direct write-off method is simpler than the allowance method in that it allows for one simple entry to reduce accounts receivable to its net realizable value. The entry would consist of debiting a bad debt expense account and crediting the respective accounts receivable in the sales ledger. The bad debt is recognized as an expense at the point when judged to be uncollectible.

When using the allowance method, an estimate is made at the end of each fiscal year of the amount of bad debt. This amount is accumulated in a provision, which is then used to reduce specific receivable accounts when necessary. Note that the allowance method is the required method for federal income tax purposes (GAAP).

Because of the matching principle of accounting, revenues and expenses should be recorded in the period in which they are incurred. When a sale is made on account, revenue is recorded along with account receivable. Because there is an inherent risk that clients might default on payment, accounts receivable have to be recorded at net realizable value. The portion of the account receivable that is estimated to be not collectible is set aside in a contra-asset account called Allowance for Doubtful Accounts. At the end of each accounting cycle, adjusting entries are made to charge uncollectible receivable as expense. The actual amount of uncollectible receivables is written off as an expense from Allowance for Doubtful Accounts.

Allowance Method Example

As time passes and a firm considers a specific customer's account to be uncollectible, it writes that account off. It debits the allowance for doubtful accounts. The credit is to the accounts receivable control account in the general ledger and to the customer's account in the accounts receivable subsidiary ledger. For example, assume Smith's USD 750 account has been determined to be uncollectible. The entry to write off this account is:

- Allowance for Uncollectible Accounts (-SE) 750
- Accounts Receivable—Smith (-A) 750

The credit balance in Allowance for doubtful accounts before making this entry represented potential uncollectible accounts not yet specifically identified. Debiting the allowance account and crediting accounts receivable shows that the firm has identified smith's account as uncollectible. Notice that the debit in the entry to write off an account receivable does not involve recording an expense. The company recognized the uncollectible accounts expense in the same accounting period as the sale. If smith's USD 750 uncollectible account were recorded in uncollectible accounts expense again, it would be counted as an expense twice.

A write-off does not affect the net realizable value of accounts receivable. For example, suppose that Amos Company has total accounts receivable of USD 50,000 and an allowance of USD 3,000 before the previous entry; the net realizable value of the accounts receivable is USD 47,000. After posting that entry, accounts receivable are USD 49,250, and the allowance is USD 2,250; net realizable value is still USD 47,000, as shown here:

- Before Write-Off // Entry for After Write-Off // Write-Off
- Accounts receivable 50,000 Dr. // 750 Cr. // $ 49,250 Dr.
- Allowance for uncollectible accounts 3,000 Cr. // 750 Dr. // 2,250 Cr.
- Net realizable value 47,000 Dr. // $47,000

You might wonder how the allowance account can develop a debit balance before adjustment. To explain this, assume that Jenkins Company began business on January 1, 2009, and decided to use the allowance method and make the adjusting entry for uncollectible accounts only at year-end. Thus, the allowance account would not have any balance at the beginning of 2009. If the company wrote off any uncollectible accounts during 2009, it would debit allowance for uncollectible accounts and cause a debit balance in that account. At the end of 2009, the company would debit uncollectible accounts expense and credit allowance for uncollectible accounts. This adjusting entry would cause the allowance account to have a credit balance.

During 2010, the company would again begin debiting the allowance account for any write-offs of uncollectible accounts. Even if the adjustment at the end of 2009 was adequate to cover all accounts receivable existing at that time that would later become uncollectible, some accounts receivable from 2010 sales may be written off before the end of 2010. If so, the allowance account would again develop a debit balance before the end-of-year 2010 adjustment.

Notes Payable

Notes Payable is a written agreement (a promissory note) in which one party agrees to pay the other party a certain amount of cash. Alternatively put, a note payable is a loan between two parties.

The following information is contained in a note payable:

- The amount to be paid.
- The interest rate applied to the loan.
- The maturity date.
- Name of the maker of the note (payer).
- Name of the payee.
- The signature of the person who issued the note with the date signed.

Notes Payable on a Balance Sheet

Notes payable appear as liabilities on a balance sheet. Additionally, they are classified as current liabilities when the amounts are due within a year. However, when the amounts are not due within one year, notes payable are classified as long-term liabilities.

An example of different accounts on a balance sheet:

ASSETS
Current Assets
Cash
Marketable Securities
Accounts Receivable
Inventory
Prepaid Expenses
TOTAL CURRENT ASSEETS
Noncurrent Assets
Property
Plant
Equipment
Copyrights
Trademarks
TOTAL NON-CURRENT ASSEETS

LIABILITIES
Current Liabilities
Accounts Payable
Short Term Notes Payable
Accrued Liabilities
TOTAL CURRENT LIABILITIES
Long-Term Liabilities
Long-Term Notes and Mortgages
Bonds Payable
TOTAL LONG-TERM LIABILITIES

OWNER'S EQIUTY
Owner's Equity
Common Stock
Treasury Stock
Retained Earnings
TOTAL OWNER'S EQUITY

Notice how notes payable can be short-term and/or long-term in nature.

Example

John borrows $100,000 from Michelle on January 1, 2017. John signs the note and agrees to pay Michelle $100,000 six months later (January 1 through June 30). Additionally, John also agrees to pay Michelle a 15% interest rate every 2 months.

The journal entries would be as follows:

Date	Account Title	Debit	Credit
Jan. 1 2017	Cash	$100,000	
	Notes Payable		$100,000
To record the borrowing of $100,000. Maturity date on June 30, 2017.			

Date	Account Title	Debit	Credit
Feb. 28 2018	Interest Expense	$2,500	
	Interest Payable		$2,500
Interest for 2 months ($100,000 x 15% x 2/12) = $2,500			

Date	Account Title	Debit	Credit
Apr. 30 2018	Interest Expense	$2,500	
	Interest Payable		$2,500
Interest for 2 months ($100,000 x 15% x 2/12) = $2,500			

Date	Account Title	Debit	Credit
June 30 2018	Interest Expense	$2,500	
	Interest Payable	$5,000	
	Notes Payable	$100,000	
	Cash		$107,500
To record the repayment of note and interest			

The Difference Between Accounts Payable and Notes Payable

The concept of accounts payable and notes payable are often mixed up. A definition of both of these terms along with their respective attributes are detailed below.

Accounts Payable

Accounts payable is an obligation that a business owes to creditors for buying goods or services. Accounts payable do not involve a promissory note, have no interest, and are a short-term liability (usually paid within a month).

Notes Payable

Notes payable is a written agreement (a promissory note) in which the borrower obtains a specific amount of money from the lender and promises to pay back the amount owed, with interest, over or within a specific time period. It is a formal and written agreement, typically bears interest, and can be a short-term or long-term liability, depending on the note's maturity time frame.

Creating an Enforceable Promissory Note

To create an enforceable promissory note, the following elements must be included:

- The loan amount.
- The repayment dates.
- The interest rate.
- Default terms.
- The names of both the lender and the borrower.
- Mailing address where each payment is mailed to.
- The borrower should print, sign, and date the promissory note.

Notes Payable vs. Notes Receivable

Both the items of Notes Payable and Notes Receivable can be found on the Balance Sheet of a business. While Notes Payable is a liability, Notes Receivable is an asset. Notes Receivable record the value of promissory notes that a business should receive, and for that reason, they are recorded as an asset. NP is a liability which records the value of promissory notes that a business will have to pay. This is analogous to accounts receivable vs. accounts payable.

Interest Receivable

Interest receivable is the amount of interest that has been earned, but which has not yet been received in cash. The usual journal entry used to record this transaction is a debit to the interest receivable account and a credit to the interest income account. When the actual interest payment is received, the entry is a debit to the cash account and a credit to the interest receivable account, thereby eliminating the balance in the interest receivable account.

The interest receivable account is usually classified as a current asset on the balance sheet, unless there is no expectation to receive payment from the borrower within one year.

The accounting treatment of interest receivable may vary, as shown in the following two examples:

- Invested funds or loan: If a business has invested funds or extended a loan to a third party, it should accrue the amount of interest receivable on the funds or loan, up until the date of the balance sheet on which the interest receivable is being stated. If there is a significant risk of non-payment, it may be necessary to create an offsetting bad debt allowance for some portion of the interest receivable, which reduces the net amount of the receivable.
- Interest charge on invoice: A company may charge interest on an invoice that is overdue for payment. In this case, the odds of collection are low and the amount is likely to be small, so it may be acceptable for a business not to accrue the interest receivable. Instead, any interest paid can be recognized on the income statement when payment is received, which means that it is never recorded as interest receivable on the balance sheet. Conversely, if there is a history of receiving a material amount of interest income from this source, a business could accrue a best estimate of the interest receivable.

Interest Payable

			Forecast Period		
FINANCIAL STATEMENTS	**2017**	**2018**	**2019**	**2020**	**2021**
Balance Sheet Check	*OK*	*OK*	*OK*	*OK*	*OK*
Balance Sheet					
Assets					
Cash	272,530	308,232	327,297	368,687	413,443
Accounts Receivable	7,807	8,158	8,485	8,782	9,045
Inventory	11,715	12,242	12,388	12,821	12,839
Property & Equipment	37,513	37,508	37,505	37,503	37,502
Total Assets	**329,564**	**366,140**	**385,674**	**427,792**	**472,829**
Liabilities					
Accounts Payable	5,338	6,205	6,279	6,498	6,507
Interest Payable	600	600	200	200	200
Debt	30,000	30,000	10,000	10,000	10,000
Total Liabilities	**35,938**	**36,805**	**16,479**	**16,698**	**16,707**
Shareholder's Equity					
Equity Capital	170,000	170,000	170,000	170,000	170,000
Retained Earnings	123,627	159,335	199,195	241,094	286,122
Shareholder's Equity	**293,627**	**329,335**	**369,195**	**411,094**	**456,122**
Total Liabilities & Shareholder's Equity	**329,564**	**366,140**	**385,674**	**427,792**	**472,829**
Check	*0.000*	*0.000*	*0.000*	*0.000*	*0.000*

Interest Payable is a liability account shown on a company's balance sheet which represents the amount of interest expense that has been accrued to date but has not been paid as of the date on the balance sheet. In short, it represents the amount of interest currently owed to lenders.

For example, if interest of $ 1,000 on a note payable has been incurred but is paid in the next fiscal year, for the current year ended December 31, the company would record the following journal entry:

DR Interest Expense 1,000

CR Interest Payable 1,000

Interest payable amounts are usually current liabilities and may also be referred to as accrued interest. The interest accounts can be seen in multiple scenarios, such as for bond instruments, lease agreements between two parties, or any note payable liabilities.

Interest Payable in Bonds

Interest payable accounts are commonly seen in bond instruments because a company's fiscal year end may not coincide with the payment dates. For example, XYZ Company issued 12% bonds on January 1, 2017 for $ 860,652 that have a maturity value of $ 800,000. The yield is 10%, the bond matures on January 1, 2022, and interest is paid on January 1 of each year.

On January 1, 2017:

DR Cash 860,653

CR Bond Payable 860,653

The issuance of the bond is recorded in the bonds payable account. The 860,653 value means that this is a premium bond and the premium will be amortized over its life.

On December 31, 2017:

DR Interest Expense 86,065

DR Bond Payable 9,935

CR Interest Payable 96,000

The interest expense is the bond payable account multiplied by the interest rate. The payable is a temporary account that will be used because payments are due on January 1 of each year. And finally, there is a decrease in the bond payable account that represents the amortization of the premium.

Therefore, on the balance sheet, the accounts would look like:

Bond Payable 850,718

Interest Payable 96,000

On January 1, 2018:

DR Interest Payable 96,000

CR Cash 96,000

Finally, the payable account is removed because cash is paid out. This payment represents the coupon payment that is part of the bond.

Interest Payable in Note Payable

Interest payable accounts also play a role in note payable situations. For example, XYZ Company purchases a computer on January 1, 2016, paying $ 30,000 upfront in cash and with a $ 75,000 note due on January 1, 2019. The interest rate is 10% and is paid on January 1 of each year.

On January 1, 2016:

DR Equipment 86,459

CR Cash 30,000

CR Note Payable 56,349

The note payable is $ 56,349, which is equal to the present value of the $ 75,000 due on December 31, 2019. The present value can be calculated using MS Excel or a financial calculator.

On December 31, 2016:

DR Interest Expense 5,635

CR Interest Payable 5,635

The interest for 2016 has been incurred but is paid on the following year on January 1, 2017, so it is recorded as a liability account in 2016.

On January 1, 2017:

DR Interest Payable 5,365

CR Cash 5,365

The account is then reduced to zero and paid out in cash.

Salaries Payable

Salaries payable is a liability account that contains the amounts of any salaries owed to employees, which have not yet been paid to them. The balance in the account represents the salaries liability of a business as of the balance sheet date. This account is classified as a current liability, since such payments are typically payable in less than one year. The balance in the account increases with a credit and decreases with a debit. The amount of salaries payable can be particularly large under any of the following circumstances:

- There is a large gap between the pay-through date of salaries paid and the end of the reporting period.
- The amount of salaries paid to any individuals in the company (such as the CEO) are quite large.
- The company is comprised largely of salaried personnel, as is frequently the case in a professional services business, such as a consulting firm.
- An employee may have been terminated, and the amount of that person's severance pay has not yet been paid.

A company may employ a large number of salaried personnel and still not have any salaries payable as of the end of a reporting period, if salaries are typically paid at the end of that reporting period. This is because there are no days at the end of the period for which employees have earned their salaries, but have not yet been paid.

The difference between salaries payable and salaries expense is that the expense encompasses the full amount of salary-based compensation paid during an accounting period, while salaries payable only encompasses any salaries not yet paid as of the end of an accounting period. Thus, the amount of salaries payable is usually much lower than the amount of salaries expense.

Equity

Equity financing is a method of raising capital by issuing additional shares to a firm's shareholders, thereby changing the previous percentage of ownership in the firm. In other words, it's the process of raising funds from investors.

Firms raise capital through equity financing by selling the ownership of their shares. An ownership stake can be given to friends and family for small businesses or to the public through an initial public offering (IPOs) for large-cap firms, leaders in their industry. The main advantage of equity financing is that firms do not have to pay back the capital or interest associated with it like debt financing.

Instead, the shareholders participate in the firm through owning the firms' shares and exercise a certain extent of control over the business decisions. Furthermore, because equity investors invest their money to the firm, they undertake the risk of business failure, expecting a higher return on investment. Therefore, they are looking for growth opportunities. Generally, equity financing is preferred when a firm is in its early stages seeking to raise funds and increase its cash flows.

Let's look at an example:

Jonathan Petersen invests $500,000 in a startup technology company with a strong growth potential to acquire 10,000 of the firm's 200,000 total shares outstanding.

After a year, the technology company grows and needs additional capital. The firm's management decides to raise the funds by issuing new stocks and giving a percentage of ownership to more investors in exchange for cash.

Jonathan agrees to invest $300,000 at a share price of $60, thereby getting another 5,000 shares. Before the stock issuance, Jonathan controlled the 5% of the company (10,000 shares of the firm's 200,000 total shares outstanding). After the equity financing, Jonathan controls the 7.5% of the company (15,000 shares of the firm's 200,000 total shares outstanding).

Several possible types of equity financing or investment exist to help out small, growing companies, such as the following list.

Family and Friends Financing

For business owners who have strong family ties or social networks, it may make sense to ask close contacts for investment funding. This type of funding, while relatively common, can be risky, especially because you are putting a relationship at risk if you cannot pay the loan back at some point.

Before asking for funding, it's important for the business owner to feel comfortable with the idea that a friend or family member might lose money.

Small Business Investment Companies

The Small Business Administration (SBA) licenses and regulates a program called Small Business Investment Companies (SBIC) that it has licensed to provide funding to small businesses. While this type of funding is very competitive, it has looser underwriting requirements than venture capital and can be a great way to get needed funding.

Angel Investors for Equity Financing

Angel investors can provide second-tier financing to businesses. They are wealthy individuals or groups who are looking for a high return on investment and are very stringent about the businesses in which they invest.

Some Angel groups, such as Southern California's Tech Coast Angels, have over 300 investors, actively seek early-stage companies for investment, and also provide technical and operational knowledge to startup ventures.

Mezzanine Financing

Mezzanine financing is actually a hybrid form of financing that utilizes both debt and equity. The lender makes a loan and, if all goes well, the company simply pays the loan back under negotiated terms.

If, however, the company does not succeed, the lender has the right to convert their loan into an ownership or equity interest. This approach allows the lender to have a claim to any future profits and protects the lender from the reality that most small businesses do fail. At the same time, it allows the business owner to keep 100 percent ownership of their own business for as long as the business is profitable.

Venture Capital

If you get a venture capitalist interested in your business, you will give up a portion of your ownership and will probably have a representative of the venture capital firm on your Board of Directors. Venture capitalists are looking for high rates of return where they invest their money. Unless your business can offer them a high rate of return, they will probably not be interested.

Royalty Financing

Royalty financing is an equity investment in future sales of a product. It is a less formal process than angel or venture capital investing. Similar to a loan, it involves a funder providing up-front cash for business expenses; the funder is then paid a "royalty" when profits start to roll in, such as a percentage of each sale.

Advantages

- Permanent source of finance

Equity financing is the permanent solution to financial needs of a company. No company's main focus or objective can be financial management only. A product manufacturing company will have an objective of producing high-quality goods and reach to its right consumer. A service provider company will ensure providing high-quality services. Equity finance provides that leverage to the management to continuously focus on fulfilling their core objectives. It keeps management away from the hassles of raising funds again and again like other sources of financing viz. debt. Debt is raised and paid back over a period of time.

- No obligatory dividend payments

Equity finance for a new company is like blessings of an angel. The main limitation of a new company is the uncertainty of cash flows. Equity mode of finance gives management a breathing space by having no fixed obligation to pay dividends. A company can choose to pay no dividend or smaller dividends as per the cash flow position.

- Open chances of borrowing

A company, majorly financed by equity, always has a controlled financial leverage ratio. Financial leverage ratio measures the ratio of financing to equity and debt. A bank or any other financial institutions require a company to invest roughly 20 to 25% of equity to finance other 75 to 80% debt. Lower levered firms have higher chances of smooth borrowing of debt in times of need.

- Retained earnings

A company develops an internal source of finance by having equity finance on board. The earnings which a company generates using the capital can be retained by the company to finance the increased working capital and other fund requirements. It obviates the other hassles of raising funds via other sources. Also, if the funds are utilized in projects with higher returns compared to what is available to the equity shareholders, the company effectively achieves its objective of shareholder's wealth maximization.

- Rights shares

A company can get required capital via an issue of rights shares from its existing capital providers which have almost nil floatation cost. Floatation cost is the cost incurred in raising funds.

Disadvantages

- Floatation cost

Financing through equity is the most difficult way of getting funds to the company. Not only does it require a lot of statutory compliances but also have other costs like fee of a merchant banker, other expenses such as brokerage, underwriting fee, and lots of other issue expenses.

- High cost of funds

Equity finance is considered to be the costly source of finance especially in comparison to debt. The obvious reason is the higher required rate of return from equity share investors. Since equity share investment is a high-risk investment, an investor will always expect a higher rate of returns.

- No tax shield

The dividends distributed to the shareholders are not a tax-deductible expense. On the contrary, the interest expense is an eligible expense for tax benefits. A 12% interest rate with 40% prevailing Tax Rate makes the effective cost of funds to be 7.2% {12% * (1-40%)} in case of debt. This benefit is not available to the equity source of financing and therefore, it is considered as a costly source of financing.

- Underwriting of shares

At the time of offering equity shares to the public, the company normally requires the appointment of underwriters. The job of an underwriter is to assume the risk of subscription. Underwriters would agree to subscribe the shares to the extent not subscribed by the general public and will charge a fee for that service. The fee may be in the form of upfront payment or maybe a discounted equity share price.

- Dilution of control

When a company raises funds via equity, it dilutes the existing shareholder's control. Percentage shareholding is reduced when new shareholders are introduced. In the case of debt financing, the control does not dilute.

- No benefit of leverage

Debt funding has an indirect benefit available to the existing owners. Since a project with the higher rate of return (12%) than the cost of debt funds (8%) would enhance the welfare of the shareholders. It is because the margin of 4% will be distributed to the existing shareholders. If the project was financed by equity, this additional benefit would not have occurred to the existing shareholders but would equally distribute between old and new shareholders.

Tangible Common Equity

Tangible common equity (TCE) is a measure of a company's capital, which is used to evaluate a financial institution's ability to deal with potential losses. Tangible common equity (TCE) is calculated by subtracting intangible assets and preferred equity from the company's book value. Measuring a company's TCE is particularly useful for evaluating companies that have large amounts of preferred stock, such as U.S. banks that received federal bailout money in the 2008 financial crisis. In exchange for bailout funds, those banks issued large numbers of shares of preferred stock to the federal government. A bank can boost TCE by converting preferred shares to common shares.

Using tangible common equity to calculate a capital adequacy ratio is one way of evaluating a bank's solvency and is considered a conservative measure of its stability. The TCE ratio (TCE divided by tangible assets) is a measure of capital adequacy at a bank.

Example of Tangible Common Equity

The formula for tangible common equity is:

Tangible Common Equity = Common Equity - Preferred Stock - Intangible Assets

Let's say Company XYZ has \$ 40,000,000 of total assets and \$ 25,000,000 of total liabilities. It has no preferred stock, but it does have a \$ 3,000,000 line item for goodwill and \$ 2,000,000 worth of trademarks.

First, we can calculate common equity by subtracting liabilities from assets: \$ 40,000,000 - \$ 25,000,000 = \$ 15,000,000.

Then we can use the formula above to calculate Company XYZ's tangible common equity:

TCE = \$ 15,000,000 - \$ 0 - \$5,000,000 = \$ 10,000,000.

Goodwill is an accounting construct with no marketable value and trademarks cannot be easily separated from the company and sold piecemeal, so these two intangible assets are subtracted from common equity to calculate tangible common equity.

Few intangible assets have liquidation value. There is one important exception: patents may indeed have value during a liquidation and are thus generally not included in "intangible assets" when calculating tangible common equity.

Significance of Tangible Common Equity

Equity, in general, is the difference between a company's assets and liabilities. Intuitively, if all the assets are sold and all the debts are repaid, common equity represents what's left over for company shareholders. However, intangible assets usually aren't worth much to anyone outside of the firm, even though they may contain tremendous value for their owners. So we back them out of the tangible common equity calculation in order to gauge the true liquidation value of a firm.

Tangible common equity as a percentage of tangible assets is called the tangible common equity ratio, which is a common indicator of bank risk and capitalization in the banking industry.

References

- What-is-a-current-asset: accountingcoach.com, Retrieved 16 April 2018
- What-are-current-assets-formula: fitsmallbusiness.com, Retrieved 25 May 2018
- What-are-examples-of-intangible-assets: accountingtools.com, Retrieved 12 June 2018
- Capitalize-trademark-accounting-purposes-60822: smallbusiness.chron.com, Retrieved 10 July 2018
- Goodwill-meaning-features-types-and-accounting-57175: yourarticlelibrary.com, Retrieved 12 April 2018
- What-are-accrued-liabilities-examples-journal-entry: patriotsoftware.com, Retrieved 11 June 2018
- Types-of-equity-financing-for-small-business-393181: thebalancesmb.com, Retrieved 28 June 2018

6

Financial Audit and Reporting

A financial audit is performed to provide an insight into the authenticity of the financial statements of a company. It ensures that all accounting standards have been met. The topics covered in this chapter address the varied aspects of financial audit and reporting, which include quarterly finance report, annual report, director's report, auditor's report, etc.

Financial Audit

In a financial audit, examiners don't just focus on instances in which the math doesn't add up in a company's master accounts. They also pay attention to the occupational environment in which accounting personnel perform tasks, paying attention to such things as staff training procedures, fraudulent reporting prevention and the importance that top leadership ascribes to regulatory compliance.

A financial audit starts with the review of a company's accounting records and ends with the publication of a report, the content of which depends on what reviewers saw during the audit and the overarching need for transparency that regulators require. Part of these requirements is that only a certified public accountant can review the books of a publicly listed company. The CPA must perform tasks in accordance with generally accepted auditing standards, heeding edicts from institutions as diverse as the U.S. Securities and Exchange Commission, the Public Company Accounting Oversight Board and the American Institute of Certified Public Accountants.

Mechanics

Before auditing an organization's financial records, reviewers agree with top leadership on engagement terms for example, items such as testing period, staff arrangements, paying for audit work and reporting guidelines. These terms are essential to prevent misunderstanding down the road, especially if personnel don't cooperate fully in giving auditors what they need to test accounts. Testing account details and balances is the bread and butter of financial auditing, the type of activity that detects inaccuracies of all stripes whether they come from error or neglect, fraudulent reporting or poor application of accounting standards. Auditors also heed internal controls around accounting and financial reporting functions to make sure the business under review has set proper measures to monitor transactions and detect mistakes.

Types

At the end of a financial audit, the reviewer-in-chief may form an opinion by selecting one of four report types: unqualified, qualified, disclaimer and adverse. An unqualified financial audit report is a clean bill of health that is, the audit team believes there's no significant error in the reporting organization's financial statements. In auditing terminology, the term for "significant error" is "material misstatement." A qualified report is similar to an unqualified conclusion, except that the audit team feels the need to inform readers about important things such as "going concern ability" and corporate accounting standards that aren't in tune with industry standards; "going concern ability" means there's doubt a company will stay in business in the foreseeable future. Auditors issue a disclaimer if they were unable to cover all grounds during testing for example, they couldn't verify substantial amounts in the corporate balance sheet. An adverse audit opinion a rarity, given its detrimental effect on a company's reputation means financial statements are misleading and don't abide by generally accepted accounting principles.

Scope

A financial audit report focuses on a quartet of accounting data summaries, along with internal procedures, senior leadership's management style and the ethical tone at the top, and the competitive landscape. Financial statements include a balance sheet, an equity statement, an income statement and a cash flow report.

Knowing how to perform a financial audit on your own books can help you to prepare for a possible external audit, keep your accounting system in order and discourage internal fraud and theft.

Gather Financial Documents

Review the systems put in place to transmit financial information to the accounting department. The first step in the accounting cycle is to gather financial documentation, such as sales receipts, invoices and bank statements, and forward it to the accounting department for processing. Without timely and reliable information, accounting records can become unreliable themselves, creating discrepancies in a company's financial records.

Look at Record-Keeping

Look into the company's record-keeping policies and check to ensure records are being stored properly. Small businesses should keep at least an electronic photocopy of cash register tapes, cancelled checks, invoices and other financial documentation until the end of the current accounting period. Make sure that archived records can be accessed quickly to shed light on any potential issues that arise.

Review the Accounting System

Identify and review each element of the company's accounting system, including individual T-accounts (debits and credits), journal entries, the general ledger and current financial statements. Systematically work through the accounting system to ensure that all necessary accounts are present, that T-accounts are posted to the general ledger in a timely manner and that the system has the ability to correct human errors, such as arithmetic mistakes.

Review the Internal Control Policies

Check into the company's internal controls policies to gauge the level of protection they provide from theft and fraud. Internal control policies include things like separation of accounting duties between different employees, locked safes for holding pending bank deposits and password-protected accounting software that tracks exactly who does what and when.

Compare Internal and External Records

Compare internal records of cash holdings, income and expenses against external records. Check the company's stored external records and compare selected transactions against internal records. Compare purchase receipts sent from suppliers for a certain month against internal purchase records, for example, or compare cash register tapes against revenue recorded on the books.

Look at Tax Records

Analyze the company's internal tax records and official tax returns. Tax records should be kept for seven years to be on the safe side. Browse through the company's tax receipts from the IRS and compare it against records of tax liabilities and taxes paid in the company's accounting records. Take a little extra time to review the range of credits and deductions claimed on the most recent tax return, looking for areas of dubious reporting, such as inflated expense numbers.

Financial Reporting

In any industry, whether manufacturing or service, we have multiple departments, which function day in day out to achieve organizational goals. The functioning of these departments may or may not be interdependent, but at the end of day they are linked together by one common thread – Accounting & Finance department. The accounting & financial aspects of each and every department are recorded and are reported to various stakeholders. There are two different types of reporting – Financial reporting for various stakeholders & Management Reporting for internal Management of an organization. Both these reporting are important and are integral part of Accounting & reporting system of an organization. But considering the number of stakeholders involved and statutory & other regulatory requirements, Financial Reporting is very important and critical task of an organization. It is vital part of Corporate Governance.

Financial Reporting involves the disclosure of financial information to the various stakeholders about the financial performance and financial position of the organization over a specified period of time. These stakeholders include – investors, creditors, public, debt providers, governments & government agencies. In case of listed companies the frequency of financial reporting is quarterly & annual.

Financial Reporting is usually considered as end product of Accounting. The typical components of financial reporting are:

1. The financial statements – Balance Sheet, Profit & loss account, Cash flow statement & Statement of changes in stock holder's equity.
2. The notes to financial statements.
3. Quarterly & Annual reports (in case of listed companies).
4. Prospectus (In case of companies going for IPOs).
5. Management Discussion & Analysis (In case of public companies).

The Government and the Institute of Chartered Accounts of India (ICAI) have issued various accounting standards & guidance notes which are applied for the purpose of financial reporting. This ensures uniformity across various diversified industries when they prepare & present their financial statements. Now let's discuss about the objectives & purposesof financial reporting.

Objectives of Financial Reporting

According to International Accounting Standard Board (IASB), the objective of financial reporting is "to provide information about the financial position, performance and changes in financial position of an enterprise that is useful to a wide range of users in making economic decisions".

The following points sum up the objectives & purposes of financial reporting –

1. Providing information to management of an organization which is used for the purpose of planning, analysis, benchmarking and decision making.
2. Providing information to investors, promoters, debt provider and creditors which is used to enable them to male rational and prudent decisions regarding investment, credit etc.
3. Providing information to shareholders & public at large in case of listed companies about various aspects of an organization.
4. Providing information about the economic resources of an organization claims to those resources (liabilities & owner's equity) and how these resources and claims have undergone change over a period of time.
5. Providing information as to how an organization is procuring & using various resources.
6. Providing information to various stakeholders regarding performance management of an organization as to how diligently & ethically they are discharging their fiduciary duties & responsibilities.
7. Providing information to the statutory auditors which in turn facilitates audit.
8. Enhancing social welfare by looking into the interest of employees, trade union & Government.

Importance of Financial Reporting

The importance of financial reporting cannot be over emphasized. It is required by each and every stakeholder for multiple reasons & purposes. The following points highlights why financial reporting framework is important –

1. In helps and organization to comply with various statues and regulatory requirements. The organizations are required to file financial statements to ROC, Government Agencies. In case of listed companies, quarterly as well as annual results are required to be filed to stock exchanges and published.
2. It facilitates statutory audit. The Statutory auditors are required to audit the financial statements of an organization to express their opinion.
3. Financial Reports forms backbone for financial planning, analysis, bench marking and decision making. These are used for above purposes by various stakeholders.

4. Financial reporting helps organizations to raise capital both domestic as well as overseas.

5. On the basis of financials, the public in large can analyze the performance of the organization as well as of its management.

6. For the purpose of bidding, labor contract, government supplies etc., organizations are required to furnish their financial reports & statements.

So we can conclude from the above points that financial reporting is very important from various stakeholders point of view. At times for large organizations it becomes very complex but the benefits are far more than such complexities. We can say that financial reporting contains reliable and relevant information which are used by multiple stakeholders for various purposes. A sound & robust financial reporting system across industries promotes good competition and also facilitates capital inflows. This in turn helps in economic development.

Quarterly Finance Report

A quarter is a three-month period on a company's financial calendar that acts as a basis for the reporting of earnings and the paying of dividends. A quarter refers to one-fourth of a year and is typically expressed as "Q."

The standard four quarters that make up the year are: January, February and March (Q1); April, May and June (Q2); July, August and September (Q3); and October, November and December (Q4). A quarter is often shown with its relevant year, as in Q1 2018 or Q1/18, which represents the first quarter of the year 2018.

All public companies in the United States must file quarterly reports, known as 10-Qs, with the U.S. Securities and Exchange Commission (SEC) at the end of each quarter. Each 10-Q contains the public company's unaudited financial statements and company operations information for the previous three months (quarter). 10-Qs are required for the first three quarters of the year. Each publicly traded company must also file an annual report, known as a 10-K, which accounts for the first three quarters with 10-Q reports, as well as the fourth quarter, and will often contain much more detailed information about the company than 10-Qs do.

Companies, investors and analysts often use data from different quarters to make comparisons and evaluate trends. Because there are four quarters in a year, one may evaluate a company's performance over time with a much higher degree of specificity than if one were doing so on a yearly basis. For instance, an investor may track a company's performance over the last eight quarters to determine if the company is consistently performing well. Certain businesses or industries, however, may often vary in performance on a seasonal basis. For example, one may expect that an ice cream or smoothie company will bring in more revenues during the summer (quarter 2 and/or 3). Therefore, an investor might track this company's performance over the past few Q3s for a better view of their progress than if the investor were looking at all four quarters of the year.

Likewise, many retail companies see a spike in business during the holiday season (Q4), so if one were tracking the performance of retail companies, comparing the performance of fourth quarters in the last couple of years may be a good decision. Box-office ticket sales are particularly tied to the time of year when the vast majority of sales taking place in the summer and during the holiday season, with the beginning of the year and the early months of fall traditionally seeing very low sales. Yet, how seasonal companies perform during off-seasons is also very important to consider, as most companies in seasonal industries are active year-round.

Quarterly report periods are often an important time for publicly traded companies, as these earnings reports may significantly affect the value of a company's stock. If a company has had a good quarter, its stock value may increase, but if the company has had a poor quarter the value of its stock may decrease. Analysts' expectations may come into play here too. If a company's earnings per share (EPS) during any particular quarter is higher than predicted by analysts, the company's stock will likely increase in value, and will likely decrease in value if its earnings per share is less than predicted.

There has been a growing chorus of executives and politicians who have been questioning the importance of the quarterly system. Warren Buffett, the CEO of Berkshire Hathaway (BRK), and Jamie Dimon, the CEO of JPMorgan Chase (JPM) have both been vocal critics of the system, saying that it puts too much pressure on companies and executives to deliver short term results to please analysts and investors as opposed to focusing on the long-term interests of the business. On August 17, 2018, President Trump joined the opposition saying he had spoken to business leaders who believe they would create more jobs and improve their businesses if they moved from a quarterly reporting system to a semi-annual one. The President asked the SEC to study the problem.

THE WHITE HOUSE

Office of the Press Secretary

FOR IMMEDIATE RELEASE

August 17, 2018

Statement by the President

In speaking with some of the world's top business leaders I asked what it is that would make business (jobs) even better in the U.S. "Stop quarterly reporting & go to a six month system," said one. That would allow greater flexibility & save money. I have asked the SEC to study!

###

Non-Standard Quarters

Not all companies use the uniform quarter standard. For example, Wal-Mart Stores' first quarter is February, March, and April; Apple Inc's Q1 is October, November, and December; Microsoft Corporation's Q1 is July, August, and September; etc. In addition, certain governments use different quarter systems. For example, the first quarter of the United States federal government's fiscal year is October, November and December, Q2 is January, February and March, Q3 is April, May and June, and Q4 is July, August and September. State governments, also, may have their own fiscal calendars.

A quarterly report for a public company typically includes an income statement, balance sheet, and cash flow statement for the quarter and the year-to-date (YTD), as well as comparative results for the prior year. Quarterly reports also include a discussion and analysis of the company's financial condition, disclosures about risk factors that may affect the value of the company, a discussion of matters submitted to a vote by shareholders during the quarter; and any other pertinent information related to the company and its business.

Generally, quarters end in March, June, September, and December, and quarterly reports are filed a few weeks later.

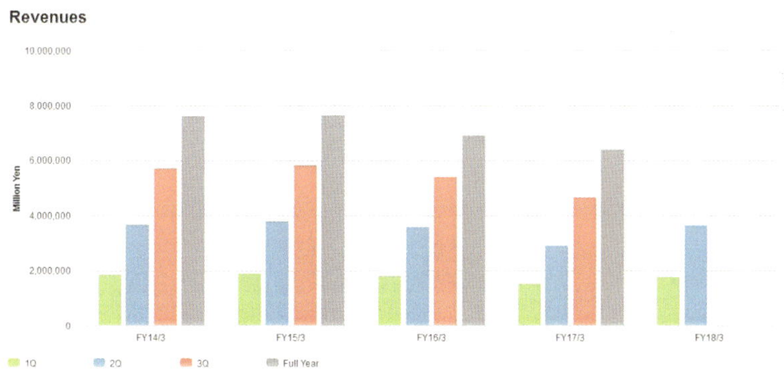

		FY14/3	FY15/3	FY16/3	FY17/3	FY18/3
1Q	Million Yen	1,887,794	1,894,465	1,820,041	1,527,779	1,796,704
2Q	Million Yen	3,700,082	3,804,036	3,605,278	2,932,620	3,657,086
3Q	Million Yen	5,725,410	5,844,124	5,416,080	4,689,023	-
Full Year	Million Yen	7,635,168	7,669,489	6,925,582	6,425,761	-

Supplied by © Euroland.com

Case Study: Henkel - Financial Report First Quarter 2012

Financial Report First Quarter 2012

The world economy grew by around 2 percent in the first quarter of 2012 compared to the prior- year period. With an increase of some 4 percent, industrial production expanded twice as fast as private consumption, which rose by around 2 percent, based in each case on data provided by Feri Euro Rating Services.

Persistently high risks such as the debt crises in Europe and the USA, and also weakening growth in Asia arising from efforts to combat inflation, continued to adversely affect economic development together with investor and private consumer confidence.

In the first quarter of 2012, the North American economy and Japanese gross domestic product grew moderately by around 2 percent versus the prior-year quarter. Economic output in Western Europe stagnated due to a moderate recession, particularly in certain Southern European countries.

The emerging region of Asia (excluding Japan) increased its economic output by around 5 per- cent. Latin America registered growth of about 3 percent. Due in particular to a lower level of demand from Western Europe, economic growth in Eastern Europe cooled slightly to just under 2 percent.

The euro depreciated slightly against the US dollar, from 1.37 to 1.31 USD, in the first three months of 2012 versus the prior-year period, due in particular to the debt crisis in Europe. Around the world, consumer prices likely rose by around 4 percent. At around 7 percent, global unemployment remains at the level encountered at the end of 2011.

Sectors of Importance for Henkel

With a rise of around 2 percent, developments in private consumption in the first quarter of 2012 remained sluggish. Consumers in North America increased their spend by about 2 percent. Consumer spending in Western Europe, and particularly in Southern Europe, likely declined slightly compared to the prior-year period. The emerging markets exhibited a higher propensity to consume with a plus of some 4 percent.

With an approximately 4 percent increase, industrial production continued to expand faster than the economy as a whole. The transport sector saw its output increase by around 6 percent. The metal industry showed robust development with an increase of around 5 percent, while the electronics sector increased production by just about 2 percent. Similarly sluggish were developments in consumer- related sectors such as the global packaging industry which grew by little more than 1 percent. Global construction output was up by around 3 percent in the first quarter of 2012.

Effects on Henkel

Despite the declining dynamism, overall economic development in the first three months of 2012 had a generally positive effect on Henkel's business performance: Robust levels of business activity in many regions of the world were reflected in disproportionately strong organic sales growth of 4.7 percent.

Growth in private consumption had a positive impact on their consumer businesses, while the Adhesive Technologies business sector benefited from the relatively strong increase in industrial production.

They were significantly affected in all three business sectors by persistently high raw material prices. However, by increasing their selling prices and maintaining their strict cost discipline, we succeeded in increasing gross margin despite the rise in material costs.

Net Assets

Compared to year-end 2011, total assets increased by 0.2 billion euros to 18.8 billion euros. Under non-current assets, intangible assets showed a decrease of 203 million euros, due essentially to currency translation factors. With property, plant and equipment remaining unchanged, capital expenditures of 92 million euros were offset by depreciation of 73 million euros and a negative currency translation effect of 15 million euros.

Current assets increased from 6.7 billion euros to 7.2 billion euros, with the increase in business volume being reflected in both higher inventories and also trade accounts receivable. Cash and cash equivalents rose by 128 million euros due to strong cash inflow in the period under review.

Equity including non-controlling interests showed an increase of 301 million euros compared to the end of fiscal 2011.

The currency translation impact arising from the decline of the US dollar since the beginning of the year had a dampening effect. Equity ratio (equity as a percentage of total assets) increased from 47.2 percent to 48.2 percent.

Developments in non-current liabilities, which came in at 5.3 billion euros, were largely influenced by a decrease in pension provisions of 117 million euros to 881 million euros. This was caused primarily by actuarial gains on plan assets. As be- fore, their non-current borrowings include three bonds: two senior bonds with a redemption value of 1.0 billion euros each, and a hybrid bond with a redemption value of 1.3 billion euros. Under cur- rent liabilities, which increased slightly to a total of 4.4 billion euros, trade accounts payable were 2,555 million euros, representing an increase versus the end of 2011 matched by developments in current assets.

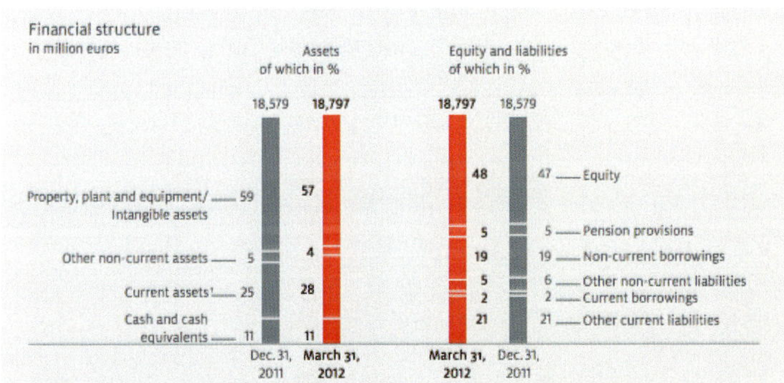

[1] Including assets held for sale.

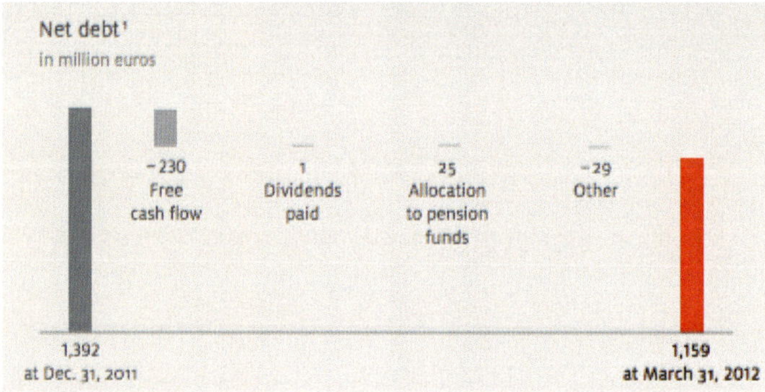

When investing their financial funds, they ensure an appropriate spread of risk. Consequently, they invest not only in vehicles that fall under the cash and cash equivalents heading within the statement of financial position, but also in interest-bearing securities and time deposits. In the future, they intend to increase the proportion of their funds allocated to such securities and time deposits. Therefore, in order to improve insight into the financial position of the Group, They have adapted 1 their definition of net debt by also including securities and time deposits, effective the first quarter of 2012. As of March 31, 2012, they have reduced net debt to 1,159 million euros.

With the decrease in their indebtedness, operating debt coverage increased to 137.6 percent in the period under review, placing it well above the target of 50 percent. Their interest coverage ratio also further improved as a result of their higher EBITDA figure.

At 385 million euros, cash flow from operating activities in the first quarter of 2012 exceeded the comparative figure for the prior-year period (173 million euros).

There was an increase in cash flow as a result of the rise in operating profit, even after taking into account higher corporate income tax payments. The outflow in net working capital was also below that of the prior-year quarter. Net working capital amounted to 8.0 percent of sales, almost matching the level that prevailed as of the end of the prior-year quarter (7.9 percent).

Cash flow from investing activities/acquisitions (–100 million euros) was affected by an increase in capital expenditures compared to the first quarter of 2011, and also lower proceeds from the disposal of non-current assets.

Cash outflow in cash flow from financing activities (–136 million euros) was significantly higher than in the prior-year period (–27 million euros). This was due to financial investment activities which led in the period under review – in contrast to the prior-year quarter – to reclassifications from "cash and cash equivalents" to "other financial assets" in the statement of financial position.

At 230 million euros, free cash flow showed an increase compared to the first quarter of 2011 (75 million euros) resulting from the increase in cash flow from operating activities. This exceeded the higher outflows arising from the balance of capital expenditures and disposal proceeds under non-current assets.

Capital Expenditures

Investments in property, plant and equipment for continuing operations amounted to 92 million euros compared to 68 million euros in the first quarter of 2011. They spent 5 million euros on intangible assets (prior-year period: 2 million euros).

A large part of these capital expenditures was attributable to the Adhesive Technologies and Laundry & Home Care business sectors. Around three quarters of the investment sum went into expansion projects and rationalization measures, for example the introduction of innovative product lines and optimization of their production structure and business processes. In regional terms, capital expenditures focused primarily on Western Europe, Eastern Europe and Asia.

The first-time consolidation of Bella Vista A/S, Silkeborg, Denmark, resulted in an addition to intangible assets in the amount of 4 million euros. Willich, Germany, increasing their shareholding from 73 percent to 95 percent.

Neither the acquisitions and divestments made nor other measures and activities undertaken have resulted in changes in their business and organizational structures.

Thanks to continuing good business performance and their improved financial profile, They regained their target ratings of "A flat" (Standard & Poor's) and "A2" (Moody's) in the second quarter of 2011. Looking forward, They intend not to jeopardize their target ratings when assessing possible acquisitions.

Employees

As of March 31, 2012, they had 46,854 employees (March 31, 2011: 48,188). The decrease is due both to the sale of their branded consumer goods business in India and the continuation of their restrictive hiring policy.

In accordance with their strategy, they continue to increase the number of employees in the emerging markets of Eastern Europe and Asia.

Research and Development

In the first three months of this fiscal year, their expenditure on research and development amounted to 102 million euros (adjusted for re- structuring charges: 101 million euros) compared to 103 million euros (adjusted: 100 million euros) in the prior-year period. Expressed as a proportion of sales, R&D expenditures decreased slightly versus the prior-year quarter to 2.5 percent (adjusted: 2.5 percent).

The development of innovative products is of key importance to their business model.

Solvency and Financial Condition Report

We have considered Irish domiciled life, non-life, health and composite companies and within this, direct writers, reinsurers and captives of all sizes were considered.

Number in sample	High	Medium High	Medium Low	Low
Life	3	10	11	5
Non-Life & Health	3	5	9	12
Composite	-	2	-	1
Total	6	17	20	18

SCR Coverage Ratio

The table below summarizes the published SCR coverage ratio of (re)insurers in Ireland, split by PRISM rating:

SCR Coverage Ratio	High	Medium High	Medium Low	Low
Average	183%	175%	218%	241%
Minimum	127%	108%	81%	123%
Maximun	361%	390%	478%	800%

As expected, the SCR coverage ratios of all high impact companies are comfortably above 100%. For below high impact companies, SCR coverage ratios vary widely across all types and sectors, with no common theme or trend evident.

SFCR user Accessibility

Overall, the purpose of the SFCR is to provide publicly available information regarding the company which can be used by policyholders, shareholders and other stakeholders. Therefore, the SFCR is expected to be understandable to the average policyholder who may not have significant knowledge of financial or insurance concepts.

This was a challenge for most companies although, in our opinion, non-life companies have generally performed better than life companies. In particular, the use of flowcharts by non-life companies to describe the Risk Management System and ORSA process allows the reader to grasp the key points of each at a single glance.

Some companies have done more than others to make these documents accessible; for example, a significant proportion of companies included a glossary of terms, explaining complex jargon in plain English.

Length and Section Weighting

The total length of the SFCR documents varied significantly with some documents as short as 16 pages while others were over 80 pages. This translated through to differences in length of each section as shown in the table below (standardized for font size).

Page count	Average	Min	Max
Summary	3	-	15
A	6	3	12
B	16	6	34
C	9	1	20
D	10	2	26
E	5	1	12
Total	49	16	88

The wide range of section lengths naturally translates into a significant variety in the level of detail in each section, even between comparable companies. In general, Section B was the longest and most detailed section while sections A and E were the shortest for all categories of (re)insurer.

Average page count	High	Medium High	Medium Low	Low
Summary	3	4	3	2
A	8	7	6	5
B	19	19	14	12
C	10	11	9	6
D	13	14	8	7
E	7	7	5	4
Total	60	61	45	37

Structure and Style

As expected, all companies covered the areas specified in the Solvency II Regulations and the order of presentation was consistent across all companies:

A. Business and performance.

B. Systems of governance.

C. Risk profile.

D. Valuation for solvency purposes.

E. Capital management.

In addition to the main sections, all companies included the required QRTs in appendices. However, the depth of detail presented and the user accessibility of that presentation varied significantly between companies, even those of similar size and type.

Larger companies and those listed on an exchange already have a significant amount of information disclosed in their Financial Statements and are naturally more comfortable with the disclosures required in the SFCR. Consequently, we found that a greater level of detail was included in the SFCR by such companies and a polished report was typically produced in line with their corporate brand and consistent with the presentational style of their Annual Report & Accounts.

Business and Performance

Across the (re)insurance industry, this section is quite factual in nature. It outlines the nature of the business written by the company and its financial performance but does not, as we might have expected, use the opportunity to 'promote' the company to readers of the SFCR.

There is significant variation in the level of detail included in this section. A large proportion of companies presented underwriting results (i.e. the numbers) by territory/line of business with no supporting commentary. For those that did include commentary, it tended to be at a high level. In general, there was very little qualitative discussion around the underwriting/investment performance of the company.

In addition to the limited commentary, there was some inconsistency in the manner of presenting the quantitative information. Most companies presented underwriting income (premiums and fees less benefits and expenses) but some companies presented internal KPIs. The lack of standard underwriting performance measures makes it difficult to compare underwriting performance between companies.

System of Governance

The CBI sent a clear message to the market that the system of governance was a key disclosure requirement. In our opinion, companies struggled to present useful information in an accessible way.

In many cases, this section was a compilation of information already included in other documents without much attention to the overall coherence and consistency of the information presented. Generally, the information presented was at the minimum factual level with no real insight into the company-specific system of governance. Some companies did include diagrams to provide clarity around the company and its governance structure but this approach was not universal. The overall feel of this section was that it was very "boilerplate".

There are a number of specific requirements to be included, some of which have not always been met. For example, a number of companies did not include the location of outsourced providers within their report and only a small minority of companies gave more information on their remuneration policy than just the general principles.

We await the CBI's view on the SFCRs but we anticipate the system of governance as being an area which companies will need to enhance as market practice emerges.

Risk Profile

High impact companies generally provided a clear explanation of the risks related to their business, how such risks are managed/mitigated and the potential impact of such risks on their liabilities (i.e. a stress).

Medium impact companies typically provided less detail or presented it in a less user-friendly manner than high impact companies but most provided details of the risks, mitigation plans and potential impacts.

Low impact companies typically had difficulty providing a clear explanation of the risks related to their business. A number of companies documented very generic risks that were not specific to their business.

One requirement which all classifications of reinsurer struggled with was the requirement to provide details of "stress testing and sensitivity analysis for material risks". While most provided the standard formula stress impacts, only a small proportion included details of any further sensitivity/scenario, stress, or reverse stress testing. The inclusion of quantitative stress or reverse stress testing information was rare. Qualitative stress or reverse stress testing information was more common but still not widespread. Companies including this information showed no particular bias between sectors but was more common among low and medium-low impact reinsurers.

Valuation for Solvency Purposes

The level of detail and structure of this section of the report varied significantly by company.

Medium-low and low impact companies were particularly light in respect of the sub-section on technical provisions (D2). Commentary in this section was often generic, repeating the delegated acts with little or no link back to the business written by the company itself. In addition, the majority did not describe the bases, methods and main assumptions used in calculating the technical provisions. In our opinion, users would have difficulty understanding how the technical provisions were calculated for a given company and comparison between companies is limited by the level of detail provided.

Overall, we would have expected to see enough detail to give users a reasonable understanding of the methodology used so this is likely to be an area where companies may need to apply more focus in the future.

Capital Management

Very few companies did more than meet the minimum requirements. In most cases, companies simply provided the required SCR and MCR information at a high level. Little discussion was provided around these figures, and most companies stated a capital management aim to continue to meet internal and external SCR coverage ratio targets.

Similar to our comment on Section A, we expect that this is an area where companies may choose to focus efforts in the future in order to expand the dialogue here, for example, to use strong coverage ratios to promote the strength of their business and brand.

Annual Report

A report created annually that provides an analysis and assessment of the financial trends of the business over the past year.

An Annual Report generally consists of:

- A description of the accounting activities seen within the report. For example, a description of the principles used for determining the accounting items in both the income statement and the balance sheet.
- Information on the events that have influenced the company's accounting throughout the year.
- A statement from management showing an accurate picture of the company's economic standing and development.
- An auditor's report, if applicable.

Not all companies are required to prepare an annual report. It depends on the company's legal form and size.

Business Finances

An annual report can help in understanding the strengths and weaknesses of a company's financial situation since it provides an outline of corporate earnings.

Annual reports can also be used to give an overview of the company's financial situation to relevant parties, such as creditors and other collaborators. It can also be used as a resource to figure out how the financial situation of a company can be improved.

Credibility and Annual Report

It is important to have an accurate and credible annual report as it is used to assess your ability to obtain credit and borrow money should your business require funding. However, the annual report does not indicate tax considerations. Those must instead be shown through tax accounting.

Director's Report

A Directors Report has remained relevant despite the emergence of new reporting tools such as the Operating and Financial Review. The quoted companies are required to include an Operating and Financial Review in their annual accounts. The Operating and Financial Review or the Management's Discussion and Analysis of Results of Operations and Financial Condition, as it is popularly known, provide a better picture of a company. The Operating and Financial Review discusses and analyzes a company's performance. Yet a Directors Report remains unique because it is a direct communication from the directors to the shareholders.

Companies are legally obliged to include a Directors Report in their annual accounts. Companies House requires companies to include a Directors Report in their annual accounts. Other documents that companies need to file with Companies House include a profit and loss account, a balance sheet, an auditors' report, notes to the accounts and group accounts if any. A directors report will give you information on all the directors of a specific company. This information can be used to judge the direction that a company may take in the future in relation to the other companies that the directors hold directorships at.

Companies House, however, does not specify the content of the Directors Report. It directs companies to follow the directives of the Companies Act 1984. A Directors Report is mandatory according to the Companies Act 1985. The Act specifies the content that should be included in a Directors Report.

Contents of the Directors' Report

Directors Reports should provide a review of the company's business.

- The Directors Report should disclose the dividend that the directors are recommending and the amount which they wish to carry to the reserves.
- The directors report should also highlight any changes to the board of directors.
- Other issues that should be included in a Directors Report are details of subsidiary undertakings, directors' interests, details of annual general meeting, statement of responsibilities and the details of the directors' remuneration report.
- The principal activities of the company.

With corporate governance becoming a critical issue worldwide, a section on corporate governance has become a fixture in the Directors Report. This section reveals the extent to which a company is complying with provisions of the revised Combined Code on corporate governance. Corporations are also including information relating to the composition of their board in the Directors Report. The number of independent directors on the board has become important after the recent raft of accounting scandals.

Although a Directors Report resembles an Operating and Financial Review in many respects, there are certain areas where it differs. The Directors Report contains additional information such as:

- Dividend recommendation.
- Details of the directors.
- Remuneration report.
- The names of the persons who, at any time during the financial year, were directors of the company.
- The principal activities of the company in the course of the year.

The Operating and Financial Review, by contrast, focuses on the operational and financial performance of a company.

In the past few years, the front-end of the annual report has become heavy with several messages from the senior management. In addition to the chairman's message, most annual reports contain a letter from the chief executive, business review and more recently, the Operating and Financial Review. The Directors Report, as a result, has been pushed to the middle of the annual report, closer to the financial statements and the auditor report.

With annual reports of most companies comprising several reports from the senior management in addition to directors information repetition of facts has become endemic. While the Directors Report continues to remain unique due to the nature of its communication, the introduction of an Operating and Financial Review may necessitate a rationalization of the messages from the senior management.

Principal Activities

The Group's principal activity is the development, patenting and sale of products based on microbial technology.

Review of the Business

A review of the business and the future developments of the Group is presented in the Chairman's.

Statement and the Chief Executive's Review

Going Concern

The directors have prepared cash flow forecasts for the Group that reflects the

Group's forecast revenues and costs. It is envisaged by the directors that existing cash resources together with these forecast revenue streams will provide adequate funds for the foreseeable future. In the event that the Group is unable to achieve its forecast revenues, the directors have a plan in place under which they will make adjustments to costs so that the business can continue to exist within its current funding arrangements. As a result, the directors have formed a view that adequate funds will be available and all its subsidiary companies for at least the next year following approval of these financial statements. The financial statements have therefore been prepared on a going concern basis. The financial statements do not contain any adjustments which would result if the Group does not generate sufficient revenue and free cash flows from its trading activities or if any future fund raising exercise was not successful.

Key Performance Indicators

Management uses a range of performance measures to monitor and manage the business. Certain of these are particularly important in the generation of shareholder value and are considered key performance indicators are as follows:

- The cash resources of the Group.
- The level of sales and repeat sales.
- The timeliness and efficiency of the research and development team.
- Manpower levels and their effectiveness.

Risks and Uncertainties

Risks and uncertainties are inherent in all businesses and our group is no exception. Risk management is seen as an important element of internal control and is used to mitigate the Group's exposure to such risks.

Commercial Risks

- Our performance depends on our continued ability to develop sales channels.
- Our performance also depends heavily on our patent protection.
- We are also affected by the lead times in conducting trials and gaining the decision to purchase.

Processes to manage the impact on the business of each of the above risks are embedded in our operations.

The directors and other senior management actively monitor these processes, and the actions which arise, to ensure risks are effectively managed.

Operational Risks

Health and safety, employer's and public liability risks are monitored by way of regular updates to our Board.

Financial Risks

The Group manages financial and treasury risk through active working capital management. Monitoring of cash flow and currency exposure is undertaken at Board level on a monthly basis.

Research and Development

The Group invests in the research and development of further anti-microbial products and has 4 employees in its research and development department. It also uses the services of highly regarded research institutions to supplement the internal resource. In the opinion of the directors, continuity of investment in this area is essential for the maintenance of the Group's market position and for future growth.

Political and Charitable Donations

The Group made a charitable donation for every year. It did not make any political donations during the year.

Disabled Employees

The Group gives full consideration to applications for employment from disabled persons where a handicapped or disabled person can adequately fulfill the requirements of the job. Where existing employees become disabled, the Group's policy wherever practicable is to provide continuing employment under normal terms and conditions and to provide training and career development and promotion to disabled employees wherever appropriate.

Employee Involvement

The directors meet staff on a regular basis to keep them appraised of important issues within the Group.

Payment Policy

Appropriate payment terms have been negotiated with each supplier and undisputed accounts are generally settled, once requested, in accordance with the agreed terms. The Company had 45 days of purchases outstanding in trade creditors.

Awareness of Auditing Information

At the date of approval, so far as each of the directors is aware, there is no relevant audit information of which the auditors are unaware and they have taken all the necessary steps to make themselves aware of any relevant audit information and to establish that the auditors are aware of that information.

Auditor's Report

An auditor's report provides an opinion on the validity and reliability of a company's financial statements.

Starting and maintaining solid, professional accounting practices is essential for the growth of a business.

When financial statements are finalized, they usually must contain an evaluation – an auditor's report - from a licensed accountant or auditor. This report provides an overview of the evaluation of the validity and reliability of a company or organization's financial statements.

The goal of an auditor's report is to document reasonable assurance that a company's financial statements are free from error.

Along with balance sheets, profit & loss statements, and directors reports, auditor's reports make up part of a company's statutory accounts.

Preparation of the Report

An audit of a company's financial statements should result in a report wherein the accountant or auditor is free to share their opinion about the validity and reliability of a company's financial statements.

In this report, the auditor should provide an accurate picture of the company and their financial statements. The auditor should also state whether they are externally or internally connected to the company.

Within the report, the auditor can share any reservations about the condition of the company's finances or relevant additional information. Reservations could arise if the auditor disagrees with something found in the financial statements, e.g. if the auditor disagrees with management about the valuation of an asset because they believe that this has a more significant impact on the financial statements.

Opinion in an Audit Report

There are primarily two kinds of opinions issued by an auditor in his / her audit report:

- Unmodified Opinion (also called unqualified report).

- Modified Opinion (also called qualified report).

Unmodified Opinion

Issued for any audit where the auditor is satisfied that the financial statements present a true and fair view of the operations and transactions in an enterprise during the period.

An audit report with an Unmodified Opinion is also known as a 'Clean Report'. An Unmodified report develops confidence among users of financial statements and annual reports of an enterprise.

It provides an impression that the financial statements are reasonably free from any misstatements and results as appearing there are true and fair.

Modified Opinion

Whenever the auditor has specific findings during his/her audit and concludes that an Unmodified Opinion cannot be issued due to the nature of findings, a Modified Opinion is issued in the audit report.

There are two basic reasons due to which an auditor concludes on issuing a Modified Opinion:

- Based on the audit and evidence, finds out that the financial statements contain a certain degree of material misstatements.
- Unable to obtain sufficient and appropriate evidences to conclude that the financial statements are free from material misstatements.

There are three kinds of modified opinions which are issued according to the findings and circumstances:

A. Adverse Opinion

B. Qualified Opinion

C. Disclaimer of Opinion.

Qualified Opinion

A Qualified Opinion is given in a situation where:

- The auditor concludes that misstatements are material but the impact is not so high that it would render the whole financial statements unacceptable; or
- The auditor is unable to obtain sufficient or appropriate audit evidence but concludes that there are indications of misstatements in the financial statements (but the degree is not high).

Example of a Qualified Opinion Paragraph in Audit Report

In our opinion, except for the incomplete disclosure of the information referred to in the Basis for Qualified Opinion paragraph, the financial statements give the information required by the Companies Act, 2013, in the manner so required and give a true and fair view in conformity with the accounting principles generally accepted in India:

- In case of the Balance Sheet, of the state of affairs of the company as at March 31, XXXX;
- In case of Profit and Loss Account, of the profit/loss for the year ended on that date; and
- In case of the Cash Flow Statement, of the cash flows for the year ended on that date.

Adverse Opinion

An Adverse opinion shall be issued by the auditor where he concludes that on the basis of evidence obtained and procedures performed, there are material misstatements in the financial statements and the impact of the same is high.

Example of a Qualified Opinion Paragraph in Audit Report

In our opinion, because of the omission of the information in the Basis for Adverse Opinion paragraph, the financial statements do not give the information required by the Companies Act, 2013, in the manner so required and also, do not give a true and fair view in conformity with the accounting principles generally accepted in India:

- In case of the Balance Sheet, of the state of affairs of the company as at March 31, XXXX;
- In case of Profit and Loss Account, of the profit/loss for the year ended on that date; and
- In case of the Cash Flow Statement, of the cash flows for the year ended on that date.

Disclaimer of Opinion

A Disclaimer of Opinion is to be issued by an auditor in cases where the auditor concludes that he/she is not able to obtain sufficient and appropriate evidences. In such scenario, the auditor is not able to form an opinion and thus, disclaims form providing an opinion on the financial statements. The impact of material misstatements and degree of the same is high enough.

Example of a Draft Disclaimer of Opinion

We were engaged to audit the financial statements of ABC Private Limited ("the entity") which comprises the Balance Sheet as at March 31, XXXX, the statement of Profit and Loss, (the statement of changes in equity) and statement of Cash Flows for the year then ended, and notes to the financial statements, including a summary of significant accounting policies.

We do not express an opinion on the accompanying financial statements of the entity. Because of the significance of the matters described in the Basis for Disclaimer of Opinion section of our report, we have not been able to obtain sufficient and appropriate audit evidence to provide a basis for an audit opinion on these financial statements.

Emphasis of Matter Paragraph in an Audit Report

In a situation where the auditor concludes that it is important to draw the attention of users of the financial statement to a particular reported item, he/she may include an Emphasis of Matter paragraph in his/her audit report. In this case, the auditor is not required to modify his/her opinion. The paragraph is added when the issue is not a key audit matter and only requires disclosure for a better understanding of the financial statements.

Example of circumstances where the auditor shall include Emphasis of Matter paragraph in audit report:

- To inform users of financial statements that the same has been prepared under a special purpose framework.
- The auditor discovers some facts after the date of an audit report and the auditor issues new or amended audit report.
- Uncertainty about the future outcome of an ongoing litigation.

Uses of Auditor's Reports

The following are some of the major uses of an Auditor's Report.

Assurance to Stakeholders

Auditor's reports are very useful for shareholders and potential investors to understand the true financial status of a company as it provides assurance from a professional auditor. This helps investors to make a fair investment decision because many do not have an in-depth financial knowledge to identify fraud in financial reports.

Verification of Internal Controls

Auditors have the knowledge and access to internal financial details to identify any fraudulent activities carried out while preparing financial statements. It is also used by government bodies to check if the financial operations of a company are genuine. Other users of the report include management, board of directors, banks, etc.

Credibility Check

The report is beneficial to banks and other creditors to ascertain the true financial health of a company. The credibility and reliability of a company is reflected in its auditor's report by checking the true performance, which will determine the ability of the company to repay loans.

Fraud Prevention

The auditor's report is extremely important to prevent fraud, as it encourages companies to prepare its financial statements with fairness and accuracy. To achieve audit level accuracy, the company would need to maintain quality internal accounting systems and employ qualified accountants. Efficient audit systems help a company to identify weaknesses and find solutions to fix them.

Limitations of Auditor's Reports

Undetected Fraud

Although audit checks are used to identify fraud, it is likely that some complicated fraud remain undetected by auditors. They cannot completely eliminate fraud. In some cases, misrepresentations of financial data occur as a result of human error, which can be counted as fraud. It is sometimes difficult for auditors to distinguish between fraud and error. Furthermore, audit results vary from one auditor to another based on the efficiency of audit methodology used and the way it is practiced by each auditor.

Emphasis on Financial Aspects

Audits focus on the financial aspects of a company's operations. Non-financial aspects are ignored while determining the credibility and reliability of a company, which might show a false image of the entity to its shareholders and other users.

Inefficient Internal Controls

The efficiency of auditing is commonly affected by the standards of a company's internal financial control. In many cases, higher level authorities in a company override controls by incorrectly recording transactions or concealing certain activities. Such internal inefficiencies challenge the efficiency of auditing.

Audit Report Format

The following is the overall structure of an audit report. You can also download the following Audit Report formats:

- Audit Report Format – Unqualified Opinion
- Audit Report Format – Qualified Opinion

Title of Audit Report

Provide an appropriate title is to be given in order to distinguish the independent auditor's report from reports and statement issued by others.

For example, the title could be 'Independent Auditor's Report'.

Addressee

Specify the party, such as the local government or shareholders, to whom the report is addressed.

For example, in a company's audit report, the report would be addressed to the Members of the Company.

Introductory Paragraph

In the introductory paragraph, the names of the financial statements audited should be provided. This usually includes the profit and loss account, balance sheet, cash flow statement, statement of changes in equity and other supportive books that were used in the preparation of financial reports.

Example: We have audited the accompanying standalone financial statements of XXX Company Limited ("the Company"), which comprise the Balance Sheet as at 31st March, 20XX, the Statement of Profit and Loss, the Cash Flow Statement for the year then ended, and a summary of the significant accounting policies and other explanatory information.

Management's Responsibility

Under this section the Auditor clearly mentions that it is the responsibility of the management to prepare the financial statements and maintain internal controls.

Example: It is the responsibility of the management to prepare its financial statements in compliance with the financial reporting framework. It needs to establish appropriate systems to minimize error, also to detect and mitigate fraud. Efficient internal controls are to be implemented and governed by management to establish quality control throughout its operations to increase accuracy in all departments.

Auditor's Responsibility

Under this section the Auditor emphasizes his/her responsibility with respect to the audit.

Example: The auditor is responsible for conducting audit in accordance with established Standards on Auditing and to express a true opinion on the financial statements. In order to check whether the financial statements are free of any misrepresentations, the auditor needs to collect reasonable evidence to support an opinion. It is the responsibility of the auditor to plan and perform the audit with professional integrity. In failing to do so, the auditor will be liable for damages to the company.

Auditor's Opinion

Under this section the Auditor expresses his opinion on the financial statements which could be unqualified, qualified, and adverse or disclaimer.

Example (if the opinion is unqualified): In our opinion and to the best of our information and according to the explanations given to us, the aforesaid standalone financial statements give the information required by the Act in the manner so required and give a true and fair view in conformity with the accounting principles generally accepted in India, of the state of affairs of the Company as at 31st March, 20XX, and its profit/loss and its cash flows for the year ended on that date.

Other Reporting Responsibilities

This can be used to mention the responsibilities other than the main responsibilities under the Standards on Audit.

Signature of the Auditor

The report is signed in the personal name of the auditor and in the name of the audit firm. The auditors also need to mention the registration number of the firm as allotted by ICAI, in the audit reports that they signed.

Date of the Auditor's Report

The report should not be dated any earlier than the final date on which the auditor has obtained sufficient appropriate audit evidence and has submitted it.

Place of Signature

The location is usually the name of the city, where the auditor signed the report.

References

- Conduct-financial-audit-10228: smallbusiness.chron.com, Retrieved 24 March 2018
- Auditors-report: indiafilings.com, Retrieved 14 July 2018
- Financial-statement-analysis, financial-dictionary, quarterly-report-2475: investinganswers.com, Retrieved 07 July 2018
- Solvency-and-financial-condition-report, financial-services: deloitte.com, Retrieved 09 July 2018
- Definition-financial-audit-reports-23964: smallbusiness.chron.com, Retrieved 12 April 2018

7

Accounting Cycle and Accrual Accounting

Accounting cycle is the process of identifying, recording and analyzing the accounting events of a company. The cycle starts when a transaction occurs and ends once it is included in the financial statements. Accrual accounting is the method which determines the performance and position of a company. This chapter closely examines the fundamental aspects of the accounting cycle and accrual accounting, such as transaction analysis, accounting cycle, cash basis and accrual basis of accounting, etc.

Accounting Cycle

The accounting cycle is the process of recording your business's financial activities. The accounting cycle looks back in time at the end of a designated period. The cycle includes several steps, starting when a transaction occurs. The cycle ends when you record the transaction as part of your financial statements.

The accounting cycle makes accounting easier, breaking your bookkeeping down into smaller tasks. It helps you see what you need to accomplish next.

You can improve consistency and accuracy by following the accounting cycle. Start and end dates allow you to manage time and set goals. You can compare one cycle to another, and reconcile bank statements.

If you use accounting software, you can program dates for your accounting cycle. The software will generate reports based on the dates you select.

Accounting Cycle Steps

Full cycle accounting can be broken down into several steps. Depending on how you do your accounting, you may be able to modify or skip some of the steps.

Many steps in the accounting cycle are meant for accrual accounting. The double-entry accounting system allows you to cross reference entries for accuracy. If you use accrual accounting, you can follow all the steps in the accounting cycle.

If you use a single-entry accounting system (cash-basis), you can still use the accounting cycle. You will begin the accounting period on a certain date, record entries, and close your books at the end of the period. You do not need to follow the steps that require you to check entries for debits and credits.

Steps of Accounting Cycle

Usually, there are eight steps in accounting cycle processes. However, you can add or subtract certain steps when necessary. Use the steps that help you stay organized and maintain accurate records.

The following accounting cycle steps can help you keep financial records:

Identify Transactions

First, separate your business transactions from all of the transactions you made. You only want to include transactions related to your company in your financial records. For example, you won't record your grocery bill as a business expense in your books.

Use source documents to identify business transactions, such as receipts and invoices. Save these kinds of financial documents to support your records. As you identify business transactions, decide which account they fall under.

Record Transactions in your Journal

The journal is where you initially record business transactions. It is a running list of financial activities, like a checkbook. Track transactions in your journal chronologically as they happen.

If you use double-entry bookkeeping, record two entries for each transaction. Enter a debit for one account and a credit for another. The debit and credit should be equal.

Post Entries to the General Ledger

The general ledger is also known as the book of final entry. General ledger entries are changes made to each account in your books. Using your journal, organize transactions into different accounts. For example, if a customer paid for a product with cash, enter the transaction under the cash account in your books.

Unadjusted Trial Balance

For your books to be accurate, the debit and credit entries must be equal. Use an unadjusted trial balance to test if your debits and credits match.

Make a note of each account balance. Add all the debit balances together and all the credit balances together. If the two totals are not the same, you might have an error in your books. Or, you might need to make adjusting entries.

Adjusting Entries

At the end of an accounting period, you might have incurred expenses but not paid for them yet. And, you might have earned income but not collected it yet. Use adjusting entries to recognize transactions that have occurred but not been recorded.

For example, you earned interest on a bank account balance. You have not recorded the interest in your books, but it appears on your bank statement. Use an adjusted entry to recognize the interest in your books.

Adjusted Trial Balance

Do an adjusted trial balance after making adjusting entries and before creating financial statements. This step tests to see if the debits and credits match after making adjusting entries.

Create Financial Statements

Once your accounts are up-to-date, create statements. The following are common financial statements for small business:

- Income statements compare your profits and losses for the period.
- Balance sheets determine progress by detailing assets, liabilities, and equity.
- Cash flow statements show money coming into and out of the business.

Use your financial statements to measure performance, make improvements, and set goals. You can also use statements to talk with lenders and negotiate terms with vendors.

Close your Books

The final step in the accounting cycle is to close your accounting books. Closing your books wraps up financial activities for the period. Do tasks like updating accounts payable, reconciling accounts, reviewing your petty cash fund, and counting inventory.

When you close your books, you should get your accounting set up for the next period. Decide which processes are moving your business forward. Create a calendar for completing future tasks. File any financial documents from the last period and get rid of old documents that are no longer useful.

Flow Chart of the Accounting Cycle

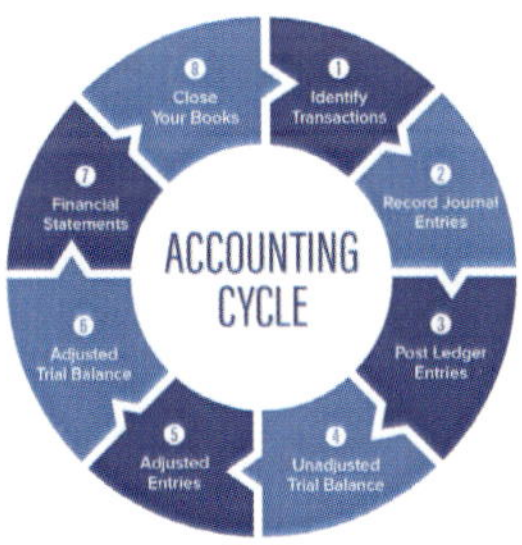

Accounting Equation

From the large, multi-national corporation down to the corner beauty salon, every business transaction will have an effect on a company's financial position. The financial position of a company is measured by the following items:

1. Assets (what it owns).
2. Liabilities (what it owes to others).
3. Owner's Equity (the difference between assets and liabilities).

The accounting equation (or basic accounting equation) offers us a simple way to understand how these three amounts relate to each other. The accounting equation for a sole proprietorship is:

$$\text{Assets} = \text{Laibilites} + \text{Ownre's Equilty}$$

The accounting equation for a corporation is:

$$\text{Assets} = \text{Laibilites} + \text{Stockholder's Equilty}$$

Assets are a company's resources—things the company owns. Examples of assets include cash, accounts receivable, inventory, prepaid insurance, investments, land, buildings, equipment, and goodwill. From the accounting equation, we see that the amount of assets must equal the combined amount of liabilities plus owner's (or stockholders') equity.

Liabilities are a company's obligations—amounts the company owes. Examples of liabilities include notes or loans payable, accounts payable, salaries and wages payable, interest payable, and income taxes payable (if the company is a regular corporation). Liabilities can be viewed in two ways:

1. As claims by creditors against the company's assets, and
2. A source—along with owner or stockholder equity—of the company's assets.

Owner's equity or stockholders' equity is the amount left over after liabilities are deducted from assets:

$$\text{Assets} = \text{Laibilites} + \text{Owner's (or Stockholder's) Equilty}$$

Owner's or stockholders' equity also reports the amounts invested into the company by the owners plus the cumulative net income of the company that has not been withdrawn or distributed to the owners.

If a company keeps accurate records, the accounting equation will always be "in balance," meaning the left side should always equal the right side. The balance is maintained because every business transaction affects at least two of a company's accounts. For example, when a company borrows money from a bank, the company's assets will increase and its liabilities will increase by the same amount. When a company purchases inventory for cash, one asset will increase and one asset will decrease. Because there are two or more accounts affected by every transaction, the accounting system is referred to as double-entry accounting.

A company keeps track of all of its transactions by recording them in accounts in the company's general ledger. Each account in the general ledger is designated as to its type: asset, liability, owner's equity, revenue, expense, gain, or loss account.

Transaction Analysis

Business transactions occur on a daily basis as a result of doing business. Items are purchased or sold, credit is extended or borrowed, income is made or expenses are assumed. These business transactions result in changes to the three elements of the basic accounting equation.

1. A transaction that increases total assets must also increase total liabilities or owner's equity.
2. A transaction that decreases total assets must also decrease total liabilities or owner's equity.
3. Some transactions may increase one account and decrease another on the same side of the equation i.e. one asset increases and another decreases.

Assets =	Liabilities +	Owner's Equity
+	+	
+		+
-	-	
-		–
+ and -		

Regardless of the nature of the specific transaction, the accounting equation must stay in balance at all times.

Transaction Analysis is the process of reconciling the differences made to each side of the equation with each financial transaction occurs. Let's look at some sample transactions to get a better understanding of how the analysis and equation work.

The accounting equation for a brand new company will look like this:

Assets = Liabilities + Owner's Equity

$0 $0 $0

Transaction 1: The owner deposits $5000 in the checking account to begin operations

Assets = Liabilities + Owner's Equity

+$5000 $0 + $5000

The asset "Cash" is increased by $5000 and the Owner's Equity is increased $5000. The business owes the owner $5000.

Transaction 2: The business purchases a computer, on credit, for $2500.

Assets = Liabilities + Owner's Equity

+$2500 + $2500 $

The asset "Computers" is increased by $2500 and the liability is also increased $2500 because the business now owns the store $2500

Transaction 3: The business purchases office supplies using $550 cash.

Assets = Liabilities + Owner's Equity

+$550

–$550

The asset "Office Supplies" is increased $550 and the asset "Cash" is decreased $550.

Transaction 4: A business purchases a building for $ 100,000 with a $ 25,000 cash down-payment and a loan for the $ 75,000 outstanding.

Assets = Liabilities + Owner's Equity

+ $ 100,000 +75,000

- $ 25,000

More than two accounts are affected by this transaction. The asset "Building" increases by $ 100,000, the asset "Cash" decreases by $ 25,000, and the liability "Bank Loan" increases by $ 75,000. The net result is that both sides of the equation increase by $ 75K.

As you can see, regardless of the transaction, the accounting equation must stay balanced.

The expanded accounting equation breaks out the Owner's Equity section into two components: Revenues and Expenses.

- Revenues = what the business earns for providing goods or services.
- Expenses = the cost of assets the business uses to generate revenues (payroll, depreciation, rent, utilities, taxes).

The business' Profit or Loss equals the Revenues – Expenses. If Revenues are more than Expenses, there is Profit. If Expenses are more than Revenues, there is Loss. The owner of the company also has the option to withdraw equity from the company in the form of drawings (proprietorships and partnerships) or dividends (corporations).

When you look at these relationships to owner's equity in terms of the accounting equation you see that:

1. Revenues increase Owner's Equity.
2. Expenses decrease Owner's Equity.
3. Drawings or Dividends decrease Owner's Equity:

The expanded Accounting Equation looks like this:

Assets = Liabilities + Owner's Equity + Revenues – Expenses – Drawings

Let's analyze some transactions involving these types of accounts:

Transaction 5: The business sells goods for $ 1,200 cash.

Assets = Liabilities + Owner's Equity

+ $ 1200 + $ 1200 (Revenue)

The asset "Cash" is increased $ 1200 and the revenue increases Owner's Equity $ 1200.

Transaction 6: The business pays its rent monthly rent of $ 950 using a company check.

Assets = Liabilities + Owner's Equity

- $ 950 - $ 950 (Expense)

The asset "Cash" is decreased $ 950 and the expense decreases Owner's Equity $ 950.

Transaction 7: The business' owner withdraws $ 2,000 for his personal use.

Assets = Liabilities + Owner's Equity

- $ 2000 - $ 2000 (Revenue)

The asset "Cash" is decreased $ 2000 and the drawing decreases Owner's Equity $ 2000.

Injection of Capital Transaction Example

As a second example of accounting transaction analysis, suppose a business is started with a capital injection of 30,000 cash by the owner.

In this example, the cash of 30,000 is injected by the owner as capital and the six steps involved in the accounting transaction analysis are:

1. This is an accounting transaction as it relates to the business and involves a monetary amount.
2. The accounts involved are the cash account and the capital account.
3. The two accounts types are an asset account (cash) and an equity account (capital).
4. Cash is increased and capital is also increased by the transaction.
5. An increase to an asset account is a debit, an increase to an equity account is a credit.
6. For each account the monetary amount is 30,000.

This can be summarized in the accounting transaction analysis table as follows:

Accounting Transaction Analysis Table

Transaction: Capital injection of 30,000 cash by the owner of the business.

Accounts	Type	Change	Dr or Cr	Amount
Cash	Asset	Increase	Debit	30,000
Capital	Equity	Increase	Credit	30,000

Account

If we are talking about an account in the context of accounting then it has a different meaning than most people are used to. The word account usually triggers thoughts of a bank account: checking or savings. In the business world, account might refer to a client.

In accounting, an account is simply a unique place in the general ledger that is used for recording a dollar balance along with a history of changes to that balance. This balance can be associated with a bank account or it can represent the amount of money owed to you by a client or customer. It could also represent your reported income, expenses or the value of assets that you own.

Account Type

Because there is so much variety when thinking about accounts we give each one a type that will determine where the account appears in different reports and how it can be used when entering income, expenses, payments and transfers.

Account Number

Account numbers are a type of short-hand for naming accounts. Accountants do a lot of data entry using the number pad on the keyboard and it is much easier to punch in a 4-digit number than it is to use the main part of the keyboard and spell it out.

Account numbers are organized so that the left-most digits represent what part of the balance sheet it is located on and the right-most digits determine what order the accounts in that section are shown.

Chart of Accounts

The chart of accounts is basically a list of all the accounts and their number that you have set up in your accounting system.

Classification of Accounts

Based on Nature

There are mainly three types of accounts in accounting: Real, Personal and Nominal accounts, personal accounts are classified into three subcategories: Artificial, Natural, and Representative.

If you fail to identify an account correctly as either a real, personal or nominal account, in most cases, you will get end up recording incorrect journal entries.

Real Accounts

All assets of a firm, which are tangible or intangible, fall under the category "Real Accounts".

Tangible real accounts are related to things that can be touched and felt physically. Few examples of tangible real accounts are building, machinery, stock, land, etc.

Intangible real accounts are related to things that can't be touched and felt physically. Few examples of such real accounts are goodwill, patents, trademarks, etc.

Golden Rule for Real Accounts

Debit what comes in
Credit what goes out

Example

The transaction below shows the interaction of two different real accounts: one is furniture and the other is cash, both of them are assets of the company and hence classified as real accounts.

- Purchased furniture for 10,000 in cash

Accounts Involved	Debit/Credit	Rule Applied
Furniture A/C	Debit	Real A/C – Dr. what comes in
To Cash A/C	Credit	Real A/C – Cr. what goes out

Amount will be 10,000 in both debit and credit.

Personal Accounts

These accounts are related to individuals, firms, companies, etc. A few examples of personal accounts include debtors, creditors, banks, outstanding/prepaid accounts, accounts of credit customers, accounts of goods suppliers, capital, drawings, etc.

Natural personal accounts: This type of personal accounts is the simplest to understand out of all and includes all of God's creations who have the ability to deal, who, in most cases, are people. E.g. Kumar's A/C, Adam's A/C, etc.

Artificial personal accounts: Personal accounts which are created artificially by law, such as corporate bodies and institutions, are called Artificial personal accounts. E.g. Pvt. Ltd. companies, LLCs, LLPs, clubs, schools, etc.

Representative personal accounts: Accounts which represent a certain person or a group directly or indirectly. E.g. Let's say that wages are paid in advance to an employee – a wage prepaid account will be opened in the books of accounts. This wages prepaid account is a representative personal account indirectly linked to the person.

Golden Rule for Personal Accounts

Debit the receiver
Credit the giver

Example

The transaction below demonstrates the interaction between two different personal accounts, one of which is a private limited company and the other one is a bank.

- Paid Unreal Pvt. Ltd. 24,000 by check

Accounts Involved	Debit/Credit	Rule Applied
Unreal Pvt. Ltd. A/C	Debit	Artificial Personal – Dr. the receiver
To Bank A/C	Credit	Artificial Personal – Cr. the giver

Amount will be 24,000 in both debit and credit.

Nominal Accounts

Accounts which are related to expenses, losses, incomes or gains are called Nominal accounts. The dictionary meaning of the word "nominal" is "*existing in name only*" and the meaning remains absolutely true in accounting sense too, because nominal accounts do not really exist in physical form, but behind every nominal account money is involved. E.g. Purchase A/C, Salary A/C, Sales A/C, Commission received A/C, etc.

The final result of all nominal accounts is either profit or loss which is then transferred to the capital account.

Golden Rule for Nominal Accounts

Debit all expenses & losses
Credit all incomes & gains

Example

The following example shows a transaction where a nominal account deals with a real a/c.

Purchased good for 15,000 in cash

Accounts Involved	Debit/Credit	Rule Applied
Purchase A/C	Debit	Nominal A/C – Dr. all expenses
To Cash A/C	Credit	Real A/C – Cr. what goes out

The amount will be 15,000 in both debit and credit.

Based on Periodicity of Flow

Assets

For assets, we have accounts receivable (which is money that is owed to the company), bank, furniture & equipment, inventory, PayPal, and undeposited funds (which is an account used to track funds received, but not yet deposited into your bank account, like a check that's sitting on your desk waiting to be deposited).

ASSETS

accounts rec.	0
bank account	0
inventory	0
paypal account	0
undeposited funds	0
land & buildings	0

All these accounts represent things that a company owns that has monetary value. For example, the accounts receivable are kind of like I.O.U.'s that were given to a business by its customers. Likewise, the desk in the office is also worth money if sold just like money in the bank account is obviously worth money.

Liabilities

For liability accounts we have accounts payable (which is money the company owes to other companies for things they've purchased but not paid for yet), bank loan, car loan, credit card, and money that's due to shareholders (which is money that the company has borrowed from its shareholders).

LIABILITIES

accounts pay.	0
bank loan	0
car loan	0
credit card	0
due to shareholder	0
mortgage	0

All these accounts represent money that the company owes. For example, accounts payable are vendor bills that need to be paid and the credit card account represents money owed to the bank that issued it.

Equity

Equity includes accounts like net income (which is technically called retained earnings), dividends, and owner's equity (or in other words, an owner's investment into the company).

Equity is the money that has been invested into the company, money that the company has made, or money the company has paid out to its owners for investing into the company. Another way to think about equity is to think of it as what's left over after you take your Assets and pay off all your liabilities. Assets - Liabilities = Equity. If we take the example of the cafe that Akko purchased, this can give us some insight into how equity is calculated. The cafe was purchased for $ 100,000, composed of a 20% down payment ($ 20,000) and an $ 80,000 mortgage. The down payment represents the equity. Assets (Cafe) $ 100,000 - Liability (mortgage) $ 80,000 = Equity (down payment) $ 20,000.

EQUITY

net income	0
dividends	0
owners equity	0

Revenue

Revenue includes accounts like cafe sales (which are items sold in the cafe), catering sales (which are for catering events outside of the cafe) and interest income (You know what interest income is, right? The 0.00001 percent interest the bank gives you for the privilege of having them loan out your money).

REVENUE

cafe sales	0
catering sales	0
interest income	0
asset gain	0

Revenue is money that goes into the business as a result of goods or services sold. Money can go into the business through a variety of methods, from an owner investing money to a loan taken out with a bank. Not all money going into a business is revenue.

Revenue can also be money received from the sale of an asset that has appreciated in value. For example, if the cafe shop was bought for $ 100,000 and sold for $ 110,000, that would be gain on the sale of an asset (revenue) of $ 10,000.

Expense

Expense includes accounts like advertising, bank fees, cost of goods sold, and office supplies.

EXPENSE

advertising	0
bank fees	0
cost of goods sold	0
office supplies	0
asset loss	0

Expenses are money that goes out of a business to pay for operations. Like revenue, not all money going out of a business is an expense. If money goes out of the business to pay back a loan, purchase an asset or as dividends to owners, these are not expenses.

And like with revenue, if an asset loses value, this can be expensed as well. So when the cafe purchased for $ 100,000 is later sold for $ 90,000, it incurs a loss on the sale of an asset (expense) of $ 10,000.

Debits and Credits

Business transactions are events that have a monetary impact on the financial statements of an organization. When accounting for these transactions, we record numbers in two accounts, where the debit column is on the left and the credit column is on the right.

- A debit is an accounting entry that either increases an asset or expense account, or decreases a liability or equity account. It is positioned to the left in an accounting entry.
- A credit is an accounting entry that either increases a liability or equity account, or decreases an asset or expense account. It is positioned to the right in an accounting entry.

Debit and Credit Usage

Whenever an accounting transaction is created, at least two accounts are always impacted, with a debit entry being recorded against one account and a credit entry being recorded against the other account. There is no upper limit to the number of accounts involved in a transaction - but the minimum is no less than two accounts. The totals of the debits and credits for any transaction must always equal each other, so that an accounting transaction is always said to be "in balance." If a transaction were not in balance, then it would not be possible to create financial statements. Thus, the use of debits and credits in a two-column transaction recording format is the most essential of all controls over accounting accuracy.

There can be considerable confusion about the inherent meaning of a debit or a credit. For example, if you debit cash account, then this means that the amount of cash on hand increases. However, if you debit an accounts payable account, this means that the amount of accounts payable liability decreases. These differences arise because debits and credits have different impacts across several broad types of accounts, which are:

- Asset accounts: A debit increases the balance and a credit decreases the balance.
- Liability accounts: A debit decreases the balance and a credit increases the balance.
- Equity accounts: A debit decreases the balance and a credit increases the balance.

The reason for this seeming reversal of the use of debits and credits is caused by the underlying accounting equation upon which the entire structure of accounting transactions are built, which is:

Assets = Liabilities + Equity

Thus, in a sense, you can only have assets if you have paid for them with liabilities or equity, so you must have one in order to have the other. Consequently, if you create a transaction with a debit and a credit, you are usually increasing an asset while also increasing a liability or equity account (or vice versa). There are some exceptions, such as increasing one asset account while decreasing another asset account.

If you are more concerned with accounts that appear on the income statement, then these additional rules apply:

- Revenue accounts: A debit decreases the balance and a credit increases the balance.
- Expense accounts: A debit increases the balance and a credit decreases the balance.
- Gain accounts: A debit decreases the balance and a credit increases the balance.
- Loss accounts: A debit increases the balance and a credit decreases the balance.

If you are really confused by these issues, then just remember that debits always go in the left column, and credits always go in the right column. There are no exceptions.

Debit and Credit Rules

The rules governing the use of debits and credits are as follows:

- All accounts that normally contain a debit balance will increase in amount when a debit (left column) is added to them, and reduced when a credit (right column) is added to them. The types of accounts to which this rule applies are expenses, assets, and dividends.
- All accounts that normally contain a credit balance will increase in amount when a credit (right column) is added to them, and reduced when a debit (left column) is added to them. The types of accounts to which this rule applies are liabilities, revenues, and equity.
- The total amount of debits must equal the total amount of credits in a transaction. Otherwise, an accounting transaction is said to be unbalanced, and will not be accepted by the accounting software.

Debits and Credits in Common Accounting Transactions

The following bullet points note the use of debits and credits in the more common business transactions:

- Sale for cash: Debit the cash account | Credit the revenue account.
- Sale on credit: Debit the accounts receivable account | Credit the revenue account.
- Receive cash in payment of an account receivable: Debit the cash account | Credit the accounts receivable account.
- Purchase supplies from supplier for cash: Debit the supplies expense account | Credit the cash account.
- Purchase supplies from supplier on credit: Debit the supplies expense account | Credit the accounts payable account.
- Purchase inventory from supplier for cash: Debit the inventory account | Credit the cash account.
- Purchase inventory from supplier on credit: Debit the inventory account | Credit the accounts payable account.
- Pay employees: Debit the wages expense and payroll tax accounts | Credit the cash account.
- Take out a loan: Debit cash account | Credit loans payable account.
- Repay a loan: Debit loans payable account | Credit cash account.

Debit and Credit Examples

Arnold Corporation sells a product to a customer for $ 1,000 in cash. This results in revenue of $ 1,000 and cash of $ 1,000. Arnold must record an increase of the cash (asset) account with a debit, and an increase of the revenue account with a credit. The entry is:

	Debit	Credit
Cash	1,000	
Revenue		1,000

Arnold Corporation also buys a machine for $ 15,000 on credit. This results in an addition to the Machinery fixed assets account with a debit, and an increase in the accounts payable (liability) account with a credit. The entry is:

	Debit	Credit
Machinery - Fixed Assets	15,000	
Accounts Payable		15,000

Other Debit and Credit Issues

A debit is commonly abbreviated as dr. in an accounting transaction, while a credit is abbreviated as cr. in an accounting transaction.

Debits and credits are not used in a single entry system. In this system, only a single notation is made of a transaction; it is usually an entry in a check book or cash journal, indicating the receipt or expenditure of cash. A single entry system is only designed to produce an income statement.

Chart of Accounts

A chart of accounts (COA) is a listing of each account a company owns, along with the account type and account balance, shown in the order the accounts appear in the company's financial statements. "Chart of accounts" is the official accounting term for the display of this information, which includes both balance-sheet accounts and income-statement accounts.

An account is a unique record for each type of asset, liability, equity, revenue and expense. The chart of accounts is a financial organizational tool that provides a complete listing of every account in the general ledger of a company, broken down into subcategories. Each chart in the list is assigned a multi-digit number to help identify the account type (e.g., all asset accounts might start with the number 1). Typically, a COA contains the accounts' names, brief descriptions and identification codes.

Using a COA, balance sheet accounts are listed first that is, assets, liabilities and shareholders' equity. Accounts in the income statement — revenues and expenses — are presented next.

For a small corporation, the chart of accounts might include these sub-accounts under the assets account:

- Cash
- Savings account
- Petty cash balance
- Accounts receivable
- Undeposited funds
- Inventory assets
- Prepaid insurance
- Vehicles
- Buildings

Liabilities account may have sub-accounts, such as:

- The company credit card
- Accrued liablities
- Accounts payable
- Payroll liabilities
- Notes payable

Shareholders' equity can be broken down into the following accounts:

- Common stock
- Preferred stock
- Retained earnings

Within the accounts of the income statement, the revenues and expenses accounts could be broken into operating revenues, operating expenses, non-operating revenues and non-operating losses. In addition, the operating revenues and operating expenses accounts might be further organized by business function and/or by company divisions. Many organizations structure their chart of accounts so that expense information is separately compiled by department; thus, the sales department, engineering department and accounting department all have the same set of expense accounts. Examples of expense accounts include cost of goods sold (COGS), depreciation expense, utilities expense, wages expense, etc.

Even a small company could have dozens of accounts in its chart of accounts. The larger and more complex the company, the larger and more complex the chart of accounts will be, but accounting software makes it easy to categorize accounting entries correctly and maintain an accurate and organized chart of accounts.

Reporting requirements can affect how a company structures its chart of accounts, but it is important to keep the COA the same from year to year to make accurate comparisons of the company's finances across time.

Here is a way to think about the chart of accounts as it relates to your own finances, which might help you better understand how it relates to a business. Say you have a checking account, a savings account and a certificate of deposit (CD) at the same bank. When you log in to your account online, you'll typically go to an overview page that shows the balance in each account. Similarly, if you use an online program that helps you manage all your accounts in one place, like Mint or Personal Capital, what you're looking at is basically the same thing as a company's chart of accounts. You can see all your assets and liabilities, all on one page.

Accruals

Accruals are earned revenues and incurred expenses that have an overall impact on an income statement. They also affect the balance sheet, which represents liabilities and non-cash-based assets used in accrual-based accounting. These accounts include, among many others, accounts payable, accounts receivable, goodwill, future tax liabilities and future interest expenses.

The use of accrual accounts has greatly increased the amount of information on accounting statements. Before the use of accruals, accountants only recorded cash transactions on these statements. But cash transactions don't give information about other important business activities, such as revenue based on credit and future liabilities. By recording accruals, a company can measure what it owes in the short-term and also what cash revenue it expects to receive. It also allows a company to show assets that do not have a cash value, such as goodwill.

Using the accrual method, an accountant makes adjustments for revenue that has been earned but is not yet recorded in the accounts, and expenses that have been incurred but are not yet recorded in the accounts. The accruals must be added via adjusting journal entries, so that the financial statements report these amounts.

In double-entry bookkeeping, the offset to an accrued expense is an accrued liability account, which appears in the balance sheet. The offset to accrued revenue is an accrued asset account, which also appears in the balance sheet. Therefore, an accrual entry will impact the balance sheet and the income statement.

Accruals are revenues and expenses that are incurred during an accounting period for which no invoices or payments were received or made. Accruals are, therefore, estimated figures since the invoice, when received, may have different numbers. When invoice has been received, a company records the amount under the accounts payable (for money owing suppliers and vendors) or accounts receivable account (for money to be collected from customers) in the balance sheet.

Examples

Let's look at an example of an accrual regarding revenue that involves an electric utility company. The utility company generated electricity that customers received in December. However, the utility does not bill the electric customers until the following month. To have the proper amounts on the utility's financial statements, there needs to be an adjusting entry to report revenue that was earned in December, which reflects the receivables that the utility has a right to as of December 31. The following month, when the cash is received, the receivables will go down, and the cash account will increase.

An example of an accrual involving an expense is employee bonuses that were earned in 2016, but will not be paid until 2017. The 2016 financial statements need to reflect the bonus expense and the bonus liability. Therefore, prior to issuing the 2016 financial statements, an adjusting entry records this accrual. The accountant increases an expense and creates a liability. Once the payment has been made in the new year the liability will be eliminated, and the cash will be reduced.

Another expense accrual occurs for interest. For instance, a company with a bond will accrue interest expense. Interest on bonds is typically paid semi-annually, but the interest expense will be recorded as the amount that has accrued as of the date of the financial statement. A corresponding interest liability will be recorded on the balance sheet.

Accrual Basis of Accounting

The accrual basis of accounting is the concept of recording revenues when earned and expenses as incurred. Accrual basis accounting is the standard approach to recording transactions for all larger businesses. This concept differs from the cash basis of accounting, under which revenues are recorded when cash is received, and expenses are recorded when cash is paid. For example, a company operating under the accrual basis of accounting will record a sale as soon as it issues an invoice to a customer, while a cash basis company would instead wait to be paid before it records the sale. Similarly, an accrual basis company will record an expense as incurred, while a cash basis company would instead wait to pay its supplier before recording the expense.

The accrual basis of accounting is advocated under both generally accepted accounting principles (GAAP) and international financial reporting standards (IFRS). Both of these accounting frameworks provide guidance regarding how to account for revenue and expense transactions in the absence of the cash receipts or payments that would trigger the recordation of a transaction under the cash basis of accounting.

The accrual basis of accounting tends to provide more even recognition of revenues and expenses over time, and so is considered by investors to be the most valid accounting system for ascertaining the results of operations, financial position, and cash flows of a business. In particular, it supports the matching principle, under which revenues and all related expenses are to be recorded within the same reporting period; by doing so, it should be possible to see the full extent of the profits and losses associated with specific business transactions within a single reporting period.

The accrual basis requires the use of estimates in certain areas. For example, a company should record an expense for estimated bad debts that have not yet been incurred. By doing so, all expenses related to a revenue transaction are recorded at the same time as the revenue, which results in an income statement that fully reflects the results of operations. Similarly, the estimated amounts of product returns, sales allowances, and obsolete inventory may be recorded. These estimates may not be entirely correct, and so can lead to materially inaccurate financial statements. Consequently, a considerable amount of care must be used when estimating accrued expenses.

A small business may elect to avoid using the accrual basis of accounting, since it requires a certain amount of accounting expertise. Also, a small business owner may choose to manipulate the timing of cash inflows and outflows to create a smaller amount of taxable income under the cash basis of accounting, which can result in the deferral of income tax payments.

A significant failing of the accrual basis of accounting is that it can indicate the presence of profits, even though the associated cash inflows have not yet occurred. The result can be a supposedly profitable entity that is starved for cash, and which may therefore go bankrupt despite its reported level of profitability. Consequently, you should pay attention to the statement of cash flows of a business, which indicates the flows of cash into and out of a business.

Cash Basis of Accounting

Businesses must choose one or the other of two possible approaches to financial reporting:

- Firstly, they may select cash basis accounting. Firms using this approach record revenue when they receive cash and record expenses when the pay cash.
- Secondly, they may choose accrual basis accounting instead. Firms using this approach record revenue when they earn it and record expenses when they owe them.

Choosing an Accounting System Impacts the Way the Firm Does Business

On first hearing the distinction between cash accounting and accrual accounting, the differences may seem minor. When the natures of the two accounting systems are better understood, however, it is clear that the accounting system choice has a profound influence on operations. Choice of system impacts the way the firm bills customers, and how it collects payments and pays its bills. And, the choice of accounting system has a profound impact on the way the firm meets reporting obligations to regulatory agencies and governments.

Most Businesses Choose Accrual Accounting

The vast majority of businesses worldwide choose accrual accounting. It is almost impossible for a public company to meet its reporting requirements using cash accounting alone. In fact, large organizations of all kinds—public and private—will not meet their own record-keeping needs using cash basis accounting only. One reason, for instance, is that only accrual accounting enables the organization to track its asset base, liabilities, and equities.

Some Businesses Choose Cash Basis Accounting

By contrast, some small privately-held businesses choose cash basis accounting because it is simple.

- This approach is more straightforward because it uses a single-entry system: each transaction results in just one transaction record entry. A double-entry accrual system, by contrast, requires at least two bookkeeping entries for each.
- Cash basis accounting is straightforward, also, because it recognizes only two kinds of transactions—cash inflows and cash outflows. Accrual accounting, by comparison, records debit and credit transactions in five different account categories.

And, with a cash basis system, keeping the firm's "books" does not require accounting or bookkeeping skills. Just about any person who can arrange figures in a table and manage a simple spreadsheet can create and use cash basis records. As a result, the cash basis approach enables some small firms to meet their record-keeping and reporting needs without a trained accountant or accounting software.

Cash Basis Means Cash Transactions Only

Cash transactions recorded in a cash basis system include physical transfer of coins and banknotes, of course, but also forms of transmission that turn into cash very quickly. As a result, the cash basis system also registers payments with written checks, credit cards, bank debit cards, and bank wire transfers.

A cash basis system, however, does not record receipt of a promissory note, creation of an account receivable, or the sending of a customer invoice.

Cash Basis Accounting Examples

Cash accounting works well with single-entry accounting, while accrual accounting works only with double-entry accounting. As a result, examples comparing cash accounting and accrual accounting are very similar to examples comparing single-entry and double-entry systems.

Single-entry cash accounting is very similar to the way that individuals use a check register for checking account checks, deposits, and balances. Users directly record the amount of each cash inflow or outflow, along with a transaction name or description.

Cash Basis Transaction Record

Tables below, show how the cash basis single-entry record might look for a few days transactions for a small business, such as a small retail shop operating as a sole proprietorship.

Three-Column Cash Record for a Small Business

Table(a), with three columns, is the briefest possible form of cash-basis transaction record.

Date	Transaction	Amount
1 June XX	Starting balance for the day	$4,520.00
1 June XX	Electricity bill for the month	($149.80)
2 June XX	Postage stamps purchased	($43.00)
2 June XX	Inventory purchased	($624.15)
3 June XX	Daily product sales	$1,040.25
3 June XX	Sales tax paid	($83.22)
4 June XX	Daily service revenues	$592.25
4 June XX	Bank interest received	$180.83
5 June XX	Customer refund paid	($42.95)
5 June XX	Ending balance for the day	$5,390.21

Three-column cash basis transaction record, for a small business. Incoming funds are positive numbers, and outgoing funds are negative numberse (in parentheses). This simple cash basis record shows transactions for five days.

Five Column Cash Basis Transaction Record for a Small Business

Table(b) with five columns is slightly more complicated than Table(a). Table(b) has separate columns for cash inflows (revenues), cash outflows (expenses), and current balance.

Date	Transaction	Revenues	Expenses	Balance
1 June XX	Starting balance for the day			$4,520.00
1 June XX	Electricity bill for the month		($149.80)	$4,370.20
2 June XX	Postage stamp purchase		($43.00)	$4,327.20
2 June XX	Inventory purchased		($624.15)	$3,703.5
3 June XX	Daily product sales	$1,040.25		$4,743.30
3 June XX	Sales tax paid		($83.22)	$4,660.08
4 June XX	Daily service revenues	$592.25		$5,252.33
4 June XX	Bank interest received	$180.83		$5,433.16
5 June XX	Customer refund paid		($42.95)	$5,390.21
5 June XX	Ending balance for the day			$5,390.21

Cash Basis transactions with a single-entry system. This version has a running balance and separate columns for incoming revenues and outgoing expenses. Incoming revenues are positive numbers, and outgoing funds are negative numbers.

The record can add additional columns, of course, to show different categories of revenues or expenses. The only structure required in the register is to include enough different revenue and expense categories to meet tax reporting requirements.

Cash Basis Accounting Sufficient: When or Where

Cash accounting can be adequate for some small businesses. Some small firms may, in fact, prefer the cash-basis approach over an accrual system.

Where is Cash Basis Accounting Preferred?

The cash approach may be preferred where all or most of the following conditions apply. The company:

- Uses single-entry accounting, not double-entry accounting.
- Has relatively few financial transactions per day.
- Does not sell on credit (does not deliver goods or services and then invoice customers for payment later).

- Requires that at the time of sale, customers must pay either by cash, written check, bank transfer, or 3rd-party credit/debit card.
- Has very few employees.
- Owns few valuable business-supporting physical assets.
- May hold some product inventory, office supplies, and cash in a bank account, but does not own buildings, substantial amounts of office furniture, large computer systems, production machinery, or vehicles.
- The company is privately held or operates as a sole proprietorship or partnership. The company does not need to publish the Income statement, Balance sheet, or other financial statements required of publicly owned companies.

Meeting Legal Reporting Needs With a Cash Basis System

Under such conditions, a cash basis system may be adequate to meet the company's legal reporting obligations. The cash basis system may be sufficient for:

- Supporting the company's income tax reporting (for which the primary data are incoming revenues and outgoing expenses, in several categories).
- Proving that the company collected and paid government sales taxes for goods or services sold.
- Forecasting future budgetary needs and sales revenues.
- Showing that the company complied with minimum wage payment and employee income tax-withholding requirements.
- Proving that the company pays its income tax.
- Providing real-time visibility and control of incoming and outgoing funds (to prevent spending over budget or overdrawing the company checking account).

Advantages to Cash Basis Accounting

Cash Basis accounting has the significant benefit of simplicity over accrual accounting:

- People with little or no financial or accounting understand the cash basis approach (and single-entry bookkeeping) readily.
- Many small companies can implement the cash basis approach without involving a trained bookkeeper or accountant.
- The cash basis approach does not require complicated accounting software. It should be clear from the examples above, for instance, that a firm can quickly create and maintain a cash basis single-entry system in a written notebook or a very simple spreadsheet.

Disadvantages to Cash Basis Accounting

Cash basis accounting cannot meet the record-keeping needs of public companies and other organizations that must file audited financial statements, such as an Income statement or Balance sheet. Nor can it—by itself—give owners and managers crucial information for evaluating the firm's financial position. Some of the essential differences between the two approaches illustrate disadvantages of the cash basis approach.

Double-entry accrual systems provide several kinds of error checking that are absent in cash accounting with a single-entry system. In the accrual system, every financial transaction results in both a debit (DR) entry in one account and an equal, offsetting credit (CR) entry in another account. For any timespan, the sum of all "debits" must equal the sum of all "credits." That is:

Total DR = Total CR

Cash Basis Systems Lack Built-in Error Checking

Moreover, a double-entry accrual system works so that the Balance sheet equation always holds:

Assets = Liabilities + Equities

These equations together are known as the accounting equation. Any departure from this equality in a double-entry accrual system is evidence of a transaction entry error somewhere in the system.

Accrual Systems Build in Error Checking

This kind of error does not exist in a cash basis single-entry system. Consider the result, for instance, if the cash basis bookkeeper mistakenly enters, say, a revenue inflow as $ 10,000 when the correct value is $ 1,000.

In a single-entry cash system, the error may not be apparent until the firm receives a bank statement with an unexpected low account balance—or an overdrawn account.

In a double-entry accrual system, however, the $ 1,000 cash deposit entry (a debit to an asset account, "Cash on hand") will be accompanied by another entry recognizing the source, e.g., a credit to a liability account (e.g., "Bank loan") or a credit to another asset account (e.g., "Accounts receivable"). If the second entry is missing, the sums of credits and debits in the system will differ, thereby revealing the error.

Focus on Revenues and Expenses Only

A double-entry system keeps in view the company's entire chart of accounts. That is, all transactions in a double-entry system result in entries in two different accounts, which may be the so-called Income statement accounts (revenue accounts and expense accounts) or the so-called Balance sheet accounts (asset accounts, liability accounts, and equities accounts).

When the company receives cash through a bank loan, as mentioned, the double-entry system records a debit for an asset account, e.g., "cash on hand" (for an asset account, a "debit DR" is an increase), as well as a credit to a liability account, e.g., "bank loans" (with a liability account, an increase is a credit).

With a single-entry system, the company may record cash received from a bank loan as incoming cash, but there is no easy way to register the corresponding liability increase (bank loan to repay). Single entry systems do not easily track the value of assets, liabilities or equities.

Cash Basis versus Accrual Basis

The difference between cash and accrual accounting stems from the fact that most business transactions involve two events:

- The seller delivers goods or services.
- The buyer pays for the purchase.

These events may occur at the same time, or there may be a time lapse between them. And, either event may precede the other.

The seller may deliver goods, for instance, then invoice the customer and wait 30 days or more for payment. Or the seller may be paid "up front," and then deliver later. For example, when a buyer leases floor space, the first payment is usually due before the occupancy period. For example, when a buyer leases floor space, the first payment is typically due before the occupancy period.

Under cash basis accounting, sellers record their expenses for delivering goods or services when they pay the cost. Similarly, sellers register cash receipts only when customers pay.

Cash Basis sellers record revenues and expenses, that is, only when they occur, even if time passes between the two events, events, including situations when they happen in different accounting periods.

Accrual Accounting Achieves Matching While Cash Basis Accounting Does Not

The generally accepted accounting principle of "Matching" is the idea that reported incoming revenues should match (report in the same accounting period) with the expenses that bring them. Otherwise, reported margins and profits are misleading. Cash basis firms that sell "on credit" will not always achieve this kind of matching.

- In contrast to cash basis accounting, the alternative—accrual accounting—achieves matching by using two pairs of entries for a single sale.
    - For accrual-basis sellers, closing the sale and delivering goods or services brings two bookkeeping entries. These are a debit to one account and a credit to another. And, receiving the customer's cash payment brings another two entries. These, again, are debit to one account and a credit to another.
    - At the same time, accrual-basis buyers record two entries when they first owe the payment, and another two entries when they pay cash.

Under accrual accounting, therefore, both sellers and buyers report revenues and expenses based on each party's first pair of entries. They state, that is, entries showing income earned by the seller and cash owed by the buyer.

Journal Entry

A journal entry is the primary record of all financial transactions of a business in chronological order. Before computer accounting software programs, the process of recording transactions was manual and recorded in a paper journal and is where the term journal entry comes from.

Journal entries are used to record daily financial transactions to analyze how financial transactions impact a business.

The journal entries are aggregated to the general ledger which is then used to construct financial statements.

A journal entry should typically include:

- Unique identifying number of the entry.
- Date of the transaction.
- Amount(s) to be debited and credited.
- Account(s) where the debits and credits are recorded.
- Name of the person making the entry.
- Whether the entry on one-time or recurring.
- A description of the transaction may be beneficial to include and provide information regarding the entry.

Below given step-by-step through the accounting cycle of double entry journal entries:

Step 1 – Recording Accounting Journal Entries with Debits and Credits

In a double entry accounting system (used by most businesses) every business transaction is recorded in at least two accounts.

One account from your small business chart of accounts will be debited which simply means the amount will be recorded on the left side and one account will be credited amount recorded on right side.

Debits and credits must balance equal.

Step 2 – Journalizing

Today most accounting is done on computers and the journalizing (recording accounting journal entries) is done in the background; however, it is still important to know the basics of double entry accounting.

- In manual accounting each financial transaction is first recorded in a book called a journal.
- In that accounting journal entry the title of the account to be debited is listed first, followed by the amount to be debited. The title of the account to be credited is listed below and to the right of the debit, followed by the amount to be credited.
- To determine which account is debited and which is credited you have to first determine what kind of account is being affected and if it was increased or decreased.

Step 3 – Recording Accounting Journal Entries using the Accounting Equation

- To determine which account is debited and which is credited memorize this basic accounting equation (the foundation of all basic accounting concepts):

  Assets = Liabilities + Owner's Equity

- Assets are on the left side or debit side and asset accounts such as Cash have their normal balances on the left side.
- Liabilities and Owner's equity are on the right side or credit side and their accounts in the general accounting ledger have their normal balance on the right side.

Step 4 – Recording Accounting Journal Entries: Increase or Decrease

- To record a business transaction in an accounting journal entry, we need to look closely at the transaction and see which accounts it involves and if it increased or decreased those accounts.
- If it involved an asset account such as Cash, you would picture that basic accounting equation above and know that its normal balance is on the left side (debit side), so if we received (increase) cash we would record the amount on the left side.
- However, if it decreased our asset account such as paying our small business bills, we would record it on second line and on the right side to show a decrease in that account.
- If the business transaction increased our liabilities or owner's equity we would record it on the right side (credit side) because those balance sheet accounts have a normal credit (right) balance.
- If the transaction decreased our liabilities or owner's equity we would record it on the left side (debit side).
- To sum it up—remembering the basic accounting equation: increase a balance sheet account by recording the amount on the same side as it's on in the equation; decrease it by recording amount on the opposite side.
- For income statement accounts such as revenue (income) and expenses, you just need to remember revenue accounts have a normal right credit balance. (Easy for me to remember—Revenue increases owner's equity and has the same normal "credit" balance)
- So following the rules above—when you increase your revenue account, you would record the amount on its normal credit (right) side and to decrease it you would record the amount on the debit (left) side.
- Expenses have a normal debit (left) balance. To increase your expense account, you would record the amount on its normal debit (left) side and to decrease it you would record the amount on its opposite (credit) side. Expenses are almost always debited.

Journal Entry Examples

Borrowing Money Journal Entry

ABC Company borrowed $300,000 from the bank

- The accounts affected are cash (asset) and bank loan payable (liability).
- Cash is increasing because we are gaining cash from the bank and bank loan payable is increasing because the company is increasing its liability to pay back the bank at a later date.

- The amount in question is $ 300,000.
- A = L + SE, A is increased by 300,000 and L is also increased by 300,000, keeping the accounting equation intact.

Therefore, the journal entry would look like:

DR Cash 300,000

CR Bank Loan Payable 300,000

Purchasing Equipment Journal Entry

- Purchased equipment for $650,000 in cash

DR Equipment 650,000

CR Cash 650,000

To learn more, launch our free accounting courses.

Purchasing Inventory Journal Entry

- Purchased inventory costing $ 90,000 for $ 10,000 in cash and the remaining $ 80,000 on the account

DR Inventory 90,000

CR Cash 10,000

CR Accounts Payable 80,000

Acquiring Land Journal Entry

- Purchased land costing $50,000 and buildings costing $400,000. Paid $100,000 in cash and signed a note payable for the balance.

DR Land 50,000

DR Buildings 400,000

CR Cash 100,000

CR Note payable 350,000

Adjusting Entries

Adjusting entries are journal entries used to recognize income or expenses that occurred but are not accurately displayed in your records.

You create adjusting journal entries at the end of an accounting period to balance your debits and credits. They ensure your books are accurate so you can create financial statements.

In accrual accounting, you report transactions when your business incurs them, not when you physically spend or receive money. Adjusting journal entries are required to record transactions in the right accounting period.

You can create adjusting entries to record depreciation and amortization, an allowance for doubtful accounts, accrued revenue or expenses, and adjustments necessary after bank statement reconciliations.

Adjusting entries fall under one of three categories:

1. Accruals: Revenues or expenses that have not been recorded, and have not been received or paid (e.g., accrued revenues and accrued expenses).
2. Deferrals: Revenues or expenses that have been recorded but not yet earned or used (e.g., prepaid expenses and unearned revenues).
3. Estimates: Non-cash items (e.g., allowance for doubtful accounts).

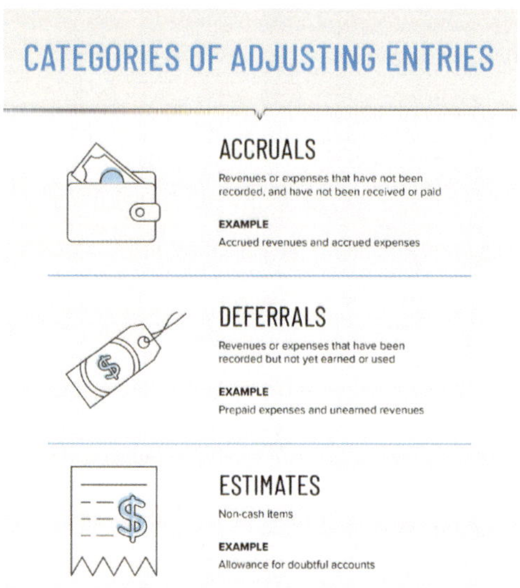

Adjusting entries can also refer to entries you need to make because you simply made a mistake in your general ledger. If your numbers don't add up, refer back to your general ledger to determine where the mistake is. Then, create an adjusting entry to reverse or alter the record.

Creating adjusting entries is one of the steps in the accounting cycle. It occurs after you prepare a trial balance, which is an accounting report to determine whether your debits and credits are equal. If the debits and credits in your trial balance are unequal, you must create accounting adjustments to fix the discrepancy.

Adjusting Entries

Prepare adjusting entries like you would any entry in accrual accounting: debit one account and credit another account.

Some accounts are increased by debits while others are increased by credits. Take a look at the following chart to help you:

ACCOUNT	INCREASED BY	DECREASED BY
Assets	Debit	Credit
Expenses	Debit	Credit
Liabilities	Credit	Debit
Equity	Credit	Debit
Revenue	Credit	Debit

Adjusting entries deal mainly with revenue and expenses. When you need to increase a revenue account, credit it. And when you need to decrease a revenue account, debit it. Oppositely, debit an expense account to increase it, and credit an expense account to decrease it.

Adjusting Entries Examples

Accruals

Let's say you operate a lawn mowing service. You mowed a customer's lawn in one accounting period, but you will not bill the customer until the following accounting period. You performed a service worth $ 1,000.

Even though you won't bill the customer until the following period, you still need to record the amount of your service in your books.

To record the amount of your services performed in one accounting period, you need to create the following adjusting entry. Debit your accounts receivable account and credit your service revenues account.

Date	Account	Notes	Debit	Credit
6/30/2018	Accounts Receivable Service Revenues	Lawn services	1,000	1,000

Creating this adjusting entry will increase the amount of your accounts receivable account in your books.

Deferrals

You run a jelly of the month subscription business. A customer pays you $300 for a 12-month supply of jelly. Because the customer pays you before they receive all their jelly, not all the revenue is earned. Instead, it is deferred revenue. However, your cash account increases because your business receives more cash.

Date	Account	Notes	Debit	Credit
1/1/2018	Cash Deferred Revenue	Payment for jelly subscription	300	300

Each month, one-twelfth of the deferred revenue becomes earned revenue, which works out to 25 per month ($ 300 / 12). Create an adjusting entry to decrease your deferred revenue account by debiting it, and increase your revenue account by crediting it.

Date	Account	Notes	Debit	Credit
1/15/2018	Deferred Revenue Revenue	One month of jelly subscription	25	25

Estimates

You set up an allowance for doubtful accounts. An allowance for doubtful accounts is a contra-asset account that decreases your accounts receivable. It estimates that some of your customers won't pay you.

Let's say you predict that you won't receive $800 of your receivables. Because a debit increases expenses, you must debit your bad debts expense account. Take a look at your adjusting entry:

Date	Account	Notes	Debit	Credit
1/5/2018	Bad Debts Expense Allowance for Doubtful Accounts	Estimated default payments	800	800

Closing Entries

Closing journal entries are made at the end of the accounting period to prepare temporary accounts for the next period.

Temporary or nominal accounts, (also called income statement accounts), are measured periodically.

The amounts in one accounting period should be closed or brought to zero so that they won't be mixed with those of the next period.

Temporary accounts consist of all revenue and expense accounts, and also withdrawal accounts of owner/s in the case of sole proprietorships and partnerships. Take note that closing entries are prepared only for temporary accounts. Permanent accounts are never closed.

Four Steps in Preparing Closing Entries

1. Close all income accounts to income summary.

2. Close all expense accounts to income summary.
3. Close Income Summary to the appropriate capital account.
4. Close withdrawals to the capital account/s (this step is for sole proprietorship and partnership only).

Closing Entries: Example

Prepare the closing entries using the following information:

Gray Electronic Repair Services Adjusted Trial Balance December 31, 2017		
Account Title	Debit	Credit
Cash	$ 7,480.00	
Accounts Receivable	3,700.00	
Service Supplies	600.00	
Furniture and Fixtures	3,000.00	
Service Equipment	16,000.00	
Accumulated Depreciation		$ 720.00
Accounts Payable		9,000.00
Utilities Payable		1,800.00
Loans Payable		12,000.00
Mr. Gray, Capital		13,200.00
Mr. Gray, Drawing	7,000.00	
Service Revenue		9,850.00
Rent Expense	1,500.00	
Salaries Expense	3,500.00	
Taxes and Licenses	370.00	
Utilities Expense	1,800.00	
Service Supplies Expense	900.00	
Depreciation Expense	720.00	
Totals	$ 46,570.00	$ 46,570.00

Step 1: Close All Income Accounts to Income Summary

Date 2017		Particulars	Debit	Credit
Dec	31	Service Revenue	9,850.00	
		Income Summary		9,850.00

In the given data, there is only 1 income account, i.e. Service Revenue. It has a credit balance of $ 9,850. To close that, we debit Service Revenue for the full amount and credit Income Summary for the same.

The Income Summary account is temporary. It is used to close income and expenses. As you will see later, Income Summary is eventually closed to capital.

Step 2: Close All Expense Accounts to Income Summary

31	Income Summary	8,790.00	
	Rent Expense		1,500.00
	Salaries Expense		3,500.00
	Taxes and Licenses		370.00
	Utilities Expense		1,800.00
	Service Supplies Expense		900.00
	Depreciation Expense		720.00

To close expenses, we credit the expense accounts and debit Income Summary.

Now for the next step, we need to get the balance of the Income Summary account. In step 1, we credited it for \$ 9,850 and debited it in step 2 for \$ 8,790. It would then have a credit balance of \$ 1,060.

Notice that the balance of the Income Summary account is actually the net income for the period. Remember that net income is equal to all income minus all expenses.

Step 3: Close Income Summary to the Appropriate Capital Account

The Income Summary balance is ultimately closed to the capital account.

31	Income Summary	1,060.00	
	Mr. Gray, Capital		1,060.00

Step 4: Close Withdrawals to the Capital Account

This step is applicable only to sole proprietorships and partnerships.

In a sole proprietorship, a drawing account is maintained to record all withdrawals made by the owner. In a partnership, a drawing account is maintained for each partner. Drawing accounts are closed to capital at the end of the accounting period.

Our example is a sole proprietorship business. Mr. Gray's withdrawals are recorded in Mr. Gray, Drawing. To close the drawing account to the capital account, we credit the drawing account and debit the capital account. Notice that drawings decrease capital.

31	Mr. Gray, Capital	7,000.00	
	Mr. Gray, Drawing		7,000.00

The purpose of closing entries is to prepare the temporary accounts for the next accounting period. In other words, the income and expense accounts are "restarted".

After preparing the closing entries above, Service Revenue will now be zero. The expense accounts and withdrawal accounts will now also be zero. The balances of these accounts have been absorbed by the capital account – Mr. Gray, Capital, which now has a balance of $ 7,260 ($ 13,200 beginning balance + $ 1,060 in step #3 - $ 7,000 in step #4).

Prepayments

Prepayments (also known as deferred expense) are assets that represents cash paid in advance for goods or services to be received later. A prepayment is related to unearned income in a sense that one company's prepayment is other company's unearned income.

The reason for deferral of expense is the accrual concept of accounting, which requires that an expense must be recognized in the period to which it relates rather than in the period in which it is paid for. Since prepayments are often made for goods or services, the receipt of which spans over two or more accounting periods, prepayments must not be simply expensed on payment date.

Prepayments are usually current assets but in extremely rare cases they may span over 12 months after year end, in which case they are classified as non-current assets.

Journal Entries

Accounting for prepayments involves the following journal entries:

1. A prepayment transaction is recorded initially by debiting an asset account (such as prepaid insurance, prepaid rent etc.) and crediting cash or bank.
2. At the end of each accounting period an adjusting entry is passed that debits expense and credits prepaid asset for the part of goods or services which have been received in that period.

Example

On April 1, 20X5, Company β pays $ 40,000 for twelve month insurance in advance. Company β's financial year ends on June 30, 20X5.

Required:

1. Journal entries to account for the above transaction on April 1, 20X5 and June 30, 20X5.

2. Balance in prepaid insurance account on June 30, 20X5.

Solution

April 1, 20X5: To record the prepayment as a current asset:

Prepaid Insurance	40,000	
Bank		40,000

June 30, 20X5: To record insurance expense for three months $[= 40000 \times 3/12]$.

Insurance Expense	10,000	
Prepaid Insurance		10,000

Balance in Prepaid Subscriptions on June 30, 20X5: \$400 – \$100 = \$300

Depreciation

In accounting terms, depreciation is defined as the reduction of recorded cost of a fixed asset in a systematic manner until the value of the asset becomes zero or negligible.

An example of fixed assets are buildings, furniture, office equipment, machinery etc. A land is the only exception which cannot be depreciated as the value of land appreciates with time.

Depreciation allows a portion of the cost of a fixed asset to the revenue generated by the fixed asset. This is mandatory under the matching principle as revenues are recorded with their associated expenses in the accounting period when the asset is in use. This helps in getting a complete picture of the revenue generation transaction.

An example of Depreciation: If a delivery truck is purchased a company with a cost of Rs. 100,000 and the expected usage of the truck are 5 years, the business might depreciate the asset under depreciation expense as Rs. 20,000 every year for a period of 5 years.

Calculation of Depreciation in Small Business

There three methods commonly used to calculate depreciation. They are:

1. Straight line method
2. Unit of production method
3. Double-declining balance method

Three main inputs are required to calculate depreciation:

1. Useful life: This is the time period over which the organization considers the fixed asset to be productive. Beyond its useful life, the fixed asset is no longer cost-effective to continue the operation of the asset.
2. Salvage value: Post the useful life of the fixed asset, the company may consider selling it at a reduced amount. This is known as the salvage value of the asset.
3. The cost of the asset: This includes taxes, shipping, and preparation/setup expenses.

Unit of production method needs the number of units used during production.

Types of Depreciation

Straight-line Depreciation Method

This is the simplest method of all. It involves simple allocation of an even rate of depreciation every year over the useful life of the asset. The formula for straight line depreciation is:

Annual Depreciation expense = (Asset cost – Residual Value) / Useful life of the asset

Example: Suppose a manufacturing company purchases a machinery for Rs. 100,000 and the useful life of the machinery are 10 years and the residual value of the machinery is Rs. 20,000

Annual Depreciation expense = (100,000-20,000) / 10 = Rs.8,000

Thus the company can take Rs.8000 as the depreciation expense every year over the next ten years as shown in depreciation table below.

Year	Original cost – Residual value	Depreciation expense
1	Rs. 80000	Rs. 8000
2	Rs. 80000	Rs. 8000
3	Rs. 80000	Rs. 8000
4	Rs. 80000	Rs. 8000
5	Rs. 80000	Rs. 8000
6	Rs. 80000	Rs. 8000
7	Rs. 80000	Rs. 8000
8	Rs. 80000	Rs. 8000
9	Rs. 80000	Rs. 8000
10	Rs. 80000	Rs. 8000

Unit of Production Method

This is a two-step process, unlike straight line method. Here, equal expense rates are assigned to each unit produced. This assignment makes the method very useful in assembly for production lines. Hence, the calculation is based on output capability of the asset rather than the number of years.

The steps are:

- Step 1: Calculate per unit depreciation:

Per unit Depreciation = (Asset cost – Residual value) / Useful life in units of production

- Step 2: Calculate the total depreciation of actual units produced:

Total Depreciation Expense = Per Unit Depreciation * Units Produced

Example: ABC company purchases a printing press to print flyers for Rs. 40,000 with a useful life of 1,80,000 units and residual value of Rs. 4000. It prints 4000 flyers.

Step 1: Per unit Depreciation = (40,000-4000)/180,000 = Rs. 0.2

Step 2: Total Depreciation expense = Rs. 0.2 * 4000 flyers = Rs. 800

So the total Depreciation expense is Rs. 800 which is accounted. Once the per unit depreciation is found out, it can be applied to future output runs.

Double Declining Method

This is one of the two common methods a company uses to account for the expenses of a fixed asset. This is an accelerated depreciation method. As the name suggests, it counts expense twice as much as the book value of the asset every year.

The formula is:

Depreciation = 2 * Straight line depreciation percent * book value at the beginning of the accounting period Book value = Cost of the asset – accumulated depreciation

Accumulated depreciation is the total depreciation of the fixed asset accumulated up to a specified time.

Example: On April 1, 2012, company X purchased an equipment for Rs. 100,000. This is expected to have 5 useful life years. The salvage value is Rs. 14,000. Company X considers depreciation expense for the nearest whole month. Calculate the depreciation expenses for 2012, 2013, 2014 using a declining balance method.

Useful life = 5

Straight line depreciation percent = 1/5 = 0.2 or 20% per year

Depreciation rate = 20% * 2 = 40% per year

Depreciation for the year 2012 = Rs. 100,000 * 40% * 9/12 = Rs. 30,000

Depreciation for the year 2013 = (Rs. 100,000-Rs. 30,000) * 40% * 12/12 = Rs. 28,000

Depreciation for the year 2014 = (Rs. 100,000 – Rs. 30,000 – Rs. 28,000) * 40% * 9/12 = Rs. 16,800

Depreciation table is shown below:

Year	Book value at the beginning	Depreciation rate	Depreciation Expense	Book value at the end of the year
2012	Rs. 100,000	40%	Rs. 30,000 * (1)	Rs. 70,000
2013	Rs. 70,000	40%	Rs. 28,000 * (2)	Rs. 42,000
2014	Rs. 42,000	40%	Rs. 16,800 * (3)	Rs. 25,200
2015	Rs. 25,200	40%	Rs. 10,080 * (4)	Rs. 15,120
2016	Rs. 15,120	40%	Rs. 1,120 * (5)	Rs. 14,000

Depreciation for 2016 is Rs. 1,120 to keep the book value same as salvage value.

Rs. 15,120 – Rs. 14,000 = Rs. 1,120 (At this point the depreciation should stop).

Care of Record Depreciation in Small Businesses

So now we know the meaning of depreciation, the methods used to calculate them, inputs required to calculate them and also we saw examples of how to calculate them. Let's find out as to why the small businesses should care to record depreciation.

As we already know the purpose of depreciation is to match the cost of the fixed asset over its productive life to the revenues the business earns from the asset. It is very difficult to directly link the cost of the asset to revenues, hence, the cost is usually assigned to the number of years the asset is productive.

Over the useful life of the fixed asset, the cost is moved from balance sheet to income statement. Alternatively, it is just an allocation process as per matching principle instead of a technique which determines the fair market value of the fixed asset.

Accounting entry: DEBIT depreciation expense account and CREDIT accumulated depreciation account.

If we do not use depreciation in accounting, then we have to charge all assets to expense once they are bought. This will result in huge losses in the following transaction period and in high profitability in periods when the corresponding revenue is considered without an offset expense. Hence, companies which do not use the depreciation expense in their accounts will incur front-loaded expenses and highly variable financial results.

Inventory and Cost of Goods Sold

Inventory is merchandise purchased by merchandisers (retailers, wholesalers, distributors) for the purpose of being sold to customers. The cost of the merchandise purchased but not yet sold is reported in the account Inventory or Merchandise Inventory.

Inventory is reported as a current asset on the company's balance sheet. Inventory is a significant asset that needs to be monitored closely. Too much inventory can result in cash flow problems, additional expenses (e.g., storage, insurance), and losses if the items become obsolete. Too little inventory can result in lost sales and lost customers.

Because of the cost principle, inventory is reported on the balance sheet at the amount paid to obtain (purchase) the merchandise, not at its selling price.

Inventory is also a significant asset of manufacturers.

Cost of goods sold is a calculation of all the costs involved in selling a product. Calculating cost of goods sold for products you manufacture or sell can be complicated, depending on the number of products and the complexity of the manufacturing process.

Cost of goods sold is a required calculation as part of your business tax return. It reduces your business income, and thus your business taxes, so it's important to get it right.

Calculating Cost of Goods Sold - Step by Step

Step 1: The Basic Components of the COGS Calculation

The basic calculation is:

- Beginning Inventory Costs (at the beginning of the year).
- Plus Additional Inventory Cost (inventory purchased during the year).
- Minus Ending Inventory (at the end of the year).
- Equals Cost of Goods Sold.

For example:

$ 14,000 cost of inventory at beginning of year

+ $ 8,000 cost of additional inventory purchased during year

- $10,000 ending inventory

= $12,000 cost of goods sold.

The COGS calculation process allows you to deduct all the costs of the products you sell, whether you manufacture them or buy and re-sell them.

There are two types of costs included in COGS: Direct and Indirect.

- Direct Costs are costs related to production or purchase of the product.
- Indirect Costs are costs related to warehousing, facilities, equipment, and labor.

Step 2: Determine Direct Costs

Determine direct costs, including:

- Cost to purchase the merchandise for resale
- Cost of raw materials
- Packaging costs
- Work in process
- Cost of inventory of finished products
- Supplies for production
- Direct overhead costs related to production (for example, utilities and rent for manufacturing facility)

Step 3: Determine Indirect Costs

Indirect costs include manufacturing materials and supplies:

- Labor (for workers who actually touch the product).
- Costs to store/wholesale the products.
- Depreciation of equipment used to produce, package, or store the product.
- Salaries of administrators, managers overseeing production.
- Equipment used for administrative work (not production).

Step 4: Determine Facilities Costs

Facilities costs are the most difficult to determine. This is where a good CPA comes in. Your CPA must allocate a percentage of your facility costs (rent or mortgage interest, utilities, and other costs) to each product, for the accounting period in question (usually a year, for tax purposes).

Step 5: Determine Beginning Inventory

Inventory includes merchandise in stock, raw materials, work in progress, finished products, and supplies that are part of the items.

Your beginning inventory this year must be exactly the same as your ending inventory last year. If it does not, you will need to submit an explanation for the difference.

Step 6: Add Purchases of Inventory Items

Most businesses add inventory during the year. You must keep track of the cost of each shipment or the total manufacturing cost of each product you add to inventory. For purchased products, keep the invoices and any other paperwork. For items you make, you will need the help of your CPA to determine the cost to add to inventory.

Step 7: Determine Ending Inventory

Ending inventory costs are usually determined by taking a physical inventory of products, or by estimating.

Ending inventory costs can be reduced for damaged, worthless, or obsolete inventory. For damaged inventory, report the estimated value. For worthless inventory, you must provide evidence that it was destroyed. For obsolete inventory, you must also show evidence of the decrease in value. Consider donating obsolete inventory to a charity.

Step 8: Do the COGS Calculation

At this point, you have all the information you need to do the COGS calculation. You can do it on a spreadsheet, or have your accountant help you.

Inventory Valuation Methods

The final item to be determined is how which inventory has been sold. There are two acceptable methods for determining which inventory is left at the end of the accounting period: LIFO (Last in, first out), or FIFO (first in, first out).

Your CPA will help you determine which method is best for your business tax situation. If you change your valuation method, you must apply to the IRS for approval. For example, if this is the first year your business is using the LIFO method, you must apply to the IRS to make this change. Use IRS Form 970 - Application to Use LIFO Inventory Method.

Cost of Goods Sold on Business Tax Returns

The process and form for calculating cost of goods sold and including it on your business tax return is different for different types of businesses.

For sole proprietors and single-member LLC's using Schedule C, cost of goods sold is calculated in Part III and included in the Income section (Part I).

For partnerships, multiple-member LLC's, corporations, and S corporations, cost of goods sold is calculated on Form 1125-A. This form is complicated, and it's a good idea to get your tax professional to help you with it.

Some Additional Tips for This Calculation

1. You can only deduct cost of goods sold if you have sales. If you purchase or make products to sell, and you don't sell any products, you can't deduct these costs.
2. If your business has less than $1 million in sales/receipts annually, you do not need to report inventory.
3. You cannot use the "lower of cost or market" method if you are using LIFO inventory valuation. You must use the "Cost" method of valuing inventory (not "lower of cost or market") if you use the cash accounting method. It is best to use the accrual method if you have inventory.

Accounting Errors and Corrections

Accounting errors can occur in double entry bookkeeping for a number of reasons. Accounting errors are not the same as fraud, errors happen unintentionally, whereas fraud is a deliberate and intentional attempt to falsify the bookkeeping entries.

An accounting error can cause the trial balance not to balance, which is easier to spot, or the error can be such that the trial balance will still balance due to compensating bookkeeping entries, which is more difficult to identify.

Accounting Errors that Affect the Trial Balance

Errors that affect the trial balance are usually a result of a one sided entry in the accounting records or an incorrect addition.

Irrespective of the reasons why a trial balance may not balance, as a temporary measure the difference in the trial balance is allocated to a suspense account and a suspense account reconciliation is carried out at a later stage.

For example, suppose the trial balance showed total debits of 84,600 but total credits of 83,400 leaving a difference of 1,200 as shown below.

Suspense Accounts – Trial Balance Difference

Account	Debit	Credit
Trial Balance Totals	84,600	83,400
Difference		1,200
Total	84,600	84,600

To make the trial balance a single entry is posted to the accounting ledgers in a suspense account.

Suspense Account Posting

Account	Debit	Credit
Suspense account		1,200

When the accounting error is identified a correcting entry is made. Suppose the difference was an addition error on the rent account, then the correcting entry would be as follows:

Suspense Account – Accounting error correction

Account	Debit	Credit
Suspense account	1,200	
Rent		1,200

Errors Which do not Affect the Trial Balance

Accounting errors that do not affect the trial balance fall into one of six categories as follows:

Error of Principle in Accounting

An error of principle in accounting occurs when the bookkeeping entry is made to the wrong type of account. For example, if a 1,000 sale is credited to the sundry expenses account instead of the sales account, the correcting entry would be as follows:

Accounting Errors – Error of Principle in Accounting Example

Account	Debit	Credit
Sundry expenses	1,000	
Sales		1,000

Error of Omission in Accounting

Errors of omission in accounting occur when a bookkeeping entry has been completely omitted from the accounting records.

If the payment 2,000 to a supplier has been omitted then the correcting entry would be as follows:

Accounting Errors – Errors of Omission in Accounting Example

Account	Debit	Credit
Accounts payable	2,000	
Cash		2,000

Error of Commission

An accounting error of commission occurs when an item is entered to the correct type of account but the wrong account. For example is cash received of 3,000 from Customer A is credited to the account of Customer B the correcting entry would be.

Accounting Errors – Error of Commission

Account	Debit	Credit
Accounts receivable – Cust. B	3,000	
Accounts receivable – Cust. A		3,000

Compensating Error

A compensating error occurs when two or more errors cancel each other out. For example, if the fixed assets account is incorrectly totalled and understated by 600, and the rent account is incorrectly totalled and overstated by 600, then the posting to correct the error would be as follows:

Accounting Errors – Compensating Error

Account	Debit	Credit
Fixed assets	600	
Rent		600

Error of Original Entry

An error of original entry occurs when an incorrect amount is posted to the correct account.

A particular example of an error of original entry is a transposition error where the numbers are not entered in the correct order. For example, if cash paid to a supplier of 2,140 was posted as 2,410 then the correcting entry of 270 would be.

A good indicator for a transposition error is that the difference (in this case 270) is divisible by 9.

Accounting Errors – Error of Original Entry

Account	Debit	Credit
Cash	270	
Accounts payable		270

Complete Reversal of Entries

Complete reversal of entries errors occur when the correct amount is posted to the correct accounts but the debits and credits have been reversed. For example if a cash sale is made for 400 and posted incorrectly as follows:

Accounting Errors – Incorrect posting

Account	Debit	Credit
Sales	400	
Cash		400

Then to correct the accounting error the original entry must be reversed and the correct entry made, this can be achieved by doubling the original amounts as follows:

Accounting Errors – Complete Reversal of Entries

Account	Debit	Credit
Sales		800
Cash	800	

The type of accounting errors that do not affect the trial balance are summarized in the table below.

Accounting Errors	Description
Error of Principle in Accounting	Correct amount, wrong type of account
Errors of Omission in Accounting	Entry missed from accounting records
Error of Commission	Correct amount and type of account but wrong account
Compensating Error	Two or more errors balance each other out

Error of Original Entry	Correct accounts, wrong amounts
Complete Reversal of Entries	Correct amount and account, entries reversed

Where possible all accounting errors should be identified and corrected, if the accounting errors are immaterial to the accounts then, as a last resort, the balance could be carried in the balance sheet on a suspense account or written off to the income statement as a sundry expense.

Preparing Financial Statements

Financial statements, though often feared as a very intimidating portion of small business accounting, are just a matter of putting the trial balance amounts onto properly formatted statements. Learn how to prepare these documents you'll need for shareholders, potential financiers and your own insight.

After you have prepared your adjusting entries in the general journal, posted the general journal totals to the general ledger, and footed the general ledger accounts, you are ready to prepare financial statements. Like most of the accounting tasks we've reviewed, your accounting software can alleviate much of the legwork.

If all adjusting entries have been made, and a trial balance done, preparing financial statements is really just a matter of putting the trial balance amounts onto properly formatted statements.

Creating the Components of a Financial Statement

The financial statements prepared for most small businesses comprise a balance sheet and an income statement.

Usually these are prepared by an accountant. But with the help of computer software, you may be able to prepare your own financial statements. If you need to prepare financial statements for a third party, such as a banker, sometimes the third party may request that the financial statements be prepared by a professional accountant or certified public accountant.

Preparing a Balance Sheet

Also called a statement of financial position, a balance sheet is a financial snapshot of your business at a given date in time. It lists your assets, your liabilities and the difference between the two, which is your owner's equity, or net worth. The accounting equation (assets = liabilities + owner's equity) is the basis for the balance sheet.

The balance sheet is prepared after all adjusting entries are made in the general journal, all journal entries have been posted to the general ledger, the general ledger accounts have been footed to arrive at the period end totals, and an adjusted trial balance is prepared from the general ledger amounts.

All amounts should be rounded to the nearest dollar, like in this example of a balance sheet for a sole proprietorship:

Beta Sales Company Balance Sheet December 31, 201X					
Assets			Liabilities and Capital		
Current Assets			Current Liabilities		
Cash	$ 12,300		Accounts payable	$ 8,900	
Accounts receivable	22,900		Wages payable	11,525	
Inventory	32,090		Total Current Liabilities		$ 20,425
Prepaid Insurance	2,500		Long-Term Liabilities		
Total Current Assets		$ 69,790	Bank Loan Payable	17,500	
Fixed Assets			Total Long-Term Liability		17,500
Equipment	100,200		Total Liabilities		37,925
Less: Accumulated Depreciation	(78,321)		Capital		
Total Fixed Assets		21,879	Tom Beta, Capital		53,744
Total Assets		$ 91,669	Total Liabilities/Capital		$91,669

Preparing an Income Statement

Also called a profit and loss statement, or a "P&L," an income statement lists your income, expenses and net income (or loss). The net income (or loss) is equal to your income minus your expenses. Your business's tax return will use a variation of the income statement to determine your potentially taxable income.

The income statement is prepared after all adjusting entries are made in the general journal, all journal entries have been posted to the general ledger, the general ledger accounts have been footed to arrive at the period end totals, and an adjusted trial balance has been prepared from the general ledger totals.

Like financial statements, don't include cents on your income statements that might look something like this:

Beta Sales Company Income Statement For the Year Ended December 31, 201X		
Sales		$ 462,452

Cost of Goods Sold		
Beginning Inventory	$ 27,335	
Add: Purchases	235,689	
Total:	263,024	
Less: Ending inventory	32,090	
Cost of Goods Sold		230,934
Gross Profit		231,518
Expenses		
Advertising	1,850	
Depreciation	13,250	
Insurance	5,400	
Payroll taxes	8,200	
Rent	9,600	
Repairs and maintenance	13,984	
Utilities	17,801	
Wages	98,852	
Total Expenses		168,937
Net Income		$ 62,581

Prepare Closing Entries to Get the Books Ready for the Next Accounting Period

After financial statements are prepared, to get your books ready for the next accounting period by clearing out the income and expense accounts in the general ledger and transferring the net income (or loss) to your owner's equity account. This is done by preparing closing entries in the general journal.

The Steps to Closing the Books

Note the distinction between adjusting entries and closing entries. Adjusting entries are required to update certain accounts in your general ledger at the end of an accounting period. They must be done before you can prepare your financial statements and income tax return. Closing entries are needed to clear out your revenue and expense accounts as you start the beginning of a new accounting period.

Preparing your closing entries is a very simple, mechanical process. Follow these steps:

1. Close the revenue accounts: Prepare one journal entry that debits all the revenue accounts. (These accounts will have a credit balance in the general ledger

prior to the closing entry.) Credit an account called "income summary" for the total.

2. Close the expense accounts: Prepare one journal entry that credits all the expense accounts. (These accounts will have a debit balance in the general ledger prior to the closing entry.) Debit the income summary account for the total.
3. Transfer the income summary balance to a capital account: Prepare a journal entry that clears out the income summary account. This entry effectively transfers the net income (or loss) of the business to the owner's equity account.
4. Close the drawing account: If your business is a sole proprietorship or partnership, close the drawing accounts (if any) by preparing a journal entry that credits the drawing account and debits the owner's equity account.

Example

You have finalized your general ledger and prepared a balance sheet and income statement for the year ended December 31, 2011. You want to get your books ready for next year. You prepare the four closing entries as follows:

	Debit	Credit
Sales	462,452	
Income summary		462,452
To close the revenue account on 12/31/2011		

	Debit	Credit
Income summary	399,871	
Purchases		230,934
Advertising		1,850
Depreciation		13,250
Insurance		5,400
Payroll taxes		8,200
Rent		9,600
Repairs and maintenance		13,984
Utilities		17,801
Wages		98,852
To close the expense accounts on 12/31/2011		

	Debit	Credit
Income summary	62,581	
Tom Beta, capital		62,581

To transfer 12/31/201X net income to the capital account		

	Debit	Credit
Tom Beta, capital	12,000	
Tom Beta, drawing		12,000
To close drawing account for year ended 12/31/201X		

After all closing entries are made, post the entry totals to the general ledger. Foot the general ledger accounts to arrive at the beginning amounts for the new accounting period. All revenue and expense accounts should have a zero balance.

References

- What-is-accounting-cycle-steps, accounting: patriotsoftware.com, Retrieved 17 April 2018
- What-is-an-account-in-accounting: kashoo.com, Retrieved 16 June 2018
- Three-type-of-accounts-in-accounting, books-and-accounts: accountingcapital.com, Retrieved 19 April 2018
- What-is-the-accrual-basis-of-accounting: accountingtools.com, Retrieved 24 June 2018
- Cash-basis-accounting: business-case-analysis.com, Retrieved 10 May 2018
- How-to-calculate-cost-of-goods-sold-397501: thebalancesmb.com, Retrieved 31 March 2018

Permissions

All chapters in this book are published with permission under the Creative Commons Attribution Share Alike License or equivalent. Every chapter published in this book has been scrutinized by our experts. Their significance has been extensively debated. The topics covered herein carry significant information for a comprehensive understanding. They may even be implemented as practical applications or may be referred to as a beginning point for further studies.

We would like to thank the editorial team for lending their expertise to make the book truly unique. They have played a crucial role in the development of this book. Without their invaluable contributions this book wouldn't have been possible. They have made vital efforts to compile up to date information on the varied aspects of this subject to make this book a valuable addition to the collection of many professionals and students.

This book was conceptualized with the vision of imparting up-to-date and integrated information in this field. To ensure the same, a matchless editorial board was set up. Every individual on the board went through rigorous rounds of assessment to prove their worth. After which they invested a large part of their time researching and compiling the most relevant data for our readers.

The editorial board has been involved in producing this book since its inception. They have spent rigorous hours researching and exploring the diverse topics which have resulted in the successful publishing of this book. They have passed on their knowledge of decades through this book. To expedite this challenging task, the publisher supported the team at every step. A small team of assistant editors was also appointed to further simplify the editing procedure and attain best results for the readers.

Apart from the editorial board, the designing team has also invested a significant amount of their time in understanding the subject and creating the most relevant covers. They scrutinized every image to scout for the most suitable representation of the subject and create an appropriate cover for the book.

The publishing team has been an ardent support to the editorial, designing and production team. Their endless efforts to recruit the best for this project, has resulted in the accomplishment of this book. They are a veteran in the field of academics and their pool of knowledge is as vast as their experience in printing. Their expertise and guidance has proved useful at every step. Their uncompromising quality standards have made this book an exceptional effort. Their encouragement from time to time has been an inspiration for everyone.

The publisher and the editorial board hope that this book will prove to be a valuable piece of knowledge for students, practitioners and scholars across the globe.

Index